To Hope + Julian,
With affection + thanks.
Gerry Izenberg

Modernism and Masculinity

Modernism and Masculinity

Mann, Wedekind, Kandinsky
through World War I

GERALD N. IZENBERG

The University of Chicago Press
Chicago and London

The University of Chicago Press, Chicago 60637
The University of Chicago Press, Ltd., London
© 2000 by The University of Chicago
All rights reserved. Published 2000
Paperback edition 2002
Printed in the United States of America

11 10 09 08 07 06 05 04 03 02   2 3 4 5
ISBN: 0-226-38868-9 (cloth)
ISBN: 0-226-38869-7 (pbk.)

Library of Congress Cataloging-in-Publication Data
Izenberg, Gerald N., 1939–
    Modernism and masculinity: Mann, Wedekind, Kandinsky through World War I /
Gerald N. Izenberg.
        p.   cm.
    Includes bibliographical references and index.
    ISBN 0-226-38868-9 (alk. paper)—ISBN 0-226-38869-7 (pbk.: alk. paper)
    1. Mann, Thomas, 1875–1955—Criticism and interpretation.   2. Wedekind, Frank,
1864–1918—Criticism and interpretation.   3. Kandinsky, Wassily, 1866–1944.
4. Modernism (Literature).   5. Modernism (Art).   6. Masculinity.   I. Title.
PT2625.A44 Z65558   2000
833′.912—dc21
                                                                            99-087470

For Zev and Benjamin

and

In memory of H. Stuart Hughes

CONTENTS

ILLUSTRATIONS

ACKNOWLEDGMENTS

It is always a pleasure to thank those who have helped in one way or another in the genesis of one's work, however they may judge the final product. Casey Blake, Laura Engelstein, Rose-Carol Washton Long, Max Okenfuss, Christine Ruane, Jerrold Seigel, and Nathan Simon read and made many valuable comments on the Kandinsky chapter, as did Robert Jensen on the version I presented at Washington University. Milica Banjanin, Oren Izenberg, and Christine Ruane gave me crucial bibliographical suggestions. I am grateful to my colleagues Lynne Tatlock and Robert Weninger for help with German translation (though I of course take full responsibility for any errors and infelicities), Paul Michael Lützeler for insights on German Modernism, and Steven Zwicker, my codirector in the program in Literature and History at Washington University, for his astringent reading and shrewd advice, always on the mark.

I am particularly grateful to the readers for the University of Chicago Press, Gail Finney and John Toews, who read the entire manuscript with enormous care and discernment, and whose detailed and insightful comments made this a better book than it would otherwise have been. The students in my seminars on Modernism and Masculinity at Washington University, graduate and undergraduate, also contributed to my revisions with their astute questions and observations. I want to thank my editors at the University of Chicago Press: Doug Mitchell, who shepherded the project from its inception, unfailingly supportive and cheerfully helpful; Erin DeWitt, my keen-eyed copy editor, most of whose suggestions I took; and Robert Devens, always quick to respond to my queries and generous with his time.

My special thanks to the Gabriele Münter- and Johannes Eichner-

Stiftung in Munich for permission to quote from Wassily Kandinsky's un-published letters to Gabriele Münter, and to Ilse Holzinger, its executive di-rector, who went out of her way to provide comfortable circumstances and extra time in which to examine the correspondence. Thanks also to Edward Macias, Dean of the Faculty at Washington University, and to Richard Wal-ter and Derek Hirst, former and current chairs of the History Department, for the financial assistance that made it possible to include color reproduc-tions in the book. My wife, Ziva, helped with a number of editorial chores, and she and my sons, Noam and Oren, and my daughter-in-law Illysa, al-ways interested and supportive, claim that I did not tax their patience too much with my immersion in the project, the latter three probably because they do not live at home.

Finally, I want to remember my teacher, mentor, and friend H. Stuart Hughes, who died this past year; it was from him I learned that subjectivity and consciousness are genuinely historical subjects and that psychoanalysis is a legitimate tool with which to study them.

INTRODUCTION

Modernism, Masculinity, Method

Locked in a literally deadly struggle with her husband over the education of
their daughter, the female protagonist of August Strindberg's 1887 play *The*   1
Father attacks her spouse's manhood by trying to infantilize him. When he   ∎
starts to cry during one of their confrontations, Laura encourages him to go
on despite his anguish over his unmanly tears. "Do you remember it was as
your second mother I came into your life?" she asks with ominous solici-
tude. "Your body was big and strong, but you had no vigor. You were a
giant-child, born prematurely—or perhaps just unwanted." The Captain—
almost always ironically referred to by his military rank rather than his
name—readily assents to both her diagnosis and her etiology: "Yes, that's
probably right. Father and mother did not want me, so I was born without a
will. Then when you and I were made one, I thought I had grafted myself on
to you. That's how you came into power." In a later exchange he puts all the
blame where he believes it really lies. "I think you [women] are all my enemies!" he bursts out. "My mother was my enemy when she did not want me
to enter the world for fear of the pain of my birth and when she failed to
nourish the seed that gave me life and made me half a cripple."[1]

   The Father is usually represented as a dramatization of the modern battle
of the sexes or as one of the canonical expressions of modern misogyny.
Though battle and misogyny are there, both characterizations miss the
essence and driving force of the drama. The "battle" is after all one-sided,
and the cause of the Captain's defeat lies less in his wife's malevolent strength
than in his own psychic vulnerability. The central themes of the play are
rather the inexorable collapse of masculinity and the psychological theory
the Captain offers that purports to explain it. A mother's desire for and nurturing love of her child are, according to him, the necessary conditions for

the development of his autonomy; without them the child lacks the self-assurance to assert his will and seeks it from maternal substitutes in adult life. Strindberg expressly reveals what Peter Gay has called "the dirty little secret" of the Victorian platitude about woman's nurturing role: "Men needed it and without it could not become men."[2]

The causes may vary—insofar as causes are suggested at all—but the same theme of manhood in jeopardy appears again and again in the texts and images of early High Modernism. Thirty years later Franz Kafka would blame his father for his own inability to fulfill the fundamental demands of manhood: "marrying, founding a family, accepting all the children that come, supporting them in this insecure world and perhaps even guiding them a little . . . the utmost a human being can succeed in doing at all."[3] He had already spectacularly documented the failure of manhood in such short stories as "The Judgment" and "The Metamorphosis"; in *Letter to His Father* he as much as said that writing itself was his poor substitute for the forms of manly independence his father had foreclosed to him. And in between the appearance of Strindberg's and Kafka's texts, Pablo Picasso visually dramatized yet another source of threat to manhood in sexual love itself; his revolutionary *Les Demoiselles d'Avignon* employed primitive blocklike figures and terrifying masks to represent woman not only as the source of deadly sexual disease but as the incarnation of dangerous otherness.[4]

If, as William Rubin claims, the formal novelty of the painting resulted from Picasso's need to forge new artistic tools to excavate the deeper strata of a psyche in crisis over relations with lovers[5]—a crisis that amounted to fundamental doubts about masculine power itself—similar conclusions could also be drawn about the aesthetic innovations of Strindberg and Kafka. Even the ostensible Naturalism of a "pre-Expressionist" play like *The Father* is an unconvincing stylistic façade. The Captain's heated paranoia is the expression of psychic rather than "external" truth—a fact Strindberg ultimately recognized formally with his creation of the "dream play," a dramatic vehicle more appropriate to the exploration of the psyche's interior.

These disparate examples of cultural creativity across Europe between 1885 and 1920 are instances of a broader underlying situation. A social and psychological crisis of masculinity helped shape both the thematic concerns and the formal innovations of the early Modernist revolution in the arts. The centrality of gender to an understanding of Modernism has been made evident by feminist scholarship over the past few decades primarily through the analysis of Modernism's patriarchal "construction," or deformation, of female identity, and of Modernist scholarship's omission of women writers and artists.[6] More recently it has been recognized that gender identities are mutually implicating, and that in an era when men still largely dominated cultural production, changing images of the feminine were reactions to disturbances in masculine identity. The terms of this new awareness remain uncertain, however, and the results thus far, while making provocative contributions to our understanding of Modernism, also raise serious questions of substance and method. I want to suggest rather different ideas about the connection between masculine identity issues and Modernist innovation by examining in some detail the interrelationship between the works and lives of three leading early Modernists: Frank Wedekind, Thomas Mann, and Wassily Kandinsky.

I begin with some preliminary considerations about Modernism, masculinity, and method. Though I use the term "Modernism" freely—and there is a vast and constantly growing literature debating its essence and scope—I do not propose to take up much space trying to define it.[7] For my purposes a somewhat standard, perhaps even conservative provisional definition not only suffices but may serve all the better to highlight the radical reorientation demanded in our understanding of even "canonical" High Modernism by attending to the issue of masculine crisis. Modernism was both formal and substantive in its thrust. It involved a break with representation in the broadest sense, the rejection of the idea that art was the portrayal of the objectively "real." Modern artists lost confidence in the real, in the official version of reality available in contemporary social ideology and Realist and Naturalist art, which they found one-sided at best and more often an outright lie. The truth of personal incoherence behind the façade of autonomy and fixed social roles showed that psychic reality could not be adequately contained within the framework of conventional social identity, even where that framework took critical account of social conflict. Beneath the ideological optimism of modern capitalist materialism lay hidden a self ravaged by suppressed longings both instinctual and transcendental, longings contemporary society could neither account for nor satisfy. Modernists reacted to such perceptions by developing further earlier Symbolist ideas of stylistic autonomy and by using radical new forms not only to explore and express these ignored dimensions of subjectivity, but also, so they hoped, to answer its yearnings.[8]

Though such a characterization of Modernism may seem elementary enough to be unobjectionable, it is incompatible with at least two other historically influential interpretations, one older and unfashionable, the other recent and distinctly modish. It is at odds with the idea that Modernism was fundamentally a formal revolution in which the arts reached their supposed maturity by finally coming to concern themselves with their true subject, the elements of their own modalities—the organization of line, color, and space on a flat surface; the orchestration of pure sound divorced from illusions of expressivity; the deployment of language as a pure play of signifiers. It is also incompatible with the contemporary Post-modernist approach that would identify the early Modernist crises of language, conventional norms, and selfhood with Postmodernist claims about the infinite fragmentation of experience, the illusoriness of the subject, and the absence of metaphysical foundations for truth. Early Modernists were concerned both with recovering a true self that was threatened or lost by uncovering its true instinctual and spiritual foundations, and reuniting that self with the world and with truth. What I propose to show is that at least for a number of canonical Modernists, the self that was to be recovered or reconstructed was the truly masculine self, and that this was to be accomplished, most paradoxically, by the masculine appropriation of ideal femininity.

Up until rather recently the "discourse of gender" in literary, cultural, and historical studies was essentially a discourse about women. If traditional scholarship had felt no need to situate masculinity historically, neither on the whole did early feminist scholarship, which even in its evolution from women's history into the study of gender as an ordering principle of culture tended to interpret the gendered character of purportedly universal categories as itself the product of a universal, homogeneous patriarchalism. This situation has changed considerably in the last decade as awareness has grown that the gendered discourses of history were the creation of historically situated men. An increasing number of works have argued that masculinity is as much a social and historical construct as femininity is, and have begun to chart the vicissitudes of "masculinities" over time.[9]

The more specific thesis of a crisis of masculine identity in Europe at the end of the nineteenth century has been almost coterminous with the general trend toward historicizing masculinity and even probably helped to instigate it. The idea seems to have originated in the assessment of the uneasy artistic and literary response to the emergence of the "New Woman" in Europe around the 1870s and '80s.[10] It first became explicit as a rubric of literary analysis,[11] but it has been taken up by recent social and cultural history to the point where it has virtually become a commonplace of periodization in the new history of European masculinity.[12] Nonetheless, the thesis is not without problems. For one thing, there seem to be rather different notions about just exactly what the crisis was. A recent study by Andrew McLaren, for example, argues that masculinity was radically refashioned at the end of the nineteenth century in response to new historical realities. "New scientific norms of male and female sexuality," he claims, "were propounded in the late nineteenth century by sexologists and psychiatrists because social transformations . . . appeared in the eyes of anxious observers to have undermined the explanatory powers of older notions of masculinity and femininity."[13] While George Mosse agrees that historical forces in the late nineteenth century threatened the modern notion of masculinity established in the eighteenth century, he argues that the new sexology, among other developments, successfully shored it up so that it prevailed until the very recent past.[14] A second difficulty is perhaps even more serious. There is real confusion in the literature of masculine crisis about exactly whose crisis it was. This is in large part because the evidence for it comes from very different kinds of sources and has quite mixed probative value.

There is greater consensus on just what idea of masculinity did come into question at the end of the nineteenth century. It was a bourgeois reworking of an older aristocratic ideal that, though importantly modified, was never totally displaced. Up to the mid-eighteenth century, honorific manhood prized the virtues of the medieval knight tempered by those of the early modern aristocratic courtier: courage, honor, military prowess, loyalty, and chivalry along with refinement of manners, cultivation, and liberality of spirit.[15] Two additional attributes are often insufficiently stressed. The role of women in defining manhood was more central than even "chivalry" suggests. Both idealizing women and protecting them were of the essence of true manhood. Women embodied the higher spirituality that men must also aspire to but could not always achieve because of the worldly, often violent nature of their other duties. In the gentler eighteenth century, women were additionally seen as the indispensable agents of the new ideal of "sociability." On the other hand, as the weaker sex unsuited for war and public affairs, women required male protection. The attitude of true men to women was one of mingled respect and contempt, though these terms do not do justice to a situation in which manliness was defined as the opposite of the "womanly" yet depended on success with women as both its badge and reward. The "aristocratic" construction of femininity also points up another neglected dimension of ideal masculinity: the importance of the spiritual in the character of the highest type of man. The ideal knight was originally the ideal Christian knight, his service devoted not only to his lord but to the Lord. Christianity tempered and

5
■

channeled the more brutal manifestations of masculinity by raising them to the level of transcendent duty; service to God was the ultimate criterion and the ultimate sanction of manliness. If the spiritual dimension of masculinity was functionally split off from the warrior and vested both in women generally and in a particular group of men whose special obligation was the care of men's souls, this was only a practical division of labor made necessary by the demands of reality; it did not alter the ultimately religious framework of true manhood.

By the middle of the eighteenth century, middle-class writers were pressing the masculinity claims of the characteristic bourgeois virtues. Aristocratic qualities were not directly challenged as much as they were supplemented, transmuted, or appropriated in a "higher" form. Productivity and economic usefulness were urged against aristocratic idleness, bourgeois domesticity and morality against aristocratic libertinism. It was now too that masculinity came to be identified with an ideal body type derived from the classical ideal, strong and muscular but at the same time sculpted, harmonious, and serene. This ideal masculine body was the necessary counterpart of the ideal bourgeois masculine character; it was both the product and the symbol of self-discipline, moderation, and balance.[16] The new bourgeois masculinity, however, was not fundamentally opposed to the warrior ethos of aristocratic manliness. On the contrary, it was argued that modernity offered a less destructive, more productive arena for the manly initiative, courage, and daring still required in the bloodless tournaments of the marketplace and political public sphere.[17] Bourgeois manliness was thus ideally a happy balance between aggressiveness and discipline; the "authentically manly man," writes Gay, "was at once self-assertive and self-controlled."[18] The value of self-control elevated the bourgeois above both the new urban lower-class male, whose supposed unbridled instinctualism constantly threatened wasteful indulgence or anarchic violence, and the by now virtually mythological dissipated aristocrat. But equal emphasis on the combative initiative of the middle-class businessman and professional was intended to appropriate the aristocratic warrior ethic for the bourgeoisie. Indeed, as historians have noted, prowess in actual physical combat did not disappear from the ideal of masculinity in the so-called "bourgeois" era. The duel was not only still sanctioned but in many places held to be the only truly "manly" way to defend one's honor even in the early twentieth century.[19]

Similarly, the feminine continued to play a central role in the definition of bourgeois masculinity. If anything there was an even sharper polarization between masculinity and femininity during the nineteenth century than previously; Victorian masculinity was almost explicitly defined as the "not-feminine." Partly this was due to increasing industrialization and the resulting separation of home and workplace that had brought about a sharper distinction between the spheres of masculine and feminine activity. But the need to insist on manly rationality and creativity as opposed to feminine emotionalism and passivity was also fueled by continuing middle-class defensiveness about the manliness of the more pacific activities of commerce. The separation of the spheres was not simply a fact of economic life but the intentional result of men's desires to keep women out of the affairs of business in order to preserve male autonomy.[20] And the conceptual polarization of masculinity and femininity was all the more important, though all the more difficult, to preserve because the guardianship of aesthetic cultivation—which was also an indispensable dimension of the lingering aristocratic ideal of manliness—was relegated to woman's sphere. Aesthetic culture was, like religion, the realm of a "higher sphere of spiritual life" that "ennobled" the "lower sphere" of gainful activity.[21] A wife's cultural involvement and attainments were necessary contributions to her husband's social standing and thus his masculinity, yet at the same time culture was a quintessentially feminine pursuit. In part because they were confined to the domestic sphere, women could pursue the spiritual inwardness that made them the humanistic and Romantic "whole beings" that men aspired to be but that their worldly striving made all but impossible to achieve.[22] The result was a deep if not always conscious bourgeois ambivalence about culture.

This was often true for religion as well. Religion still exercised an important role in the creation of true manliness in the nineteenth century. Whether it was in the ideal of self-control, tenderness and compassion toward the weak, fighting the good fight for virtue against sin, or sacrificing oneself heroically for a higher purpose, the morality that underlay bourgeois manliness was often at least nominally Christian.[23] Yet religion was also largely the preserve of women, whose domestic charge included transmitting its values to their children, and religious feelings were often seen as feminine.

It is this "bourgeois" ideal of masculinity, already fraught with inner tensions, that is supposed to have fallen into crisis toward the end of the nineteenth century. The evidence for this crisis is derived from quite disparate sources: late-nineteenth-century economic developments that purportedly altered, and weakened, middle-class male economic roles; political and social challenges to the exclusivity of other male bastions of power, such as politics; attacks by critics on the decline of virility amid the softness of mod-

ern urban commercial and consumer society; "symptomatic" cultural phe-
nomena such as the appearance of modern sexology that ostensibly point to
anxiety about traditional masculinity. None of these sources, however, offers direct testimony of a subjective *sense* of crisis within middle-class European men themselves. What signs there are of such internal feelings come
largely from literature and the arts, and even there it is often unclear how
much is inferred from the work and then explained in circular fashion by
positing the economic and social developments that must have produced
those feelings in its creator.

The idea that the late nineteenth century saw an enormous concentration in finance and industry that transformed the independent entrepreneur
into the salaried manager of the large corporation with baneful consequences for bourgeois power goes back to the Frankfurt School.[24] This
transformation is supposed to have undermined the average bourgeois
male's sense of autonomy and mastery in work and, by making him increasingly dependent, delegitimized the authority he claimed at home over his
wife and children. In a parallel argument, Anneliese Mauge attributes the irrational male panic over the modest inroads of the New Woman into public life that she discerns in French novels and writings on the "woman
question" after 1870 to the growth of large-scale industrialism in France at
the expense of a traditional economy. Individual initiative was increasingly
replaced by "anonymous groups" and machines. The factory and machine
technology strangled the individual creativity of the artisanate; the growth
of large enterprises turned the salaried engineer into a cog in a machine no
different from the unskilled laborer. A contemporary observer argued, she
notes, that the great majority of civil professions had been reduced to simple routines that even the most "mediocre" female brain could learn in a few
years, while another lamented that material life had become ever more nar-
row and limited, devoid of all initiative.[25] But whatever the validity of these
economic analyses—and few are derived from detailed empirical historical
investigation—their actual impact on the consciousness of middle-class
businessmen and professionals is completely inferential. Mauge offers a list
of fictional characters—business owners, merchants, professionals—who
in keeping with her analysis of the decline of a sense of masculine agency
pride themselves not on their vocational prowess but on their acceptance of
the constraints of reality. But they are of course all literary creations, and
they offer the testimony not of their actual social models but of their literary creators.

We have also become familiar in the last two decades with the idea that
the rise of large-scale social and political movements on the right and on
the left challenged—and, in at least one dramatic case, overthrew—the

political power of the well-to-do middle class in Europe. The age of mass politics that followed the extension of the franchise in Europe in the fifteen years after 1870 ended the upper-class monopoly of politics and with it the putative political confidence of the middle class. In his widely acclaimed *Fin-de-Siècle Vienna,* Carl Schorske argues that this development caused middle-class writers and intellectuals to turn away from the hope of exercising power in the public sphere and turn anxiously instead to an exploration of the psychic interior and its conflicts. While Schorske's work does not deal explicitly with a crisis of masculinity, his analysis would seem to have obvious implications for the male identities of his figures, implications that have more recently been explored by others.[26] Once again, however, the unquestionable historical facts of the rise of mass political power on the left and right and its attack on bourgeois liberalism say nothing directly about their impact on the male identities of the bulk of middle-class men.

There is at least one body of evidence that does seem to focus explicitly on a crisis of masculinity in the late nineteenth century. The proponents of the new nationalism and imperialism in various European countries had taken up the warrior ideal of manliness with renewed vigor in the decades after the unification of Germany and Italy, because in the uneasy jockeying for power and security that ensued, the nation obviously required the virtues of the fighter to protect or extend it.[27] Observers concerned with the preservation and promotion of these virtues became increasingly anxious about the softening of masculinity in the new urban world of consumption and luxury, or the undermining of the physical fitness of the lower classes who manned the armies of workers in the unhealthy conditions of its factories.[28] The poor performance of British soldiers against the Boer farmer militias inspired an outburst of fear about the loss of virile strength in modern civilization and such remedies for it as the creation of the Boy Scout movement. Fear of depopulation in France as birth rates declined in absolute terms or fell below those of national adversaries also raised the specter for some of a decline of masculinity. But these expressions of fear about modernity's impact on manliness were warnings from the outside, alarms raised by observers worried about national strength, not expressions of a sense of anxiety within the observers about their own sense of masculinity. The crisis of virility they saw was always somebody else's.

More persuasive if indirect evidence for a widespread sense of internal anxiety about masculinity is to be found in the systematic efforts to conceptually split off the "unmanly" behavior of some men—and the "unwomanly" behavior of some women—through the scientific catego-

9

rization of pathology in the later nineteenth century. The rise, and even more the popularity, of "sexology"—the classification of types of sexual deviancy epitomized by Krafft-Ebing's *Psychopathia Sexualis*—suggests at the very least that a great deal of attention was being paid to sexual "aberration" and malfunction. Contemporary concern about "degeneracy"—the supposed weakening of the physical and mental constitution of men because of the rapid pace of modern life and its ever greater demands on human energy—led both to the psychiatric classification of such mental diseases as "neurasthenia" and to a typology of mental illness implying a radical difference between the pathological and the normal.[29] The insistence of the psychiatrists Charcot and Freud that hysteria was a male as well as a female disorder caused a near-hysterical reaction on the part of many psychiatrists. Perhaps the most obvious sign of masculine anxiety in this regard was the designation of homosexuals as a "third sex," a species of effeminate male that was not truly masculine but constituted a distinct gender.[30]

Exactly how these developments actually expressed general male anxiety about masculinity, however, is not made wholly clear in the literature. Economic and ideological modernization in the later nineteenth century unquestionably made homosexuality more socially and politically prominent by promoting the growth of homosexual subcultures in the sheltering pluralism and anonymity of large cities and by implicitly supporting the assertion of homosexual rights to self-expression without criminal penalty. A further psychological hypothesis is needed to explain why, however, greater homosexual visibility was a threat to the masculinity of heterosexual males and how this threat lay behind the medical pathologizing of homosexuality: heterosexual men feared their own effeminacy and projected it onto the homosexual as other, thus expelling it from themselves. The same would be true for the argument that masculine anxiety lay behind the new psychiatric classification of mental illness. While such explanations are psychologically plausible, based on clinical understanding of how psychic defenses function for individuals, they remain at best suggestive hypotheses in the absence of corroborating evidence from the testimony, direct or indirect, of the authors and consumers of sexology.

Undoubtedly the most telling of the apparent cultural symptoms of anxiety about threats to masculinity is the male reaction to women's emancipation movements in the late nineteenth century. The vast majority of men opposed these movements, and there is plenty of evidence showing that many men were terrified by them far out of proportion to their size or the threat they realistically posed to male prerogatives in education, politics, or the arts.[31] The opposition ranged from politicians to poets. One

10
■

conservative Reichstag deputy unwittingly acknowledged the truth of Strindberg's perception about women's role in creating masculinity when he used the argument that women's greatest glory was in raising competent men to oppose a Social Democratic bill allowing women to join political organizations.[32] Most contemporary arguments against rights for women were far less flattering. Otto Weininger's notorious *Sex and Character* was only the most extreme example of the arguments used to denigrate women that were unleashed by fears of contemporary feminism. Characterizing maleness as "being" itself, the totality of human qualities, and femininity correspondingly as nothingness, Weininger openly avowed that the motive behind his analysis was to put a stop to the unnatural claims of women to equality with men put forward by the female emancipation movement.[33] But it was also Weininger who exposed the connection between opposition to women's equality and anxiety about masculinity with the contradictory claim—not unique to him during the period—that all human beings were bisexual. The very structure of *Sex and Character* in fact suggests that the extremist polarization of masculinity and femininity in the second part of his book was a masculine protest against his acknowledgment of the partial femininity of all men in the much shorter first section. Weininger's homosexuality does not lessen the representative significance of his book. While it offers uniquely powerful evidence for a subjective connection between homosexuality, femininity, and fear for one's masculinity, all across Europe *Sex and Character* was enormously popular with heterosexual men, who found Weininger's radical differentiation of the sexes quite compelling.

11

If they did, it was because the contemporary sense of masculinity depended so heavily on its opposition to femininity. Men could be "men" only if women remained "women," and the actual power of the women's movement mattered less than what it betokened for the future. If women could be as educated, as economically productive, as politically active as men, there was no real difference between masculinity and femininity other than reproductive roles; it thus made sense to defend traditional masculinity by trying to reduce femininity to nothing but that role and its attendant requirements. Already threatened by loss of autonomy and power with the growth of the large-scale corporation, men, it has been argued, turned for compensation to the family, where the law itself might, as in France, give power explicitly to the husband and father.[34] But the changing role of women made the family a weak support for traditional masculinity. "As for the erosion of the bourgeois family, not least by the emancipation of its female members," Eric Hobsbawm argues, "how could it fail to undermine the self-definition of a class which rested so largely on its maintenance . . . a class for which respectability equated with 'morality' and which depended so crucially on the perceived conduct of its women?"[35] "Its women" could only mean of course that the self-definition of the class was its masculine self-definition.

Once again, however, for all its plausibility, Hobsbawm's language is the language of surmise. This is hardly surprising. The vast majority of men were not given to self-reflection on their masculinity, nor in a position to leave written records of it if they were; the age of polling, not to speak of general male self-consciousness about the issue of masculinity, was still far off. And though wholly understandable, it is an unfortunate state of affairs for the thesis of a general crisis of masculinity at the turn of the century. Subjective evidence for it is the weakest type available, though it would seem to be logically the most important, for a crisis of identity is by its very definition a crisis of subjective consciousness. It is partly for this reason that works like Weininger's, though not expressly autobiographical, take on additional significance. The fact is that not only the subjective but much of the "objective" evidence of a crisis of masculinity that we have is from or about writers and artists, whose occupations entail some degree of self-consciousness and self-observation as well as the sustained observation of others. The fin de siècle notion of the "demonic woman" or "femme fatale," for example, rests almost completely on her depiction in literature, painting, and opera in the works of Wilde, Beardsley, Strindberg, Klimt, Wedekind, and Strauss, to name some of the better-known purveyors.[36]

Such evidence for masculine anxiety is more direct, but it is also evidence about a special case. It is difficult to know how representative artists were of the middle class as a whole, not only because of the problems of obtaining evidence about masculine identity from social history, but because the masculinity issues of artists were arguably unique. The male artist qua artist felt increasingly "unmanned" in the face of the rise of new economic power as well as the continued dominance of the older warrior ideals. Not only had he become dependent on the market during the nineteenth century, a shift that underlined and intensified his chronic dependency because of the impersonality and remoteness of the marketplace in comparison with aristocratic or clerical patronage; not only did he have to make his way in a materialistic civilization whose "philistine" emphasis on utilitarian productivity seemed to make it at best indifferent to aesthetic values—the artist's very enterprise allied him with "feminine" values because the realms of the emotional and the aesthetic were delegated, or relegated, to the feminine sphere within the bourgeois division of labor. If the business and professional middle class felt unease about the manliness of its commercial pursuits, this was a fortiori true of the artist, who could not defend the virility of his vocation with an ideology of material usefulness, wealth production, or the combative fortitude these demanded. The artist had to fight for masculine recognition itself, and on two fronts: alongside his fellow bourgeois, for recognition of their mutual claim to manliness against the proponents of the warrior ethic; and against him, for recognition of the idea that artistic creativity was genuine productivity in a materialist culture.

Significantly, the few studies that look at a crisis of masculinity among Modernist artists focus on their highly ambivalent identification with femininity. In his work on Viennese Modernism, Jacques Le Rider argues that it was the attraction-repulsion of Viennese artists and intellectuals to the femininity within themselves, a part of all males through early identification with their mothers, that inspired a large part of the literature, art, and cultural criticism of the turn of the century. The cause of the heightened attraction of internalized femininity lay in the stresses of modernization, which these writers experienced and interpreted as a "too-exclusive affirmation of the values connected with the masculine element."[37] The price of the scientific and technical rationality that had given modern men "mastery over the object" was that it also pulled them away from a sense of "being," of harmony with the whole. Since men identified the sense of being with femininity, where it is supposedly self-evident, the artist's identity crisis manifested itself as "a crisis of the masculine element and nostalgia for the 'lost' feminine element—lost as a paradise is lost."[38] But as this very "cult of the feminine" was antipathetic to their masculinity, they reacted with a "'masculine' protest against the femininity that they discovered in themselves, or against the feminization of modern culture."[39]

Rita Felski argues along similar lines in *The Gender of Modernity*. Reacting against the characterization of nineteenth-century modernity as "masculine" by both contemporary and present-day observers, she points out that fin de siècle writers like Oscar Wilde identified with a vision of aestheticized, feminized modernity as an alternative to the "prevailing forces of positivism, progress ideology and the sovereignty of the reality principle. . . ."[40] Femininity had been associated in the modernizing narrative with a premodern ideal of plenitude, harmony, and oneness that tragically but necessarily had to be disrupted for the development of individuation, mastery of the world, and progress. In reaction, nostalgia for the "redemptive maternal body" was a "recurring and guiding theme" in the self-constitution of those artists protesting against modernity.[41] Wilde and others subverted modern bourgeois masculinity by identifying with the feminine, but their appropriation of femininity demanded at the same time

13
•

that it be reconceptualized, lest it completely subvert their own masculinity as well. For the male aesthete, therefore, "proper" femininity was no longer to be identified with vulgar nature and the tyranny of the body, to which women were biologically subjected. In aestheticist texts, natural beauty became artifice and spontaneous emotion became conscious display. In a reversal of the conventional sense of modernity and femininity, the "aesthete's performance of femininity is depicted as authentically modern precisely because of its self-conscious transcendence of the constraints of corporeality."[42] When men *perform* the feminine, it is masculine.

These provocative suggestions about the Modernist's conflicted appropriation of femininity open up large new possibilities for understanding both the inner contours of the Modernist's masculine crisis and certain features of Modernist texts. They are simultaneously, however, too particular and too general. Le Rider, for example, argues that the Viennese crisis of masculine identity was accompanied by, was in fact "closely, perhaps indissolubly linked with," a crisis of Jewish identity at the end of a century of emancipation.[43] But whatever the connection between the two—the structure of the argument seems to imply a causal relationship that Le Rider never actually claims—such a link between masculine and Jewish identity crises is too restrictive even for Vienna. It undoubtedly fits Otto Weininger, the subject of Le Rider's previous study, in whose book the relationship between antifeminism and self-hating anti-Semitism is explicit, and the hypothesis is buttressed by the fact that so many of the major figures of the Viennese fin de siècle were Jews or of Jewish origin. But problematic masculinity played a crucial role in stimulating the painting of the Viennese artists Gustav Klimt and Egon Schiele, neither of whom was Jewish.[44] Nor are any of the figures in the present study. Whatever role membership in a minority group singled out by the majority culture for hatred and exclusion may have played in inducing a sense of "feminine" weakness and passivity in certain writers, it could not have been a necessary cause of masculine self-doubt among Modernists throughout Europe. Similarly, Felski limits her discussion of Modernist "feminization" to a few fin de siècle aestheticists, none of them conventionally considered High Modernists, and acknowledges that this small group was "by no means representative of writers as a whole, let alone of the broader cultivated public."[45] The self-consciously flamboyant preoccupation of aestheticism with dress, cosmetics, display, and emotion seems to lend itself to a feminizing interpretation in ways that other Modernist concerns do not immediately suggest. But Le Rider's work demonstrates that the cultural crisis of masculinity was not confined to fin de siècle aestheticism narrowly defined.

If these discussions are too limited in their scope, they also suffer from overreliance on theoretical frameworks at a very high level of abstraction. Le Rider draws on the psychoanalytic object relations theory of D. W. Winnicott for his fundamental conception of identity, according to which the "feeling of self" must rest on "the feeling of being" that is always identified with the mother.[46] He relies further on highly schematic Adlerian version of Freud for his understanding of the two different possible outcomes of the conflicted feminine identification he sees in his writers. "In the first case the excessive authority of the father figure would trigger an attempt to replace him with a feminine object, a mother figure," he suggests, in what he openly offers as hypothesis; "this gives us Schreber and . . . Otto Gross. The 'law of the mother' (matriarchy) would then substitute, in a more or less illusory way, for 'the law of the father.' In the second case, the loss of the father figure would send the ego back to its (feminine) object and trigger a 'masculine protest,' a desire to 'save the father,' defend him . . . against threats which most likely come from the female. This second case would be Otto Weininger."[47] Felski draws on sociological rather than psychological theory, but the line of argumentation is very similar. The terms of her analysis are determined by Georg Simmel's argument that modernity, which demanded individuation and aggressive energy, was masculine, while the feminine represented a premodern ideal of non-individuated plenitude. In arguing that some Modernists identified with rather than repudiated the feminine, she retains Simmel's characterization of femininity.

Both Le Rider's and Felski's notion of the feminine seem to a great extent a priori rather than derived from detailed readings of Modernist texts and lives. In the case of Le Rider's explicitly psychoanalytic hypotheses, the problem is even more obvious because the concepts he employs seem to refer by their very nature to the writer's subjectivity, though little biographical information is given to underpin them. The hypotheses thus hover uncertainly between implied psychodynamic processes within authors and psychoanalytic readings of characteristics of their texts, attempting to catch both with their roots deeply in neither.

Nevertheless a psychobiographical approach is not only legitimate; it is necessary if one is to speak plausibly of a "crisis of masculinity" in Modernism. This is obvious if the argument is meant, as it seems to be, causally. Without evidence of a subjective sense of masculinity endangered, the claim that certain features of Modernist works are the result of a crisis of masculine identity is circular and vacuous. But even if the concept refers only descriptively to what is going on in the works, knowledge of the artist's life is crucial for their most complete understanding. It is of course hard to imagine an artistic theme as fraught as masculinity and femininity not having resonance in the life of the artist. But this "resonance" is more than an empirical likelihood. The artist's life is not an entity apart from his work, an organic, somehow unfashioned process. It is a construction shaped by formal and historical values, as much "art" as art is an aesthetic and thematized reworking of life. Biography is not the underlying reality to which a work of art ultimately "refers," like the roman à clef supposedly deciphered when the real-life models for its characters are discovered. It is a parallel text, governed by the same issues that govern the work however much its outcome may differ, for it is often a text in counterpoint to the life. Life and work mutually inform one another, each often supplying the hidden or suppressed text of the other; each is therefore an indispensable source for interpreting the other. This is a fortiori true for Modernism, one of whose central concerns was, after all, the exploration of hitherto ignored or suppressed subjectivity.

16

The figures in this study, Wedekind, Mann, and Kandinsky, explicitly invited readers and viewers, both in their artistic works and in their theoretical writings, to construe their subjectivity as a crucial part of the context of their art. For that same reason, they also felt the urgent need to conceal the most intimate personal details of their lives. But just the fact that they were bent on personal concealment in their work makes recourse to their lives even more useful to its understanding. Kandinsky's autobiographical "Reminiscences" explicitly tells us that the artistic quest that resulted in his discovery of abstraction was a struggle with omnipotent, feminine nature for an independent creative identity. But without the evidence of his intimate letters to his lover, we would not know how the personal, erotic dimension of his conflict with the feminine concretely shaped his development as an artist as well as a man, providing a key both to his stylistic evolution and to individual paintings. The publication of Mann's diaries and notebooks has already radically revised our estimation of the significance of homosexuality for his fiction, just as the appearance of Wedekind's diaries has illuminated the deeper structure of the ambivalence toward women evident in his plays, which has posed such problems of interpretation for his work.

The biographical approach cannot mean reduction of the life to purely intrapsychic or intrafamilial dynamics because social, political, religious, and cultural factors condition family and individual identity. Wedekind's conflict with his father and intense attachment/identification with his mother were not simply aspects of a "timeless" or even abstractly "bourgeois" oedipal struggle, but one conditioned by the peculiar contradictions of late-nineteenth-century German liberalism, embodied in the marital and generational tensions within the Wedekind family. Kandinsky's most intimate feelings about love show clear marks of his cultural situation as a member of the Russian intelligentsia. But by the same token, the broader cultural forces can only be speculative factors in relation to the work they purport to explain whose causal connection misses a crucial link unless we can show they were actually lived, and mediated, by individual artists, and how they shaped their creative concerns.

In the cases of the three figures in this study, detailed examination of the interrelationships of work and life substantiates the idea that the artists' crises of masculinity involved their relation to femininity. But for none of them did femininity represent the nostalgic ideal of pre-individuated "being," even where it was in some way identified with the maternal. Very much the opposite was the case, especially for Wedekind and Kandinsky—Mann's case is somewhat more complex. It was precisely their sense that "the feminine" embodied both autonomous creative power and connection with the whole of being, the union of the best of modernity with the best of premodernity, that drew them to it. Contrary to everything that might have been expected in view of the prevailing stereotypes of femininity, these artists implicitly and even explicitly identified the ideal feminine with Nietzsche's *Übermensch,* the human being of the future. Free from transcendental dependency, the "ideal feminine" lived in her body, legislated her own values, and created her own forms, as Zarathustra had preached. The attraction of these artists to the feminine in this sense was not a nostalgic yearning for a regressive return to undifferentiated fusion, a search for ultimate security that meant dissolution of the self, but a quest for a restoration of their own creativity through an appropriation of the feminine. At the same time, however, the feminine also represented the quite un-Nietzschean, indeed anti-Nietzschean idea of totality; to appropriate it would mean not just human self-sufficiency, but godlike wholeness.

17
■

The sense of masculine vulnerability and weakness that drove the artists' quest for a restoration of masculine power stemmed from a combination of personal and social factors, not the least important of which was the corrosive doubt they all felt about the power and value of art itself. Inevitably, however, their idealization of the feminine as the way to rejuvenation exacerbated their sense of masculine vulnerability and led to inescapable ambivalence toward femininity. They needed to assimilate it in order to regain masculine and creative power, but they were afraid of being consumed by the object of their desire and losing not only their autonomy but their very selves. Their ambivalence was heightened by the contradictory but intelligible circumstance that the artists also retained the prevailing image of femininity as weak, passive, and dependent. This was a partly a defense against their own idealization of the feminine, but it backfired to the extent that appropriating the feminine also implicated them in all the traditional stigmas of weakness and passivity, the very dilemma they were trying to escape. Their aesthetic enterprises can be seen as a series of strategies for refashioning masculinity by incorporating the feminine while navigating the ambivalence that a venture so conceived necessarily produced. It can easily be argued that they did not reconcile the inherent contradictions of that venture either logically or existentially. Aesthetic success, however, depends neither on logical nor psychological consistency. Their efforts produced an aesthetic revolution.

The "nominalist" method I pursue in this book dictates that generalizations can only follow detailed individual analyses, and even then they must be subject to qualification and exception. Other than my initial sense that all three figures in this study gave some evidence of a crisis of masculine identity, I did not choose them because I knew or even suspected in advance that their crises were similar, or that they bore a similar relationship to their art. In fact, as will become abundantly evident, the differences are as striking and as important as any similarities. I chose the three because they represented a spectrum of the arts—drama, fiction, and painting—and because geographically and culturally they constituted a community of difference within unity. All three figures lived for a significant part of the time covered in this study in Munich, though none of them originated from there; Wedekind was born in Hanover and grew up in Switzerland, Mann moved from Lübeck to Munich after he finished gymnasium, and the Russian Kandinsky came to Munich from Moscow at age thirty. Though a significant part of their prewar work—only Wedekind did not survive the war— was done in Munich, much of it was also done elsewhere. They were and considered themselves to be both Müncheners and cosmopolitans. Some of their work is importantly related to Munich, with which all three had a love-hate relationship, but they were not "local artists." Despite the existence of a well-defined artistic community and cultural infrastructure in Munich,[48] they do not comprise even the kind of relatively settled and inbred community we associate with Viennese Modernism, though Viennese homogeneity and parochialism can be exaggerated. Wedekind and Mann were closely acquainted with one another, and more or less on good terms, except for the brief period that Mann spent on the Munich censorship board; neither of them knew Kandinsky, so far as I have been able to ascertain. They were members of a European community of artists who like many others traveled a good deal both within Germany and across Europe, living in different locations for months at a time. As a group, then, the three offer the opportunity to take account of the common Munich context yet at the same time to see their masculine dilemmas as representative of a wider cultural situation, with implications for Modernism across the whole of Europe.

Frank Wedekind and the Femininity of Freedom

Gerhart H[auptmann] thinks that I am not altogether deficient in love, he considers me capable of self-sacrifice, etc. That I readily grant him, but for me such feelings denote weakness rather than strength.
        —Frank Wedekind, *Diary of an Erotic Life*

Why should anyone trust a man who for the price of a ticket serves up to the whole world what he ought to fight out with himself at home?
        —Frank Wedekind, *Censorship*

A people that is ripe for Wedekind is lost.
        —Thomas Mann, *Notebooks*

Frank Wedekind's dramatic Modernism is not just a matter of literary interpretation after the fact. The writer himself announced it in a contemporary polemic, appropriately enough a theatrical encounter with the iconic figure of nineteenth-century Naturalism in the German drama. Wedekind had a deeply personal reason to be enraged with Gerhart Hauptmann. In a moment of anguish he had confided to Hauptmann the story of the bitter confrontation with his father over his future vocation in which he had hit his father in the face, only to see the event appear virtually undisguised in a Hauptmann play shortly afterward. But Wedekind's brilliant revenge lampooning of Hauptmann in his own play *The Young World* (*Die junge Welt*, 1889) went well beyond personal grievance. It was also intended as an aesthetic manifesto. In the play, the Hauptmann figure Meier almost destroys his marriage by living it with notebook in hand, taking down everything his wife says and does, including her complaints that he takes down everything she says and does. One of the play's spokesmen for Wedekind successfully effects a (no doubt temporary) marital reconciliation, at the cost to Meier of a lecture on the right way to write. "Your realism has caused you to forget literature [*Poesie*]," Karl tells him. "The true writer [*Poet*] doesn't write by spying on people but by enjoying them. . . . True literature has never yet come between lovers. The writer after all writes only because he lives, because he loves, because he enjoys his existence."[1] That the shaft aimed at Hauptmann was not just occasional is attested by another jibe in the same spirit directed some years before at the avatar of Naturalism in the novel, Émile Zola. In his 1886 essay on wit, Wedekind had remarked in passing—not quite on topic but not wholly irrelevantly—"Zola and the Realists date the beginning of literature from Zola's appearance; other authorities assert that it is precisely at that point that it ceases to be literature."[2]

These attacks do more than display Wedekind's satiric wit, though his wit, not to be underestimated as mere entertainment, is one of the essential features of his Modernism. They propose, or at least intimate, an aesthetic philosophy. But the alternative to Realism implied in *The Young World,* the aesthetic of enjoyment, can't be taken at face value. Wedekind's relationship to "enjoyment" was far more tortured than Karl's words imply, and its complexity affected the style and the substance of all his work, not excluding the play in which the exhortation to enjoyment appears. A more accurate approach to his aesthetic is suggested by an offbeat metaphor quite characteristic of Wedekind's style. In an early essay "Thoughts on the Circus," he did a little riff on a flirtation between a circus trick rider and a philosopher. The trick rider was Wedekind's muse, the ideal embodiment of the intrepid instinctual life; the philosopher represented the intellect that could recognize, appreciate, and articulate the ethic of instinctual action. "Out of such an unheard of misalliance," Wedekind concluded, teasing himself about his own literary productions, "emerge deformed changelings from which every decent historian of literature turns away with justified horror."[3]

More accurately than he could know in 1887, he was predicting the judgment of his "misbegotten" dramas by many a contemporary critic, let alone the bureaucratic guardians of official culture who would so frequently censor his works. Informed by serious ideas, yet displaying the lightness, the breathtaking daring, the flexibility, and not least the coquetry and sensuality of the trick rider, Wedekind's dramas defied the rules of Realism and the well-made play in ways most of his contemporaries were not ready for. The main elements of his style have been well catalogued by later critics: the "*Aneinander-Vorbeireden*" style of dialogue, in which characters talk past, rather than with, one another; speeches with little resemblance to actual spoken language; the genre-bending mixture of deeply tragic scenes with moments of hilarious farce; the "grotesque montage" of his plot structures, which renounce any attempt at unity, verisimilitude, or closure.[4] But the "misalliance" of Wedekind's flirtation metaphor is more than the incompatibility of high seriousness and circus, instinct and reason. It is neither accidental nor inconsequential that these abstract polarities are figured in the metaphor as male and female. The fundamental misalliance to which Wedekind implicitly attributes his dramatic progeny is the misalliance of man and woman, more exactly for the writer, of male author and feminine muse. His metaphor thus goes to the heart not only of the Modernist style of his plays but to their thematic concerns. The dissonant mixture of high and low, logos and eros, classic drama and vaudeville slapstick reflects the unreconciled conflict of the author with the feminine and with his own masculinity.

It has always been recognized that Wedekind's theater is riven by deep contradiction. Early works like the unfinished fragment *Elin's Awakening* (*Elins Erweckung,* 1887) and Wedekind's first great play *Spring's Awakening* (*Frühlings Erwachen,* 1891) seem to celebrate the naturalness of sensuality and the liberation of instinct in the teeth of a repressive traditional society—the very titles suggest a manifesto. *Elin's Awakening* introduced as the symbol of liberation a figure calculated to rub bourgeois ethical sensibility raw, the wholesome prostitute who enjoys her work. She would achieve her apotheosis a few years later in *The Solar Spectrum* (*Das Sonnenspektrum,* 1893–94), which presented prostitution as an escape from prudery and hypocrisy to a happier life. (The "spectrum" refers to the array of young prostitutes, dressed attractively in every color of the rainbow, cheerfully awaiting the client's choice.) On the other hand, *Death and the Devil* (*Tod und Teufel,* 1905) literally turns on the sudden realization of its two main characters that the female desire for sexual gratification is nothing other than masochism, self-willed enslavement to physical and psychological suffering. More than a decade separates the first version of *The Solar Spectrum* from *Death and the Devil,* but there was no real change in Wedekind's view of sexuality over that time; free sensuality and sadomasochism are simultaneously present in his work from the very beginning. As the young adolescent Wendla in *Spring's Awakening* struggles with her attraction to her school friend Melchior, utterly ignorant of its sexual nature, her first request of him is that he beat her. When he doesn't hit her hard enough, she goads him on until he finally complies with a savagery that horrifies him.

The other contradiction in Wedekind's work, until recently less frequently noted, is between vital, healthy female sensuality and the destructive femme fatale. The first was long overshadowed by the figure of Lulu in his dramas *Earth Spirit* (*Erdgeist*, 1895) and *Pandora's Box* (*Die Büchse der Pandora*, 1902). For decades Lulu was typed by the words of the ringmaster who introduces her as a snake in the prologue to *Earth Spirit* that Wedekind added to the second edition of 1903: "She was created to stir up great disaster / To entice, to seduce, to poison / To murder, with no one being the wiser."[5] The recent publication and staging of the original manuscript from which the two published plays were carved out, *Pandora's Box: A Monstertragedy* (*Die Büchse der Pandora: Eine Monstretragödie*, 1894, 1989) have made the contradiction impossible to ignore because the Lulu of the original play appears to be rather less demonic than her later incarnation. The differences between the two versions, however, can be overstated.[6] Like the contradiction between "healthy" natural sexuality and sadomasochism, that between feminine free sensuality and the feminine desire to dominate is present from the very beginning. It is an essential key to Wedekind's work. For while his project undoubtedly aimed at a kind of liberation, his image of liberation was embodied in woman, a problematic circumstance bound to create the most profound ambivalence toward women. That circumstance also derived from a crisis of masculine identity that Wedekind felt deeply within himself and perceived in various segments of the society around him.

Trick Riders and Tightrope Walkers

> *Elasticity! . . . I fell from the rope tower three times, I was married seven times, I was fatally in love seven times seventy times. There isn't a bone in my body I haven't broken. But show me the situation I can't master!*
>
> —Frank Wedekind, *Franz Schwigerling, or, The Love Potion*

Because so much emphasis has been placed on Wedekind's preoccupation with sexual expression, the larger idea of freedom he puts forward in his early essay "Thoughts on the Circus" needs close attention. There are actually two somewhat different conceptions of freedom presented there. The first is exemplified by the circus trick rider ostensibly of either sex. "What can be thought more beautiful, more sublime," Wedekind claimed, "than an Arabian ridden by a woman and a Trakehner ridden by a man?"[7] But the initial reference to male and female riders and the description that follows of the two breeds of horses identified with femininity and masculinity prove deceptive. The essay goes on to describe only the female rider. Both the choice and the omission are significant.

The contrast between the Arabian and the Trakehner offers an important but by itself misleading insight into Wedekind's gender ideals:

> In the Arabian, absolutely everything is grace, elegance, charm and elasticity. The wonderful balance of the individual parts determines the total impression of the body, the unified yet free figure. The full but supple rump atop the delicate, yet sinewy and powerful limbs, the cool little head with its great glowing eyes, the slim, gently-bowed neck under the thin mane fluttering in the wind, the tail upraised and carried with pride—all this unites into a picture full of nobility and beauty, for which there is no equal in the whole world of animals. . . . The Trakehner on the other hand presents an appearance of decidedly more masculine character. The consciousness of strength and of pride reined in only with strenuous effort confronts us in his very essence. The eyes flash with fire, the nostrils are wide open. The strongly arched neck with its thick mane carries an expressive head that thrusts itself up from a deep chest. The straight, somewhat short body, the longish cruppers, the muscular, not too high masses of the limbs indicate speed and stamina. His thoroughly artful gait and poses allow one to conclude that he has a high degree of intelligence.[8]

The details Wedekind described constitute, for all the idiosyncratic energy of his descriptions, fairly conventional gender stereotypes, and the prevailing norms would seem to imply the superiority of the male attributes. Other clues in the essay, however, point to the very opposite.

The "female" Arabian horse is characterized not only by charm and grace but also by "elasticity," the most important of all character traits for Wedekind. Elasticity is the distinguishing principle of the circus ring, but its greater significance is metaphorical: it stands for a cultural ideal. It is "the plastic-allegorical representation of a form of life wisdom, exactly the one we children of the nineteenth century need the most, because for us the old, comfortable pilgrimage . . . has given way to a restless, agitated steeplechase over endless obstacles and pitfalls." Wedekind elaborated on the idea with the example of a circus gymnast's leap, the play version of the driven steeplechase of everyday life: "A bold, swift, decisive take-off at the favorable moment of excitement; a light, laughing jump; and when the foot touches the ground, a pleasing bending of the knee, so that one doesn't fall on one's nose; wonderful virtuosity in small things, to achieve effects that will astound the world—are those not timely mottoes?"[9] This idea is retrospectively illuminated by the prescription for freedom that Günter Grass in *The Tin Drum* put into the mouth of another entertainer in much more tyrannical circumstances, the "musical clown" Bebra, leader of a theater troupe entertaining German soldiers during World War II: "We must perform and run the show. If we don't,

25

others will run us." The only way the individual—the artist—can prevent himself from being overwhelmed by society and its self-destructive ideologies is to play at what the world takes seriously and entertain it with one's dazzling skill at the game. And in Wedekind's description of trick riding, elasticity is an attribute not only of the female Arabian horse, but also of its female rider. "These measured, rounded movements," he continued, "the flexible, swinging gait, the coquettish planting of the feet, whose joints move with unbelievable elasticity—none other than the skilled rider [*Reiterin*], who, with her attractive smile holds the rein with delicate fingers more gracious than imperious, more permissive than commanding, none other will seem to be able to do justice to such an animal in all its uniqueness."[10]

Clearly there is more to the aesthetic of elasticity than sensuality; it is a prescription for living freely, energetically, and daringly, yet with a concern for grace and harmony of spirit as well as body. Wedekind made the ideal of mind-body unity explicit in his description of the movements of his other exemplary female circus artist, the tightrope walker. "The step with which the artist [*Künstlerin*] brings her exercise to a close, the choice of her poses and the way she shapes each one into a self-contained genre-painting, the precision of her rounded movements, all of this is able to make us momentarily forget the boundaries between the bodily and the spiritual."[11] For Wedekind, the body was not just flesh and physical susceptibility; the human desire for wholeness expressed itself physically as well as psychologically in the urge for aesthetic form in bodily movement. The quest for the physical embodiment of spiritual transcendence was, according to Wedekind, the very principle of ancient dance, which in the past had inspired the Israelites with courage through their wanderings in the desert and helped the Greeks honor their gods at their most solemn festivals. But modern dance had lost its poetic-religious soul—what Wedekind expressly called its "feminine essence"—under the influence of contemporary Realism. Emphasizing acrobatics and athleticism over fluid form, it tried to impress with a machinelike ensemble precision that rather resembled a Prussian military drill.[12] As dance evolved into the masculine opposite of its original spirit, the circus tightrope walker had taken over the dancer's former role of enacting the unity of body and spirit.

The second conception of freedom in "Thoughts on the Circus" was also represented for Wedekind by the tightrope walker. To bring out her peculiar virtue, Wedekind compared the risks she undertook with those of the trapeze artist. The trapeze artist is supported by ropes attached to a pole anchored in the ground, the tightrope walker by nothing but her own skill. The trapeze artist loses her balance only if the ropes tear, while the tightrope walker "falls with remorseless inevitability the first second she forgets herself."[13] The high point of the tightrope walker's skill was thus reached when she moved from the taut high wire of the circus ring to the much slacker rope used to cross the Niagara gorge. "The artist no longer possesses any firm point of support," Wedekind pointed out in another essay, "as a result of which she has to look for it inside herself. Her balancing act thus becomes to an extent a double one. Through the movement of her upper body she holds her own weight in equilibrium, while through the hardly noticeable movements of her foot she controls the tightrope which will give way with the slightest loss of balance."[14]

In his polemical ardor, Wedekind did not scruple at interpreting his own metaphors. All human beings are idealists, but there are two quite different kinds. The first project their ideals into the heavens, so that they feel themselves, like the trapeze artist, sustained by supports outside and above them. They are so convinced of the absolute objectivity of their ideals that they feel superior to the rest of humanity, though if their beliefs collapse under a blow of fate, neither doctor nor psychiatrist can help them. The second kind are the practical idealists who construct an image of relative wholeness out of whatever life circumstances they find themselves in, and then strive energetically to attain it. This ethical approach clearly derived from two distinct philosophical traditions, the pragmatic and the Nietzschean. "Tightrope ethics" are concrete and practical, rather than abstract, rooted in the actual life conditions of human beings; they do not demand the unnatural or the humanly impossible. They are also self-consciously created by those who live them. Tightrope ethicists take responsibility for their own choices, knowing that there can never be an external guarantee of their rightness and that there is therefore always a danger of plummeting to disaster. But the compensation for the risk is a sense of mastery and utter self-sufficiency that command the awed respect of those too terrified to undertake it themselves.

Though the two ethical approaches were philosophically derived, the choice between them seemed more determined for Wedekind the writer not by their relative philosophical merits but by criteria of aesthetics and historical appropriateness. "We have long possessed a comparative anatomy, a comparative linguistics and science of law," he wrote, "is it not time to broach a comparative aesthetics? Abstract-sublime and real-practical idealism! Stable and labile equilibrium! It will hardly be in doubt which of these two ways of leading one's life is to be preferred in the age of steam and electricity."[15] If the reference to "the age of steam and electricity" seems a little like ad-speak—Wedekind spent seven months after the rupture with his father supporting himself as director of advertising for the Swiss soup company Maggi—it was a style shared by later Modernist manifestos, and Wedekind's desire to situate his aesthetic historically was certainly genuine enough. His drama intended a *Kulturkampf* waged on two fronts: against the authoritarianism and reli-

27

gious puritanism of traditional society, but also against modernity itself, though from squarely within its own premise of freedom. Wedekind's battle was expressly cultural, not political, as its circus venue makes clear. That venue was of course neither original with nor unique to him. Since the beginning of the Industrial Revolution, the circus had figured as a nonpolitical, countercultural haven within modern capitalist industrialism, a place where, as in Charles Dickens's *Hard Times*, imagination, sensuousness, vitality, and variety could be kept alive amidst the drab utilitarian homogeneity and grim single-mindedness of a profit-grubbing society. It emerged again in the work of cultural critics with Germany's rapid industrialization in the late nineteenth century, in such places as Wedekind's plays and essays and the Expressionist paintings of Ernst Ludwig Kirchner, a representation of the life possibilities that bourgeois civilization was crushing out.

But the critique of economic modernity does not by itself explain why Wedekind fixed specifically on *female* trick riders and tightrope walkers as the embodiments of his counterethic, or why he identified the religious-poetic essence of the dance as feminine. As much as the circus, the feminine itself was the very embodiment of Wedekind's image of liberation. The apparently universal qualities that he defined as freedom—sensual expressiveness, the integration of body and spirit, inner-directed ethics, psychological self-sufficiency—he also defined as feminine. Why this was so is a fundamental question about Wedekind; it obviously created enormous problems for him. What could the essentializing of freedom as inherently feminine mean for a male? How then could men win freedom except through women? Whatever "freedom through women" might mean concretely, what were its implications for male identity, and what could that goal bode for male-female relationships? And what, finally, did his identification of femininity and freedom entail for Wedekind's attitude to contemporary women's own self-definitions and their demands for freedom as expressed in the women's movements of the times?

Feminist Antifeminism

> *You ought to know that to demean a woman to the status of a worker is to express contempt for all human feeling. . . . It is sad enough that the world is full of misery. Is that a reason to make it completely desolate and expel from it the last remnant of human worth, of nobility, of idealism?*
>
> —Frank Wedekind, *The Young World*

Wedekind gave his first answers to all of these questions in *The Young World*, which, as it turns out, was as much a reckoning with the contemporary women's movement as it was with literary Realism; the critiques of both are in fact closely related. It quickly becomes apparent in the play that the young playwright was himself walking a tightrope, trying to balance his respect for women's demands for equality and dignity against his own ideas of what would truly give it to them. The lengthy prologue poses the problem that the rest of the play is meant to work out. A group of young women in a Swiss finishing school has been caught with a contraband copy of the *Decameron,* which the headmistress has confiscated. Outraged at what they regard as a violation of their rights, they concede that the fault is partly their own because they have acquiesced in an education whose sole purpose is to prepare them for marriage and domesticity. They form an organization based on a commitment not to marry until the most crying abuses in the education of young women are remedied. In the opening scene Anna, the most determined of the group, firmly reminds them of the resolution they passed at their founding meeting: "That in the future the young girl should receive an education which will enable us to satisfy not only the demands that the young man makes upon a girl, but the ones that an educated person makes upon herself."[16]

While the girls' male teacher is an officious oppressor, a dry run for the more vicious schoolmaster buffoons of *Spring's Awakening,* the more important whipping boy for retrograde patriarchalism is again the hapless would-be Realist writer Meier. His first speeches are outrageously broad caricatures of what Wedekind took to be widely prevalent attitudes about women's roles, spoken out of a blissfully unaware and whiningly self-pitying narcissism. "Misunderstood by his best friends, condemned and outlawed by his relatives, misperceived by his times," Meier declaims, the writer "stands in loneliness, a stranger among strangers. . . . If woman has a vocation to fulfill, it is that of supporting man in his holy suffering—she would otherwise be to a certain extent superfluous." When one of the young women angrily protests that a woman too can become a writer, Meier responds blithely that women are useless for the public sphere, then continues with ever-mounting offensiveness:

> Thoughtful nature, ladies, has intended you as man's compensation for his pitiless battle with time, with the elements. That is the justification of your existence. Show yourselves worthy, dear ladies, of the overabundance of charm with which kind nature has enabled you to fulfill your office. No one demands more from you; anything over and above that is evil. We are born fighters; our sphere of conquest is creativity, our reward in the world beyond. You, dear ladies, are the oases on our wanderings through the desert, in whose shades bubble crystal-clear springs for our refreshment. (23)

Meier's words echo in an episode described in one of Wedekind's diary entries the year the play was written: "On the way home I'm foolish enough to let myself be drawn into a defense of higher education for women against the medical student Geise. And, sure enough, he treats the matter with all the sheer stupidity you could imagine, as was only to be expected."[17] Women were not officially admitted into German universities until 1901. The middle-class feminist movement in Germany concentrated during the 1870s and 1880s on the improvement of women's education generally and on the admission of women into the medical profession in particular,[18] and Wedekind may have been particularly exercised on this issue because his father was a doctor. But here Wedekind converted the bitter male opposition to women's educational advancement into the sexism of the insecure writer anxiously concerned about his manhood in the explicit terms of the contemporary language of masculinity—the true man as heroic warrior and conqueror. In the play, "stupid" antifeminism is extended beyond Meier's supercilious contempt for women into what the dramatist sees as its logical counterpart: a readiness to use anyone for his own purposes, which Wedekind linked directly to Meier's literary style. When Anna hears how Meier betrayed Karl by writing down his confidences and putting them in a play, her sardonic reaction is a moral indictment of a style she sees as the inevitable aesthetic of any authoritarian society. "When Realism has outlived itself, its representatives will earn their living as members of the secret police" (76).

Wedekind made yet another feminist gesture in the play through Anna's scathing repudiation of conventional marriage in response to Meier's pretentious prattling about engagements. Claiming that people get engaged without adequate moral preparation, Meier has written a high-minded poem about spiritual love for his fiancée to recite, a device to raise his own impending betrothal to a higher level (her friends will help her sabotage it by dressing her as sensual Amor instead of cerebral Psyche). Anna is full of scorn. "People get engaged in fifty out of a hundred cases out of pure desperation, at least as far as the young girl is concerned, because she hasn't learned anything else," Anna claims. "In that way her life happiness turns into hollow-eyed necessity, a gloomy refuge. She learns nothing more than renunciation, nothing more than saying yes yes, than subordinating herself and denying her own individuality. Let the state bring up the children, each to its own appropriate vocation, as is already happening in many American communities; take away excessive responsibility from the man and take the chains off the woman, and all family misery will come to an end" (62). The accuracy of her critique of contemporary female education is demonstrated repeatedly throughout the play, as one by one each of the friends who once subscribed to it get married and fall victim to the fate Anna describes. She herself tries to avoid this fate by studying medicine and going off to help women in India. It comes as a shocking surprise to everybody, then, when at the very end of the play Anna reveals that she too is married. She has married Oscar, a doctor friend who accompanied her to India to get away from the disappointment of his rejection by Ricarda, another of the original group of school friends, with whom he is deeply in love.

Anna's marriage, however, is not quite the betrayal it might seem, for she has in fact succumbed not to desperation or convention but to Wedekind's philosophy, as represented by Oscar, another of the Wedekind figures in the play. It is Oscar who remonstrates with the most stubborn feminists, Ricarda and the even stauncher Anna, in explicitly ideological terms. Trying to persuade Ricarda to give up her schoolgirl resolution and marry him, he argues, "You shouldn't believe that you can satisfy your thirst for activity by joining organizations. You least of all. You cling to life. You are seeking personal satisfaction, and that you will not find until you have learned to forget completely your demanding little ego—No one has dared to try to rectify the eternal laws of nature without being punished" (39). To Anna, on her way to India, he insists, "As a doctor you ought to know that to demean a woman to the status of a worker is to express contempt for all human feeling, it is barbarism. . . . It is sad enough that the world is full of misery. Is that a reason to make it completely desolate and expel from it the last remnant of human worth, of nobility, of idealism with scorn and contempt?" However sexist this sounds to the contemporary ear, Wedekind's denunciation of women's organizations and women's work must also be read in the context of his bitter condemnation of the human cost of modern market society and the bureaucratic, militarized German Empire. As he saw it, contemporary feminism sought nothing better than to join the life-denying "steeplechase" that men were already trapped in. In this respect, he wasn't being hypocritical in condemning women's desire to work; as an artist who had himself opted out of bourgeois work, he was not denying women prerogatives he wanted to preserve for himself. On the contrary, precisely because they had not yet been deformed by modernity, he believed women represented the last best hope for preserving the whole personality that modern life was destroying, though not by remaining traditional hausfraus.

But Wedekind did not stake out his reformist position without a good deal of self-irony. The character who expresses the greatest optimism undercuts it with his actions. When Karl asks Meier's disgusted wife Alma whether she won't be lonely if she divorces him for his behavior, she retorts that it will take Europe centuries to learn that love that is not freely bestowed is both impossible and immoral. In an outburst of reformist enthusiasm, Oscar goes even further: "That humanity under free institutions will remain fresh and energetic to its last breath! That life will increase a hundredfold in

31

value!"—to which Anna sarcastically responds, thinking of the miserable marriages around her, "This is certainly the right place to sing the praises of such a utopia!" It seems for a moment as if Oscar gets the last word. "There was once a time," he declares to her, "when people were open enough and faithful enough to their convictions to defend such a utopia with flaming enthusiasm" (86). And Anna herself must have at least some faith in that utopia; she has married Oscar, after all. But in the scene before the exchange just cited, Oscar has tried to proposition Ricarda to run away with him for a tryst, though he is married and Ricarda is about to marry Karl. All is not well in Oscar's personal utopia of freely willing and equal sexual partners. He does not seem to be fulfilled with the independent Anna, and her skepticism about his vision seems well founded.

What is the source of the play's ambivalence about the liberation of women? In her thought-provoking analysis of the origins of the femme fatale in fin de siècle art and literature, of which she holds Wedekind's Lulu to be the most famous German example, Carola Hilmes argues that both the idealizing and the demonizing of women spoke to the dilemma of many European men toward the end of the nineteenth century. With their socioeconomic roles diminishing in importance, middle-class men looked to family and spousal love to compensate for lost authority just as women were starting to look outside the home for their fulfillment and creating their own movements to demand it. At the same time, wanting greater sexual liberty but inhibited by the traditional moral strictures meant to keep sexual license in check, men projected their pressing sexual desire onto women, casting themselves as the passive objects of aggressive female initiative. Women thus became the ambivalent objects of male fear and hatred as well as of worship and lust.[19]

But even if Lulu can be classified as a femme fatale—and I have suggested that the label is problematic even for the Lulu of the originally published plays—Wedekind's circus essays and *The Young World* suggest a rather different view of woman, the feminine ideal, and female emancipation. And there is a further difficulty of a theoretical nature, with broader implications for cultural analysis. The virtue of Hilmes's broad-brush picture is that it offers a sociohistorical explanation for a cultural theme that was more than the obsession of a single artist. But her mode of analysis offers a narrative about the state of mind of individual writers that is produced either by theoretically assuming a general social model for the individual case or by inferring the state of mind in a circular fashion from the very texts it is supposed to explain. Invoking only the most general developments in family and society leaves out the individual histories that mediate between social factors and individual cultural production, and that offer the only evidence possible of real causal connection between them. Wedekind certainly observed and responded to the social pressures around him, but he also lived his own version of contemporary social issues within his family. His experience offers a rather different picture of the strains and fault lines within German bourgeois society in the second half of the nineteenth century than the one Hilmes sketches.

The School of Women and the School for Women

> *When one of us said "I," she always meant her whole self from the top of her head to the tips of her toes. We felt our selves in our legs and feet almost more than in our eyes and fingers. I don't remember how any of the girls spoke. I remember only how each one walked.*
>
> —Frank Wedekind, *Mine-Haha*

33
∎

Friedrich Wilhelm Wedekind, Frank's father, was virtually an archetype of the midcentury German liberal bourgeoisie, in whom all of the class's characteristic social, ideological, and psychological contradictions appear in their most blatant form. A physician and idealistic radical democrat who had actively participated in the revolution of 1848, he immigrated to the United States after the disappointment of its hopes, made his fortune in land speculation in San Francisco during the gold rush, and promptly helped form a vigilante organization to provide the law and order necessary to protect his new wealth in the raw frontier town. A man of puritanical moral convictions and a patron of high culture in the German community of San Francisco, he became infatuated with a young married music hall performer less than half his age, began an affair with her, then forced her after their marriage to give up her stage career and return with him to Germany as a respectable hausfrau. Eight years later, when Bismarck declared the new German Empire, Friedrich Wilhelm left Germany to avoid having his sons serve in the Prussianized Imperial army (and to remove his wife from the temptation of flirtatious younger men), bought an isolated castle on a hill in Switzerland, and lived out his life like the Junkers he despised, the authoritarian and increasingly reclusive lord of an unhappy manor.[20]

That the marriage played itself out in front of the children at Schloss Lenzburg as a "daily catastrophe"[21] was hardly surprising. Emilie Wedekind resembled her husband only in the independent-minded adventurousness of her early life. The talented and beautiful daughter of a creative businessman and political radical who had spent time in prison for revolutionary activity, she sailed from Germany at age sixteen to join her married sister in

Valparaiso after her father's death, the only female on board ship, warding off a rape attempt along the way. When her sister's husband went bankrupt shortly afterward, she and Sophie, a trained concert singer, decided to try to support the family with their singing until they could get to San Francisco, where Sophie's father-in-law lived. With husband and new baby in tow, the two sisters made their way up the west coast of South America appearing in concerts together in port cities along the way. Tragically, Sophie died of yellow fever during the trip and was buried at sea, the father-in-law in San Francisco proved as feckless as his son, and Emilie, at eighteen, found herself supporting her sister's family with singing and acting engagements in San Francisco's German community. When her brother-in-law and nephew finally departed for Europe, she was left alone, though apparently neither helpless nor frightened. The memoir she wrote in her seventies—an earlier one from 1886 written at the request of her son is lost—suggests the formidable self-possession, self-conscious femininity, and unabashed narcissism of the young woman:

> From the time I could get the applause—in contrast to earlier, when next to my sister I wasn't even noticed—I found great satisfaction in my vocation. In addition my awareness that my looks won unusual attention and recognition increased my self-confidence and afforded me security when I appeared onstage. I would not have been a woman if I did not enjoy hearing that people liked me and admired my beauty. . . . I swam in a sea of satisfied vanity like a fish in clear water and wished only that it would last for a long time.[22]

Emilie's obvious pleasure in her independent life, however, did not stop her from marrying a man she didn't love, partly as protection against constant propositions and gossip, but partly also in the hope of financial support for her advancing career as a music hall singer. Nor did her marital status in turn prevent Friedrich Wilhelm Wedekind, who had become her family doctor, from falling in love with her. Despite moral reservations about her disreputable surroundings and social reservations about her status and education, the repressed forty-five-year-old bachelor was overwhelmed by the talent, vivaciousness, and youthful sexuality of the twenty-one-year-old actress and singer. He began to court her with promises of respectability, the more seductive since her husband had proved a financial failure and exploiter. Friedrich Wilhelm's diary speaks explicitly of an affair behind her husband's back before he finally pressed her to divorce. He was especially anxious to marry her because Emilie had begun to take on dramatic roles in English—she could perform in five languages—a step that promised a respectable career and ultimate financial independence. Saddled with her husband's considerable debts, however, Emilie apparently saw marriage to this pillar of the community as the best way out of her problems. The price was the renunciation of her career. In a diary entry Friedrich Wilhelm noted Emilie's talent and accomplishments, but also what he called *"une certaine froideur du coeur."*[23] Rolf Kieser suggests that the coldness was the wall of ice Emilie built around herself to protect the last remnants of her independence from her controlling husband-to-be. Whatever the case, this was not a match made in heaven, as Emilie Wedekind acknowledged years later in her memoir. Externally, she wrote, her marriage had proceeded in a settled, orderly fashion, but "internally there were disturbances and battles, which . . . arose mostly because the differences in age, education and cultivation between me and my husband were rather too great. . . . I had only one passionate wish, to make the father of my children happy and to show him my gratitude by fulfilling my duties to the utmost. Unfortunately, I did not succeed, and as more children came with the years, my heart, all my feelings and thoughts turned to these dear beings."[24] One might well imagine the impact of such a personality turning the full force of her frustrated abilities and desires on her children while maintaining her protective coldness.

In an autobiographical sketch written when he was thirty-seven, Frank Wedekind noted the age difference between his parents and commented dryly, "This fact strikes me as not altogether devoid of significance."[25] It was certainly significant for him, and not only because the age difference between the still youthful mother and the aging father he knew as he grew up intensified the oedipal entanglements that unquestionably affected Frank's relationships with both of them. When Emilie Wedekind was not managing the affairs of the castle, she was introducing her children into the bohemian world of her past, regaling them with stories from her early life and encouraging them to stage plays and music hall acts in which she was an enthusiastic participant, while her husband lowered in his study. These performances continued into Frank's young adulthood, as a diary entry from 1888/89, when he was twenty-four, vividly describes: "Mother puts on a cloak of Genoese velvet with gold braid that reaches down to the ground. In this outfit she dances a *samaqueca* on the Smyrna carpet with incomparable verve and suppleness. . . ."[26] A dream reported in the diary some months later testifies to the highly ambivalent effects these performances had on him: "Last night I was haunted by a vile dream in which our home appeared in a most unedifying light. It had turned into a sort of cabaret, in which Mother and Donald [his younger brother] were the principle figures and performed all sorts of tricks. I was sitting in the audience" (July 27, 1889). It takes little psychological sophistication to hear Frank protesting rather too much that it was Donald, not he, doing tricks with his mother. The dream's paternalistic condemnation of the "unedifying" cabaret per-

35
■

formance sounds an ironic note in view of Frank's future career as a cabaret performer. For Frank, Emilie Wedekind was both an erotic and an ideal object, a pole of attraction and of identification. But in the context of his father's politics, both of these took on broader cultural significance.

The sexual ambivalence that had both drawn Friedrich Wilhelm to Emilie and made him reject her way of life dramatizes the limits of even the most advanced liberalism in the mid-nineteenth century. "Victorian" civilization in the broad European sense, not least its German "Biedermeier" version, might encompass economic and even political freedom, but—whatever actually went on in the bedroom[27]—could not accommodate the *idea* of sexual freedom, which threatened to undermine the behavioral restraints it believed necessary to make an individualistic society safe from anarchy as well as to distinguish the middle from the dissipated lower and upper classes. Even less could it accommodate the idea of the sexual woman, which threatened to disrupt the saving balance between the economic world of aggressive, sink-or-swim competition and the domestic world of emotional security, moral education, and piety. But as his family functioned, Frank identified as much with his mother as with his father. If in his father he had the very model of ascetic classical liberalism, in Emilie he had a—literally—dramatic example of an obviously sexual woman whose freedom of personal expression had been constrained by the contradictions of his father's patriarchal liberalism. His identification with her was reinforced by his own sense of being a victim of its paternalist contradiction, to which he once gave very direct expression when some adolescent friends questioned him about his atheism. Asked what he thought of the proposition that one couldn't raise young children without religion, he answered, "The father very well could and should refer the first of the ten commandments to himself: I am . . . etc. and thou shalt have no other God beside me." (In antic spirit he went on to suggest how one might elaborate the cult of the father with a prayer, which he begged his correspondent not to take as parody: "Dear Father, who art upstairs in Thy study! Hallowed be Thy name! . . . Thy will be done in our thoughts and deeds. Give us this day our daily bread, and forgive us our sins. Save us from temptation and deliver us from evil. For Thine is the kingdom and the power and the glory forever."[28]) On the other hand, if both innate talent and identification with his mother drew him to the world of art rather than commerce or politics, he saw himself, in his father's spirit, as a political artist, though one far more consistent in his quest for freedom than his father. In a letter accompanying the gift of a drawing of Byron's head to his "erotic aunt" Bertha Jahn (of whom more later), he gave a description of the Romantic poet that encapsulated his own ideal self-image: "a man who stormed through the world in an unceasing cyclone of the most intense passions, fought on the battlefield of poetry, love and politics, and finally, still in the bloom of his years, in the fullness of physical and spiritual strength, died an enviable death offering himself up as sacrifice to liberty. . . . For these reasons he is my ideal."[29]

But of the battlefields he mentioned here, the overtly political involved him the least. It is possible to interpret Frank's particular engagement with liberty in what look like contradictory ways. Viewed strictly politically, it could be seen as a retreat from his father's activism on behalf of democratic ideals, the kind of turning inward that according to the now-contested but still vigorous *Sonderweg* theory of German history was characteristic of the political surrender of the post-1866 German bourgeoisie to Bismarckian authoritarianism. From another perspective, however, Wedekind's agenda was the unfinished business of middle-class liberalism, the extension of the idea of freedom from economics and politics to the family, sexuality, and the metaphysics of morals. The two points of view are not necessarily incompatible. There is at least one passage from a letter Wedekind wrote at age twenty that seems to repeat the ideological commonplaces of post-1848 and especially post-1870 European liberals who had become frightened of politics in the age of the masses. Reflecting on his cousin's assertion that his thought had undergone a "revolutionary change," Wedekind spun out a conservative political metaphor:

> Every heart is after all a little world, a little state, in which one regime dissolves another in quite stormy fashion. The strict ministry (I mean that of modest understanding) usually doesn't have much to say about it, and is made deathly still by the enthusiastic screaming of the raging masses, or even actually put to death on the high guillotine. So it goes, here and there, up and down, everyone shouting liberty, equality, and fraternity until suddenly a world-conquering hero comes along and with powerful voice demands quiet. In an instant the masses are won by the power of his speech and those who praised the republic to the heavens now greet absolute despotism with jubilation.[30]

Wedekind came of age in Switzerland, which despite its republicanism and willingness to accept foreign political exiles was hostile to radical political agitation, especially by noncitizens, and monitored it closely. The passage breathes the spirit of antipathy to the French revolutionary mobs, whose government had annexed Switzerland, and to the "world-conquering" despot Napoleon, who ratified French rule. On the other hand, Switzerland, unlike Imperial Germany, was tolerant of cultural radicalism. Zurich became a haven for German expatriate writers during the harshest years of Wilhelmine repression and a center of radical artistic experimentation (as it also was for other international expatriates like James Joyce and the

Dadaists—though also Lenin—through World War I); it was in Zurich that Wedekind met writers like Hauptmann and did his literary apprenticeship.

But in one sense these considerations miss the essential. Wedekind's "liberalism" was inescapably defined by its enmeshment from its very beginnings with issues of masculinity and femininity. From his adolescence on, freedom for Frank Wedekind was both a psychophysical and a metaphysical concept, embodied in woman and taught him by women who wittingly and unwittingly, theoretically and experientially, were the mentors of both his philosophical and his sentimental education.

Wedekind's astonishingly accomplished adolescent juvenilia—some of the poems he wrote as early as age fourteen were published later with only light revisions—already display two central themes of his adult work: the erotic woman as the essence of life and the inescapable but onerous divinity of man after the death of God. They represent the impact on him of four extraordinary relationships with four unusual women—his mother; her friends Bertha Jahn, whom he dubbed his "erotic aunt," and Olga Plümacher, his so-called "philosophical aunt"; and his cousin Minna, three years older and the only one at all close to him in age. Kieser, quoting from another context, nicely describes the young Wedekind as practicing "polymothering [*Vielmütterei*]," though these unquestionably maternal relationships with older women offered much more than conventional maternal love.

His own mother was the living counterexample to the prudish pieties and constricting sexual norms of German Swiss small town life and the German Swiss gymnasium—microcosms of the wider German culture—that he would savage unforgettably in *Spring's Awakening*. It was through her open sensuality that Wedekind understood their falsity. The cycle of poems he wrote at twenty that traced the evolution of kissing from its earliest stages to its highest development, the sensually passionate kiss of adult love, begins with "The Mother's Kiss." It preserved the same ambiguity toward his mother's sexuality as his dreams, insisting on the childlike innocence of a mother's kiss while clearly presenting it as the first in a progression of ever more explicitly erotic experiences. There was no such ambiguity, however, in his relationship with Bertha Jahn, his "erotic aunt," a widow twenty-five years his senior who bore a strong resemblance to his mother and to whom "The Kiss" cycle was dedicated. He had been infatuated at a distance with younger married women before; Bertha he courted avidly in poetry and in person for more than a year, and the evidence indicates that she ultimately returned his love.[31] That there is even a question about whether it was physically consummated is a measure of the erotic directness and intensity of their exchanges. But there was more to the relationship than the sexual. "The Mother's Kiss" reveals another essential dimension of maternal love for the adolescent Wedekind, thinking back to childhood on the threshold of adulthood. When his mother would kiss him good-night and say a prayer over him, according to the poem, he would babble "Our Father" (the Lord's Prayer) to himself but he did not really know what he was saying, because "she was my God, my spirit and my Savior."[32] Mother was not only erotic but absolute being, the source of both sensual stimulation and metaphysical security.

Wedekind's relationship with the remarkable Olga Plümacher, his "philosophical aunt," was platonic but no less influential. A self-taught philosopher who had published books on Schopenhauer and Eduard von Hartmann, Olga schooled Frank's untutored speculative instincts, offering him what his traditional classical gymnasium education could not. It was she who introduced him to the most advanced philosophical currents of the day, not only to Hartmann's idea of the unconscious and the cosmic pessimism he had derived from Schopenhauer, but to the as yet little known Nietzsche (of whom she was critical for his attacks on Schopenhauer). Wedekind quickly declared himself to be a "pessimist," though less out of adherence to an abstract philosophical system than because that system supported his native skepticism about human nature and his constantly honed sensitivity to hypocrisy and self-deception. "Brothers, let us all be robbers / Let us plunder, burn and kill," one of his gymnasium poems begins rather bombastically, then explains, "For the all-powerful regime / That constrains human living / Is more suited to beastliness / Than to ideal striving."[33] But he was also alert to the disjunction between the stoic implications of philosophical pessimism and his sexual obsessiveness, as he self-mockingly indicated in the last verse of a poem written at the time of the affair with Bertha Jahn: "You mock life and like to fancy / You stand so sublimely above; / But when you see a girl's gleaming limb / You're struck by the fever of love."[34] Nietzsche's influence on Wedekind was equally immediate but more profound and longer lasting, as the circus essays and the dramas show. Wedekind took a more favorable view of Nietzsche than his mentor did, perhaps because the idea of the death of God matched his domestic experience: internally contradictory, issued from the distance of Friedrich Wilhelm's withdrawal from family interaction, his father's commandments had lost much of their legitimacy, if not their force. Having labeled God a lie and chased him out of the temple, Wedekind wrote in another of his poems, he had to face the horrifying ecstasy of knowing himself to be both man and God.[35] But perhaps as significant for Wedekind as Olga's ideas was what she represented. In her Wedekind encountered a woman who engaged him purely on the level of mind, who showed him that women could be as powerful intellectually as sensually and had something to teach him other than the body.

It was an ambiguous lesson. Despite his apparent erotic and intellectual successes with these older women, despite their obvious responsiveness to him, Wedekind was not able to believe either that he possessed them or that he had personally attained what they possessed. Women remained an enigma and an ideal out of his reach. His encounters with them were desperate efforts to prove to himself and to women what he knew, and what they supposedly denied: that women were sexual beings and not inherently unavailable. When a friend once asked him to suggest questions for debate, Wedekind, then eighteen, responded with the suggestion, "What does a beautiful girl feel when she considers her body without outside interference? . . . Are the feelings the same as or different from those of a young man looking at the same beautiful female body? . . . If it can be shown that the girl's feelings are the same as, or even just similar to the young man's, the innocence of the female totally collapses, is completely impossible—that would be a great discovery!!!"[36] This letter was written not long before his seduction of Bertha Jahn. But the report of his flirtation with his cousin Minna that followed a few years afterward shows that despite Bertha, he felt the need to continue his quest for the exposure and conquest of women. The diary entries that document the campaign—it was nothing less—were rewritten for publication (the originals are unavailable) and present a rather different picture from the more sensitive and egalitarian spirit of the cousins' correspondence from that time. Wedekind represented himself in the diary as a cool sexual adventurer carrying out research on a flighty, boy-crazy girl. "I keep wondering," runs the first entry in the series, "how I might best talk her into an exchange of affections during the winter." When, having been drawn in, "Wilhelmine" (Minna's fictionalized name) jealously notices kiss marks on his neck, he cheerfully admits, "as a consolation, that she isn't the only one, but merely a representative: that precisely what intrigues me is to view her primarily as a type, and only then as an individual." And when she says later that even if he wanted to marry her, she wouldn't consent, he replies that to win her, "I need only give free rein to my idealism; its effect on her would be all the more infallible since she has known me only as an idle fellow."[37] Plainly, Wedekind's goal was not the seduction of Minna for herself but for the experimental proof that any woman could be seduced once one was able to figure out what would get to her.[38] He seemed quite unaware that the very project testified to the maddening superiority and elusiveness of the experimental object.

Wedekind's idealization of adult women made him fearful of them. His diaries describe compulsive womanizing, almost exclusively with prostitutes, while constantly complaining of impotence. "Piccolo [his term for his penis] is docile," he noted wryly but in obvious distress just a few months after the Minna episode, "as if he didn't exist. I can't think what's the matter with him. Whether he's reached the ultimate stage of development, or whether he will some time or other rise up in hitherto unsuspected glory. There is a peculiar irony in the fact that it is actually the individual who aspires to evolve into a universal human being who lags behind the merest machine, however restricted its development, precisely in this most human of all functions."[39] This was not an isolated incident. During the period in Paris when he conceived and began the first version of the Lulu plays, impotence was a chronic problem. It may well have been a function of the oddity of his liaisons, which were not quite what might have been expected from the stereotype of the bohemian roué. Though he did frequent a number of prostitutes, he had a more or less stable, relatively long-term relationship with at least one of them that had strikingly, and amusingly, domestic overtones. Six months into the relationship, for example, he described the following scene:

> We go up to my room, where I make some tea. As usual, Rachel strips to her vest straight away, and sprawls on the divan. We carry on chatting until two o'clock. She begins to dance a cancan and climbs on to my shoulders, and, heavy as she is, I carry her round the room. She's enough to make one's mouth water, and, unusually for me, I'm pretty much in love with her. We get stuck into each other, she inflicts a number of love bites on me, and in spite of my false teeth I manage to leave a suggestion of the same on her thigh. When we get into bed, she draws the curtains as close as she can. . . . Exceptionally, I find I'm more potent than otherwise, but afterwards I fall asleep instantly, with a "bon soir, ma petite femme," to which she replies with a "bon soir, mon mari." (December 18, 1892)

Rachel defied the usual stereotype in other ways as well. She had chosen to have a child with a previous lover, she told Wedekind when they met, and was apparently a devoted mother. The child had been born prematurely and had to be carefully tended under glass to be kept warm and fed with a medicine dropper. It was with a nursemaid in the country, but Rachel was planning to take it back and keep it with her in the city (June 12, 1892). These were significant details for Wedekind to note and record. They suggest the importance to him of her domesticity, and by that token a possible reason for his unreliable potency.

At any rate, it will not surprise a contemporary reader that his original observation about "Piccolo's" refusal to function immediately follows the description of the "vile" dream of his mother's cabaret performance. And just before that passage, Wedekind had remarked that his work was going desperately slowly and that whenever he got bogged down like that, he was "overwhelmed with sadness, thinking of my father and what I did to him." He was thinking not only about the confrontation three years before in which he had hit his father in the face, but about the fact that shortly after their reconciliation a year later, his father had died; in his mind, the two events were connected, perhaps even causally. The oedipal thread of the sequence of associations in the diary entry reads like a textbook case—or a parody.

But the same diary entry points to the unmistakable and critical historical dimension of the oedipal situation that further undermined Wedekind's masculine self-confidence. In an apparent non sequitur after describing the cabaret dream, he remarked, "Not infrequently I'm also plagued by doubts as to whether my work is work, after all." The violent confrontation with his father had been over his career. He had gone off to Munich in 1884 to study law but had spent his time instead attending the theater and working on his first play, as a step toward a full-time literary career; when he was discovered, a blowup was inevitable. More was involved in the doubt about the value of his literary work than a son's self-punitive internal submission to the father he had rebelled against with such violent consequences. Frank's doubt was about the value of art itself; to call into question whether it was "really" work was to identify with the standards of utility, material productivity, and science that virtually defined the bourgeoisie in the nineteenth century, the standard that had been invoked to establish its claim to equal worth with, if not superiority to, the aristocracy. But that same standard was also the bourgeoisie's claim to masculinity. The manliness, the *virtu* of the traditional aristocracy, rested in large part on its historical identity as warriors, those responsible for the eternal task of protecting the community. Against that the bourgeoisie, unable to reject warrior values completely for both philosophical as well as social reasons,[40] had to insist not only on their own indispensable utility as creators of society's wealth but on the marketplace as the moral equivalent of war, for which the qualities of courage and initiative were equally necessary. By these criteria, art, whose concern was feeling and whose métier was sensibility, was highly suspect. That in pursuing a career in literature and the theater Wedekind was choosing his mother's path against his father's made its effeminacy almost literal.

The play Wedekind worked on while not studying law in Munich, *The Quick-Sketch Artist, or, Art and Money (Der Schnellmaler, oder, Kunst und Mammon,* 1886), wrestled with precisely this issue by pitting the sensitive, languishing artist against the businessman as philistine and con man. It was a theme that in numerous variations, not least the conflation of the two identities of artist and con man, would occupy Wedekind to the end of his life. Its mixture of the burlesque and the deadly serious became the hallmark of Wedekind's theater; what reads much of the time like a trivial, though very funny, situation comedy or farce is constantly jarred by moments of deep feeling and near tragedy. Fridolin, a young, as yet unrecognized painter, is in love with Johanna, the daughter of a factory owner, but will not marry her until he can support her. Her father is contemptuous of him and conspires to have her marry a supposed chemist with whom he has entered into a joint business venture but whose "discovery" of potato sugar is completely bogus. Johanna's brother Thomas is Fridolin's ally but sees no future for him in art; he advises him, in what becomes a refrain throughout the play, to give up painting, become a salesman, and come to work in the family business so that he can make money and enjoy life. Fridolin rejects the advice out of hand; it is not poverty that makes him suffer, he asserts, but the terrible necessity of prostituting his art day after day making sketches for a dehumanized crowd to earn a crust of bread. He pledges faithfulness to his "high goddess" art until death, which may in fact be imminent since he is haunted by the thought of committing suicide if his serious work is not soon recognized. Fridolin's recurrent evocation of death is simultaneously moving and lugubrious; Wedekind's irony spares no character, not even his alter ego. The play of course ends as a good comedy should; the hero sells his masterpiece *Prometheus Unbound* [!] to the Royal Art Academy, the villain is exposed, and the lovers are united. But the last-minute triumph of artistic talent over money does not efface the picture of the artist painted throughout the play as moody, unstable, and desperate—in short, unmanly.

43

Wedekind's masculine crisis can be seen as an exacerbation of his father's conflicts not simply in familial but in generational and social terms. His father held together the contradictions of the midcentury bourgeois liberal without being aware of them and without paralyzing internal conflict but at a great price to his family and ultimately to himself. In the son, the fault lines in the masculine self-confidence of the father's generation were put under enough additional pressure to produce an upheaval. Frank strove both to be more consistent than his father in his idea of freedom and to integrate within himself the free sensuality his father had tried to possess externally through his wife. Yet at the same time, in his undoubted, if conflicted, admiration for his father, he acceded to the prevailing definitions of manliness. This juggling act made his identification with and idealization of everything his mother and her surrogates represented doubly problematic for his sense of himself as a man. His father, the paternalistic successful professional and businessman, had not been able to hold his mother; how could he, her son—closer to her in temperament but by the same token less manly—hold her, or anyone like her?

His recurrent impotence was not the only symptom of this dilemma. His difficulties in coping sexually with adult women lie behind some of the most bizarre entries in the diaries that in altered form later found their way into one of his strangest published works. He recalled an anecdote from Krafft-Ebing's compendium of sexual perversions *Psychopathia Sexualis* about a prostitute walking on her hands and collecting money by holding her legs slightly apart, then suddenly thought of her as his daughter. He went on to fantasize about teaching the daughters he would have in the future to do the same. "A pity," he remarked with typically dry self-irony, "that the money-collecting bit doesn't go too well with my role as a father. A pity there's a limit there, a pity the whole business encroaches on the area of sex, it would be so nice if it could be done with a proper gravity, with dignity and love." But he had more than images to persuade him that his fantasy did encroach on sex; as he fantasized, he noticed that "Piccolo, otherwise somnolent, is suddenly painfully sensitive. . . . He's up and ready in a trice" (August 8, 1889). For the next few days, the fantasies of training daughters were elaborated to include tightrope walking and revolving peep shows with two girls and a dog. An abruptly interpolated denial allows their repressed sadism to surface for a moment: "NB There is no punishment, only kindly encouragement with a slender switch that I draw across her abdomen." Little wonder that he wrote at the end of the entry: "I think it's high time to put a stop to this feverish fit. I'm afraid I might go mad in the end."

A month later the fantasies had not stopped. On September 5 he described a dream in which his father appeared as a meek, wraithlike figure. He didn't reproach his son for anything that had happened since his death but looked beseechingly at him and timidly expressed the wish that he had been allowed to live out his few years in peace. This bit of wish fulfillment, reversing the power relationship with his father, was immediately followed by more fantasies about the training of a daughter. These were in a more reflective vein that clearly betrayed the confused mix of idealization and identification with the feminine and the need to control females that underlay his obsessive fascination with the whole subject.

> I'll urge her as far as possible to live for the enjoyment of her fellow-creatures, so that she'll be endowed with the happiest childhood any person can possibly have. . . . And from the first dawning of consciousness her very own spiritual life will unfold within her, independent of us all, untrammeled as a god, autonomous, childishly fanciful combinations of elements of reality, an innocent and innocuous patrimony which will not vanish without trace, like some trivial trumpery concocted from fairy-tales and tinsel, for once the body has developed to its harmonious maturity, once aspirations have assumed a more positive character, then an integrated sphere of ideas, at least equally harmonious, will be born from that womb, a sphere of ideas which embraces the nocturnal side of life, as well as its bright side, without being . . . sullied. (September 5, 1889)

Mens sana, it would seem, *in corpore sano.* Wedekind's educational ideal aimed at producing the personality he longed to be but was not, the fully au-

44
.

tonomous person who successfully integrated imagination and hard-headed realism, mind and body, good and evil. Its less wholesome contradictions, however, are obvious. The ideal young girl was not only to live for the enjoyment of others but was to be fashioned by a controlling Pygmalion. These contradictions were inevitable given that the ideal personality was necessarily female. Projected onto the feminine other, it could be achieved for the masculine self only by domination.

Though diary records of the fantasies soon disappear, they remained with him. A much-elaborated version became his one attempt at a novel, the fragment *Mine-Haha, or, On the Bodily Education of Young Girls* (*Mine-Haha, oder, Über die körperliche Erziehung der jungen Mädchen*, 1895). The dilemma created for Wedekind by his equation of freedom and wholeness with fresh unspoiled femininity, his consequent ambivalence toward it, and the resulting sadomasochism of his attitude toward young girls provide the key resolving the puzzle of a work that has produced radically conflicting readings. *Mine-Haha* purports to be the autobiographical reminiscences of an eighty-four-year-old retired schoolteacher Helene Engel who has recently committed suicide. It describes her education in a unique school for young girls, breaking off at the point where she and her cohort leave the school to enter the world. The work is presented as edited by Wedekind, to whom Engel had shown it because she had read his *Spring's Awakening* and thought he would be interested in seeing another work along the same emancipatory lines; the reference implies that the novel is Wedekind's answer to the miseducation described in the play.

The educational institution for girls is located in a walled garden that has the characteristics of both idyllic refuge and prison. It is a world without visible adults; the younger girls are trained and supervised by older girls, who have themselves gone through the earlier stages of the process. Wedekind's preoccupation with girls learning to walk on their hands reappears with obsessive frequency, but the more general emphasis is on perfecting bodily movement and flexibility in preparation for dancing. Indeed, the girls' individuality is expressed wholly physically. "Everyone thought and felt like everyone else," Helene recalls; "we could tell one another apart only through bodily differences. When one of us said 'I,' she always meant her whole self from the top of her head to the tips of her toes. We felt our selves in our legs and feet almost more than in our eyes and fingers. I don't remember how any of the girls spoke. I remember only how each one walked."[41]

The erotic point of the education is overt, if more subdued than in the diaries. The girls are being prepared to dance and act in a pantomime before an outside audience of well-to-do men; the performances provide the financial support for the institution. Roles are allocated by audition after the years of preparation; the acolytes undress, then dance and sing for the older girls, who have already performed. For the pantomime the girls, still pre-pubescent, wear skimpy costumes and take up suggestive poses without provocative intent but whose effects on the male audience they are aware of, not without embarrassment. The all-female environment breeds the temptation of homosexuality, but it is ruthlessly checked; girls who succumb become the maids who take care of the house and are not allowed to leave. The girls stop dancing with the onset of their menses. At that point they leave the school to be handed over to the world of boys without any sexual preparation, though the anxiety they feel does not seem to last very long. Helene closes her memoir:

> I would like to remind my fellow-students of the anxious horror that we all once experienced for the entertainment of an insensitive crude world drunk with lust, even if the powerful, unanticipated destinies of life very soon allowed us to think back on those terrors only with mocking smiles. Perhaps society is not wrong to turn through its educational practices the practical activity of all our powers into completely different directions within a few days; perhaps I am committing a crime if I dare to offer a word in favor of the more delicate feelings with which nature starts all of us out. But the older and calmer I get, the less can I shake my belief that the world could in fact be ordered less brutally than it is. (132)

These last words seem to imply that the benign effects of an ideal education in a school that respects and nourishes natural feeling are countered, if not undone, by an unreformed world. They recall the utopianism of Oscar's ideas about raising people in free institutions in *The Young World,* and even more specifically Anna's notion of having the state take girls away from their parents in order to raise them to recognize and realize their own unique vocations. It was this vision of a socialized education breaking the destructive stranglehold of the bourgeois family on its children that led Leon Trotsky to praise *Mine-Haha* as a progressive tract despite its apparently purely "aesthetic" concerns. Other critics, however, have seen in Wedekind's educational notions, if not outright pornography, at least the delectations of a voyeur. In general, critics have remained sharply divided as to whether the book describes a utopia, an alternative childhood similar to some of the ideas expressed by Moritz in *Spring's Awakening;* a dystopia, a nightmare world of rigid control; or is simply a grotesque satire of the way young women are actually brought up.[42] Only the last of these views need be discounted, and it is not necessary to choose between the first two. It is hard to imagine a contemporary ethical standpoint from which *Mine-Haha* would not be a "dystopia," but the more interesting problem is how both genuine liberation and sexual manipulation can inhabit the same design. Behind the contradictory attitude toward girls lie the ambiguities of Wedekind's masculine identity. Even more than the picture of a destructive adolescent educational system or the supposed implications for a healthier one, it is the question of masculine identity that also lies at the heart of the first of Wedekind's great plays, *Spring's Awakening.*

The True Nature of Masculine Sexuality

> *Girls enjoy themselves . . . like the gods in* their *bliss. . . . By comparison, a* man's *satisfaction seems . . . shallow, stagnant.*
>
> —Frank Wedekind, *Spring's Awakening*

The plot of *Spring's Awakening* is quickly told. It is a story of young adolescents struggling both with pubertal urges in a culture that denies adolescent sexuality and with the demands of a draconian educational system in which failure ends all hope of bourgeois respectability. Two young classmates die in the play, fourteen-year-old Wendla Bergmann at the hands of an abortionist and Moritz Stiefel by his own hand, unable to face his parents' anticipated disgrace and fury because of his failing grades. The unwitting mover in both deaths is Melchior Gabor, the brooding, philosophically questioning youth at the center of the play. He impregnates Wendla, deceived by her mother about the connection between sex and conception, in a fumbling, ambivalent, but fiercely urgent sexual exploration. He also writes a sex education pamphlet for the bewildered Moritz that intensifies the struggling youth's sexual distraction. When Melchior is found out, he is blamed for both deaths and his father persuades his initially resisting mother to commit him to a reformatory. He escapes, but, consumed by guilt for Wendla's death, he is tempted by the ghost of Moritz to join him in suicide. The intervention of a mysterious masked man, who offers him a view of morality that moderates his guilt, enables him to opt for life instead of death.

Spring's Awakening is subtitled *Tragedy of Childhood.* Together the titles suggest a natural blooming nipped in the bud with disastrous results. In a letter to a critic written shortly after the play was completed, Wedekind described its point as an attempt to depict the phenomenon of puberty poetically in order to help educators, parents, and teachers judge it more humanely and rationally;[43] the reformist intention of the play has since become a staple of interpretation. There can be no doubting Wedekind's bitter social satire; parents and teachers are exposed as at best stupid or ignorant buffoons, at worst criminally self-righteous hypocrites who de-

stroy young life to evade the truth of their own impulses or any responsibility for damage they themselves have caused. But if the play is unambiva-
lent about what it rejects, it is most uncertain about what it affirms. The
reformist implication of the attack on the sexual miseducation of children
is both undercut and displaced by even more troubling issues that suggest
there is no simple alternative. The manifest outrages of Wendla's death,
Moritz's suicide, and the scapegoating of Melchior overshadow the fact
that sexuality, far from being unambiguously natural and healthy, is both
psychologically and morally suspect in the play. And the climax, the appearance of the man in the mask and the pronouncement of his saving
message, turns not on the social issues it seemed to dramatize but on the
problem of male identity—on the question of how to affirm the (male)
self in the face of the morally ambiguous nature of male sexuality and the
unambiguous demands of ethics.

    The notorious first meeting between Wendla and Melchior introduces
the themes of feminine masochism and male sadism that would continue to
haunt Wedekind's literary imagination. Wendla wants to know what it feels
like to be beaten. She incites an initially reluctant Melchior until he complies with a savagery that shocks them both. Their fright, however, proves no
obstacle to their subsequent sexual encounter, and again, though Wendla
feels fulfilled, even ecstatic in its aftermath, Melchior has no doubt that it
was a rape—not only because Wendla initially said no, but because Melchior knew his own intentions. He has come to believe that there are no un-
selfish motives, that people are deterministically driven by what gives them
pleasure; consideration of Wendla had nothing to do with his lust. Nor are
masochism and sadism simply the confused urges of the sexually ignorant
and uninitiated. Ilse, a former classmate who has left school to live the free
life of an artist's model, betrays the same contradictions as Wendla. She is
virtually the sexual prisoner of a group of artists who took her under their
"protection" after some terrifying episodes with a psychotic artist and the
police, and whom she cheerfully describes as apes, pigs, and hyenas, but she
insists that she "wouldn't want to be tied to anyone else if the world were full
of archangels and millionaires."[44]

    Nonetheless it is both true and not incidental that it is the girls who live
their sensuality with any real joy, despite their masochistic proclivities; the
only exception, tellingly enough, is the brief moment of homosexual tenderness shared by two of the boys. Though critics have attributed the sadomasochism of Wedekind's adolescents to the sexual fantasies inevitably
engendered by a repressive and patriarchal society,[45] the capacity for authentic pleasure seems for him to be inherent in femininity itself. Moritz,
who as the final scene clearly shows is Melchior/Wedekind's alter ego, is

48

certainly speaking for Wedekind when he describes the impact of Melchior's sex education pamphlet on him. He tells his friend:

> I was most affected by what you wrote about girls. Girls enjoy themselves . . . like the gods in *their* bliss. . . . A girl keeps herself free of everything bitter till the last moment. She then has the pleasure of seeing all heaven break over her. She hasn't stopped fearing hell when suddenly she notices paradise in full bloom. Her feelings are as fresh as water springing from the rock. She takes up a chalice, a goblet of nectar, which no earthly breath has yet blown upon and—even as it flickers and flares—she drains it! By comparison, a man's satisfaction seems to me shallow, stagnant. (32)

A dithyrambic fantasy, no doubt, but one made more intelligible by the gender universe of the play. Aside from the prudish hint that girls don't masturbate, *Spring's Awakening* offers the first clear insight into some of the personal-social reasons why Wedekind saw his human ideal embodied in the feminine. There is not a humane or authentic adult male in the entire play. The most significant negative model of masculinity is Melchior's father, whose ostensible rationality and sober rectitude are much more sinister than the cartoonish ridiculousness of the gymnasium professors and much more powerful in their effects. With chilling self-certainty he castigates his wife's "imaginative" methods of child rearing, which he contrasts with his own "serious principles," for abetting Melchior's complete depravity. Only someone "rotten to the core," he pontificates, someone whom "we clinicians" (one remembers that Wedekind's father was a doctor) describe as corrupted with extreme "moral depravity" could have composed the pamphlet Melchior wrote (63). Mrs. Gabor's sharp response is as significant as her husband's pompous judgment. "It takes a man to talk like that," she counters, arguing that the pamphlet actually demonstrates her son's childlike innocence. "It takes a man to let himself be blinded by dead words. It takes a man to see no further than his nose. . . . To find moral corruption here, one must have the soul of a bureaucrat, one must be wholly ignorant of human nature . . ." (64).

Wedekind once acknowledged that the parental dialogue in this scene echoed the tone and content of arguments between his own parents. Again, however, the significance of the exchange goes beyond individual biography. Mrs. Gabor's refrain—"It takes a man"—is an indictment not only of her husband but also of contemporary masculinity. It isn't that men alone deny their children's sexuality, as Wendla's mother proves so fatefully. But men alone reify their moral principles, treating them the way bureaucrats treat regulations, not as ends serving human purposes but as ends in themselves, and so dehumanize themselves and others, even their own children. Mrs. Ga-

49

bor's accusation parallels Nora's charge against her husband in *A Doll's House,* which similarly goes to the heart of the contradictions of late-nineteenth-century liberalism. Torvald, the principled liberal bourgeois, puts the abstraction of the law, which his wife broke only to save his life, above her, utterly oblivious to its original purpose of protecting the individual. It is his inability even to consider her intentions in his utter condemnation of her conduct, let alone his supposed feelings for her, that convinces Nora that he can never have loved her, for all he can see are abstractions, not persons. Through Mrs. Gabor, Wedekind generalized Ibsen's accusation. Men are but abstractions of human beings, out of touch with the body and its vitality, unable to relate to others as feeling subjects. They rationalize their fears and prejudices as "science," their ideologies masquerading as clinical judgments. Worse, they are hypocrites, and cowardly ones to boot. When Melchior, responding to the masked man's offer to take care of him, momentarily confuses him with his father, the mysterious figure informs him, "At this moment your father is seeking solace in the doughty arms of your mother" (81). Men not only indulge what they morally condemn, but do so like dependent children, using their wives for maternal comfort and consolation.

This impulse is one Melchior knows at firsthand. His idealization of femininity is countered by his powerful fear of the femininity in himself. It is both psychologically and dramatically significant that though it is Melchior who has written the praise of feminine enjoyment, it is Moritz who quotes it and professes to have been moved by it. He goes even further: he virtually expresses wistful envy of the female orgasm. "Believe me, Melchior," he tells his friend, "to have to suffer wrong is sweeter than to do wrong. To let oneself undergo a sweet wrong undeservedly seems to me the essence of earthly bliss" (31). This description of sexual climax invokes the stereotypes of feminine sexual innocence and male violence; Moritz is expressing a desire for the quintessential passive feminine experience. Though Moritz's fate was based on the suicides of two of Wedekind's schoolmates, through the character of Moritz Wedekind was exorcising the demons that their deaths excited in him. Like Moritz, Wedekind also struggled academically and was actually held back at one point, facing the terrors of educational failure. In the play, Moritz talks about how he would raise his children so that they are not soft and full of shame as he and Melchior are as a result of their upbringing. How to raise children is a girl's concern, as the next scene, in which Wendla and her girlfriends talk about their dreams of raising children, seems to suggest; but the link to Wedekind's thoughts in the diaries about raising his future children is obvious. Moritz is made to bear all the adolescent boy's ambivalent shame and fear at facing his sexuality, emotions that are stigmatized in the play as feminine; at one point, when Moritz refuses to confront Melchior's matter-of-fact descriptions of sex and is overcome with emotion, Melchior tells him straight out that he is like a girl (13). Moritz's suicide is the cowardly, unmanly way out of his failure at what it takes to be a man, epitomized in his inability to face disappointing his parents. His very mode of suicide, blowing off his head, is an act of emasculation, a symbolic castration.

It is the fear of his own attraction to the glory of feminine sexual passivity that explains Melchior's sadism. If he is not to be a woman, like Moritz, constantly afraid of the world and of himself, he must enact the exact opposite of femininity. If women invite the "injustice" of sexual attack, he must be the unjust sexual attacker, a tough, virile male who takes what he wants whether it is offered or not. Despite his belief in the superior bliss of female experience, he must reassert traditional masculinity; indeed, he must exaggerate it. Through Melchior's relationship with Moritz, Wedekind explored the femininity within males that so threatened traditional masculinity it had to be expelled violently.

Because the prevailing ideal of bourgeois masculinity must be affirmed, fathers, for all their rigidity, hypocrisy, and weakness, can't be dismissed. Most obviously they have the power, both legal and psychological, to enforce their unreason on their sons, as Mrs. Gabor's ultimate submission shows. But paternal power is not just external; it is internalized by the sons. Melchior's wistful question to the man in the mask—"Are you my father?"—as well as his touchingly sad acknowledgment that he would not necessarily recognize his father's voice point to his yearning for a father who would care for him and show him how to be a man, a yearning for his own father in fact, cold and rejecting as he is. And even that cold and emotionally absent father is an abiding internal presence for Melchior. He is present first of all in the internalized ethical judgment that makes Melchior ready to punish himself more drastically than his father would, but he is present even more fearfully in the very impulse that rouses Melchior's guilt—the masculine will to exploit women for his own needs that, for all their difference, he shares with his father. What makes that sadistic will and the ensuing guilt so much the worse is precisely the supposed female penchant for exploitation that invites violence without legitimizing it.

What Melchior does not share with his father is the lack of self-awareness that allows his father to compartmentalize his inconsistencies and sustain his masculine authority and self-confidence. Committed to the liberation of the body, whose reality he has learned from women—committed, therefore, to the liberation of female sexuality from the constraints of the puritanism that would destroy it—he can't hide from himself the contradiction of his own need to subjugate and control the female body. That conflict renders him not

51

only guilty but immobile, bereft of potency. The seductions that the headless Moritz offers him in death are putatively the seductions of omnipotence. The dead see everything and hence are above everything, he says; they see the timidity of idealistic youth, the terrors of emperors, the deceptions of lovers, the battle of God and the devil for superiority. These are the temptations of masculine power. Melchior is not deceived; if he agrees to die, it will not be because he believes death is the way to power but to the oblivion he deserves.

If he is to live, he needs an ethical formula that will enable him to heal the moral and psychological breach created by his masculine impulses. That is what the masked man purports to give him. Melchior did not kill Wendla by making her pregnant, he tells the boy. She was "superbly built" for child-bearing; it was the abortionist's pills that killed her. In any case, the moral philosophy by which Melchior condemns himself is based on a fundamental error. He has judged himself not only by an external idea of moral obligation, but by one that is at best only half of morality. "I take our morality to be the real product of two imaginary factors," the masked man asserts. "The imaginary factors are 'I ought to' and 'I want to.' The product is called 'morality.' Its reality is undeniable" (83).

The moral formula that the man in the mask offers Melchior is somewhat opaque, but decipherable enough to reveal its logical inadequacy as a solution to the problem posed by Melchior's masculinity. By describing moral commands with the pseudo-mathematical term "imaginary factors," the masked man presumably means that they are limiting cases, theoretically absolute demands that can't ever be realized in their purity in practice because they must be tempered by other absolute demands. Behavior can't be governed solely by the "I ought" any more than it can by the "I want"; the first suppresses life and the second leads to evil and anarchy. Authentic human morality is thus the tightrope between them. But in the case of Melchior's "stirrings of manhood," as he and Moritz had delicately put it earlier, there can be no compromise "product" because what he wants—his exploitive desire—is in outright conflict with what he ought. In an ironic foreshadowing of his own tragedy, Melchior had earlier argued that the outrage of Faust's transgression against Gretchen wasn't getting her pregnant; Faust would be no less culpable if he had simply broken her heart by abandoning her after promising to marry her. It was Faust's callous selfishness that was the crime. By his own criterion, then, Melchior is to blame in Wendla's case even if it was not her pregnancy that killed her. The selfish and sadistic nature of his sexuality makes desire itself intrinsically morally problematic; it is, after all, for his rape of Wendla, not his impregnation of her, that he feels most guilty. Though the masked man's moral prescription saves Melchior's life in the play, it is even more a deus ex machina than the figure of the masked man himself. The latter is successful as an anti-Realist dramatic innovation, but the hollowness of the masked man's moral formula marks it as a conceptual, psychological, and social failure.

Wedekind's first reckoning with the problem of masculinity in the face of the reality of masculine sexuality as he understood it ironically served not to solve it but to parse its elements more clearly. Contemporary bourgeois morality had discredited itself by its authoritarian, and hypocritical, denial of sexual freedom. It had turned the morality that was supposed to protect the self against self-expression, especially that of others. Women, excluded from the serious world of work and law, were the last repository of authenticity and free physical expression. But envying women undermined masculine self-confidence. To complicate matters, because the feminine also retained its stereotypical attributes of passivity, weakness, and masochism, male identification with femininity was terrifying. It provoked a hyper-masculine reactive drive to conquer and possess rather than identify with the feminine. This sadistic drive, in turn, further discredited masculine integrity without enhancing masculine strength. The masculine crisis that *Spring's Awakening* so acutely dramatized undermined the play's liberationist thrust. The exposure of these dilemmas opened the way for Wedekind's greatest exploration of the crisis of masculine identity and its putative resolution in the idealized, desired, feared, and finally hated woman.

53
•

The "Demonic" Ideal

I am not searching for [se]X, I am searching for woman.
—Frank Wedekind, unpublished diary entry

The rediscovery of the previously unpublished "Ur-Lulu," *Pandora's Box: A Monstertragedy,* is still fresh enough[46] that it must inevitably be considered under the shadow of the two published plays Wedekind carved from it—the plays that for much of her literary existence have defined the figure of Lulu. For obvious reasons, most attention has been paid to the changes that her character underwent between the two versions. There seems to be a consensus that Lulu is a softer, more sensually innocent creature in the original, and that the murderous femme fatale of enduring reputation is a creation of Wedekind's later revisions, though the change has been variously explained and variously assessed. Eric Bentley, for example, while preferring the "First Lulu" to the later plays on grounds of style and structure, does not make the change in Lulu a central issue and offers an essentially biographical explanation for it that is peripheral to the import of the play. In conversation with him, Bentley reports, Wedekind's daughter Kadidja attributed the change to the affair her father had with August Strindberg's estranged second wife, which—somehow—caused Wedekind to move closer to Strindberg's more misogynistic views of women.[47] For Ruth Florack, on the other hand, author of the most extended study to date of the original play, the changes in the figure of Lulu are nothing less than a fundamental subversion of its original meaning. The first Lulu, she argues, is not a character in the naturalistic sense at all, a woman to whom one can ascribe psychological motives, but a complex artistic construct made up of heterogeneous roles from French boulevard farce and cabaret and diverse fragments of a utopian vision of life as unconditional sensuality.[48] The central subject of the original play is the reification of sensuality that was created by the ever-intensifying utilitarian rationality of contemporary bourgeois society, a trend evident in the popular and pseudoscientific discourse of sex around the turn of the century. To the modern mechanization of sexuality as a physiological reaction of the "body-machine" or as a commodity for manipulation or sale, Wedekind opposed the idea of an unconditional, anarchic, and diffuse sensuality that fulfills itself completely in each ever-changing moment.[49] That he then turned Lulu from the signifier of a new ideal into the incarnation of the conventional fin de siècle femme fatale is the result of his frustration with his lack of dramatic success, and his consequent surrender to censorship and the public taste.

Wedekind himself is on record with the protest that the image of Lulu as femme fatale was overdrawn, even erroneous. He criticized the performance of the actress who first made the role of Lulu in *Earth Spirit* famous for not capturing his intentions. He had imagined Lulu as spontaneous and childlike, he claimed; what he saw instead was craftiness. His objection, of course, leaves open the possibility that there was something in the character as written to motivate the actress's interpretation, though he was always to claim that the best Lulu interpreter was his wife Tilly, a "child of nature"[50] like Lulu herself. The debate over Lulu, however, has obscured another equally important change between the first and the later versions of the play. The role of Alwa Schöning, the young playwright who in many ways represents Wedekind, is larger and more central in the original. In act 3 of the *Monstertragedy,* for example, his dalliance with Lulu is prolonged, explicitly sexual, and clearly the occasion of his father's death; he marries Lulu immediately afterward, and we later learn that she had actually slept with him on the day of her wedding to his father, before the ceremony, dressed in her bridal gown. In the two-play version, the marriage of Alwa and Lulu emerges only in the last act of *Pandora's Box* as an afterthought, and the incestuous tryst of the wedding day has turned into a mere fantasy. Alwa has a much reduced role in the orgy leading to his father's death, which, as the cli-

54
■

max of the self-contained play *Earth Spirit*, makes Dr. Schön (the name was shortened in the later plays) the most prominent male character of the first part of the restructured drama. The diminution and alteration of Alwa's role and the excision of the most blatantly oedipal material, as much as the changes in the character of Lulu, are crucial to understanding how problems of masculine identity shaped the entire Lulu project.

Lulu is a girl of unknown origins, rescued at age five from the streets, where she sold flowers to support her ominous "protector" Schigolch, by the journalist Dr. Schöning. Though Schöning has been having sex with her since her adolescence, he has married her off so that he can make a socially more respectable match after the death of his first wife. Lulu appears in the first act as the wife of the elderly Dr. Goll, who has commissioned a portrait of her from the young artist Schwarz. When Goll dies of a stroke after catching the artist and his model in flagrante, Lulu marries Schwarz; he in turn commits suicide when he learns that she has been carrying on an affair with Schöning. Despite his earlier declared intention of breaking with her, Schöning marries her too, only to discover her arranging trysts with his son and other paramours while he is supposed to be gone. In a jealous rage he tries to force her to kill herself, but she shoots him to death instead. Married now to Alwa, she flees to the demimonde of Paris with an entourage of sleazy characters all trying to exploit her and the one person who apparently loves her unselfishly, the lesbian Countess Geschwitz. Paris becomes untenable when one of the blackmailers reveals her whereabouts to the police, and the last act finds her in London, reduced to supporting herself, Alwa, Schigolch, and Geschwitz through prostitution. The final customer of her first evening is Jack the Ripper, who in the grotesque climax of the play kills Alwa, Geschwitz, and Lulu and cuts out Lulu's uterus as a keepsake.

Who is Lulu? Both as "real event" and as symbol, the mystery of Lulu's origins inevitably provokes the question of her identity. Florack's approach, Lulu as mere "signifier," denies the very validity of the question; much feminist criticism, with which Florack takes issue, has claimed, in an argument oddly convergent with hers, that Lulu has no character of her own. As the changing names she is assigned by the men in her life serve to show, she is nothing but a screen for their projections. That her identity is constantly constructed and reconstructed by males is clearly true. But to end with that observation is to stop short of the crucial question: *Why* do men fashion her as they do? And why, in the process, do they so completely miss Lulu's own reality?

Wedekind certainly assigned her a dramatic reality, both through her speeches and actions and through his stage directions. The play's point of view is not that of its male characters, or not that alone. Lulu's reality is un-doubtedly kaleidoscopic and contradictory, in part because Wedekind's at-titude toward her was contradictory (and would become even more so in the later versions), in part because contradiction is the psycho-logic of the female character produced by the conditions in which she is placed. But she is neither the figuration of innocently anarchic sensuality nor a cipher. She is narcissistic, playful, sensual, seductive, manipulative, a betrayer, even in the *Monstertragedy*. She takes the initiative as much as she responds to the initia-tives of her men. But her apparent agency, perhaps even her very sensuality, is at least in part the recoil of a trapped and desperate existence using the only means available to her to gain her ends. It is only in the perception of her men, in relation to their needs and fantasies, that Lulu is a free spirit.

Her ever-changing identity as Lulu, Nelly, Eve, Mignon represents a set of fantasy solutions to a series of problems of masculine identity. What her second husband Schwarz says of her—"I saw in her . . . my savior!"[51]—could have been said by any of the men in the play, including Jack the Rip-per. In fact, as Schöning points out, her first husband Goll did say it, and if Schöning himself doesn't do so explicitly, his behavior shows that he be-lieves it. Lulu supplies, in fantasy at least, what each male lacks for his sense of masculinity. Taken together, the qualities they see in her, the attributes they project onto her comprise Wedekind's diagnostic chart of the infirmi-ties of bourgeois masculinity at the end of the nineteenth century.

To Dr. Goll, physician and high-level bureaucrat, Lulu is the answer to his failure to live up to the male physical ideal—he is a "fat dwarf of a man"—and to the impotence of aging. Christened by him Nelly, she is the child he has never had, "the unfinished—the helpless—to whom a fatherly friend may not be dispensable just yet" (39); but she is also the sexual woman he keeps dressed in a slip during the day—"pure bordello style"—and has dance for him in a different costume every evening. Her dancing supplies him not only with vicarious sex but with an aging man's fantasy of infinite possibility. It is Goll who has commissioned Schwarz to paint her as Pierrot, though the symbolism of her Pierrot costume resonates for all the men in the play. Goll seems most taken by the androgyny of the traditional literary figure;[52] in response to Schwarz's questions about the costumes in which she dances for Goll, Lulu makes a point of describing only one in any detail, that of a fisherman. The androgyne is an image, perhaps the ur-image, of the ideal of human totality, since within it sexual otherness, so often in hu-man imagination Otherness incarnate, is absorbed into same. But given Wedekind's idealization of the feminine, the androgyne was perhaps also the inevitable symbol for the possibility of male appropriation of the ideal that femininity represented—the female male.

The painter Schwarz sees Lulu in the Pierrot costume as "magic, fairy tale incarnate," completely at one with her costume.[53] Her magic for him is partly that she *is* an incarnation. There appears to be no space between her and her role, or rather, she seems not to be playing a role at all; she is who she is, identical with herself. Schwarz himself is not. A poor man of modest origins in a highly stratified and class-conscious society, he aspires to be what he "is" not. Since he believes that Lulu, as the wife of a high medical official, is from the upper bourgeoisie, she could confer her status on him. "She has class" is his first observation about her. But more is at stake in her social standing than social status. Without the self-confidence of social status, Schwarz's very manhood is uncertain. At age twenty-eight he has never had sex, and though that is partly the choice of his lower-middle-class puritanism, he is embarrassed about it because it means he "lacks the guts to live. To love" (64). For Schwarz, Lulu is Eve, the ur-woman; possessing her confers absolute identity, in the literal sense of sameness through time, and absolute masculine power. "Ever since I've had you," he tells her explicitly, "I've known what I am, and got recognition for it. I've you to thank for my self-confidence, my pride as an artist, my joy in creating art. . . . It's the way you are: you bloom, you fade for me! Your body lives for me! Yes, I had to fish you out! *I was man enough . . .*" (68–69; italics added). Man enough, at least, to marry her—though he was initially so frightened of his inadequacy that when Goll's death gave him his chance with Lulu, he fantasized resurrecting the old man and giving him his own youth so that Goll could take her on again. But not "man enough" to consummate his marriage; though Schwarz desires Lulu, his repressive lower-class sexual values demand that she remain chaste and spiritual. "With just my arms uncovered," a frustrated Lulu tells Schöning contemptuously, "he runs wild like a Zulu, crash bang. . . after which he has nothing left for me but a few snorts" (82). Small wonder that when he learns of her origins, and above all that she is not a virgin, he is destroyed. "Be a man," Schöning urges him, accept her as she is; she is, after all, worth half a million marks. But it is his ideal Lulu who *makes* him a man. Without *that* woman, there is nothing left of his manhood, and therefore no recourse but death.

57

Schöning's fatal attraction to Lulu seems at first harder to explain as a response to precarious masculinity. An influential writer for a newspaper in the prime of middle age—in *Earth Spirit* Wedekind made him its editor in chief—worldly and cynical, he is neither impotent like Goll, nor naïve and inexperienced like the twenty-eight-year-old Schwarz, whom Schöning deftly skewers as young for his age. He has exploited Lulu sexually since her pubescence, but at the beginning of the play seems to want nothing more than to be rid of her so that he can marry a young girl of high society to enhance his own status. It was undoubtedly in part to fill the yawning gap between Schöning's repudiation of Lulu in act 2 and his marriage to her before act 3 that Wedekind added the notorious scene to *Earth Spirit* in which Lulu makes him break off his engagement in an abject letter to his fiancée dictated by "the woman who masters me."[54] More than anything else in *Earth Spirit,* it was this cold exercise of manipulative power that gave Lulu her reputation as femme fatale. But though the scene displays Lulu's emotional hold on Schön(ing) more dramatically than anything in the *Monstertragedy,* it doesn't explain it.

One clue to her power over him can be found in the opening scene of the original, omitted in *Earth Spirit.* Schöning is trying to convey to Schwarz the essential spirit of his recently deceased first wife, whose portrait he has commissioned Schwarz to paint from a photograph. He describes her as humble, too much the wife and mother to accept the homage of a portrait during her lifetime, yet a higher being untouched by anything low and trivial, one he looked up to for half his lifetime with "childlike reverence." His worship of this paragon of Victorian domesticity begins to explain his fascination with Lulu. Despite his worldliness, Schöning is no less a prisoner of the Victorian sexual split than Schwarz. His description of his wife resembles Schnitzler's picture of middle-class marital inhibition in *Reigen* and Freud's analysis of the sexually taboo respectable woman in "On the Universal Tendency to Debasement in the Sphere of Love." Schöning's high-minded wife, he unwittingly reveals, was as unthinkable sexually as a mother would be. Lulu fulfills all the Freudian qualifications for facilitating male potency. She is of disreputable origins, hence degraded, and unabashedly sensuous. Furthermore she is young, dependent, and controllable; Schöning has trained her sexually for himself since her girlhood. But if she has become in turn his master, there is more to his enthrallment than physical lust.

The social, political, and economic foundations of Schöning's power in the world are far less secure than his bearing and position suggest. The hints are subtle but their significance broad. That he wants to marry the daughter of a baroness points to the existing status hierarchy that afflicts his self-confidence no less than Schwarz's, if at a different social level. Perhaps an autobiographical allusion to the aristocratic pretensions of Wedekind's father in buying Lenzburg Castle, Schöning's aspiration is in any case symptomatic of the social anxiety of the class from which Friedrich Wilhelm Wedekind came. As for his occupation as journalist, Schöning may be able to manipulate public opinion—Lulu sarcastically advises him to draw a veil over Schwarz's suicide, as he has over so many other events—but he has no real control over an unsettled world whose constant upheavals threaten middle-class stability and power. At the very moment when Schöning is anguishing over the threat to his marriage plans created by Schwarz's suicide, Alwa rushes in with the announcement that the Reichstag—the emblem of the German middle class's political achievement—has been dissolved and that all is confusion at the newspaper office because no one knows how to handle it. Just a year later, the revised *Earth Spirit* raised the ante not only by elevating Schöning's position to editor in chief, but by heightening the political instability of the environment. At two junctures in that play, each concerned with a husband's discoveries of Lulu's infidelities, the news is announced that a revolution has broken out in Paris and that no one at the newspaper knows what to write. Wedekind wrote the *Monstertragedy* as well as its first revision *Earth Spirit* in Paris, between 1892 and 1895. "Revolution in Paris" had been both the reality and the symbol of a political world turned upside down since 1789, but at the end of the century, with the memory of the Paris Commune, the more recent near-coup of General Boulanger in 1888–89, and the increasing visibility of organized socialism, revolution meant popular threat to middle-class power, the threat of the unknown but restive masses who had been brought into the political arena in Western Europe by the recent extensions of the franchise. Bourgeois men, the plays suggest, have no more control over the political world than over their women—or perhaps they feel an intensified need to control women because of the threat of loss of control elsewhere.

59
∎

And the economic basis of their power is no less precarious than their hold on politics. The reason for Lulu's infidelity in her marriage to Schöning is that he can't be home to spend time with her because he has to tend to business. In the *Monstertragedy* he is at the command of the newspaper, always out covering events. *Earth Spirit* offers an indictment of economic conditions from a more financially elevated level. Editor Schön has invested all of his money in the stock market. When Lulu begs him to spend more time with him, he protests, "You know I have to be at the Exchange. I'm never free today. Everything I own drifts on a sea of chance" (92). His anxiety evokes the state of mind of the monied middle class ever since the stock market crash of 1873, the first in the history of the modern industrial era, which not only ruined many investors and inaugurated a depression that lasted until 1896, but exposed the structural precariousness of the new financial-industrial economy to the shocked optimists of the *Gründerzeit*. The dramatic evolution of the character Schöning suggests that there can be no such thing as real freedom, let alone security, in the new world of industrial and financial market capitalism.

Thus though Schöning knows the truth about Lulu better than anyone else, though he calls her a whore, his knowledge and disdain are as little a protection against his need for her as Schwarz's naïve idealization. Her apparent amorality and detachment seem to be her freedom, and the promise of his. Her sexuality and youthful energy are his hope for vitality and renewal. Even her brazen domineering is an attraction, because it is proof of power. As she taunts him at one point, he didn't marry her; it was she who married him. He never admires her more than in the costume she puts on to entertain her lovers. "You've come to us from the far side of the sunset," he tells her as he interrupts the tryst she's arranged simultaneously with his son and the acrobat Rodrigo. "On a flying trapeze"—again the image of the free circus performer. "Were it not for your big, round, little-girl eyes, the way you move your hips would create a major scandal," he adds, remarking on her seductive combination of innocence and sexual knowingness. And when she saucily responds that it's nobler to show off her hips than to conceal them, he concedes with the ultimate accolade, "Beauty conquers shamelessness. Your very flesh signifies *self*-conquest." Her response—"My very flesh IS Lulu" (116)—confirms his implicit identification of Nietzsche's overman, the self-overcoming human being who can live without transcendence, with the feminine body. The Nietzschean reference becomes explicit a few lines later when Schöning tells her to shoot herself with his gun. "If you'd also brought your riding whip," she responds playfully, apparently assuming he's joking, "it would have led you to different conclusions." This masochistic invitation is not the reversal of power it might appear. Lulu seems to be inviting her husband to exert his mastery over her, making her self-sufficiency his. In the context, however, it is a meaningless, even contemptuous invitation; her previous behavior has shown him just how much she is not his. He, however, is hers, and can't imagine not having her. In *Earth Spirit,* when Lulu coolly responds to his plaintive accusations that she has mistreated him, "You can get a divorce," it is meant as a taunt; divorce is not an option for him. "Is divorce possible when two people have grown so together that half of him is cut off in the division?" he asks, clearly speaking for himself (104). Schön(ing) does not have the inner resources to complete himself; he fought the temptation to dependency for a long time, but once having allowed himself to admit his need for Lulu, he can't accept the possibility of separation. Of course he seems prepared to kill her, or rather have her kill herself, but that is not the same as being abandoned by her. His rage is the murderous anger of the helpless child who does not have the power to kill the one upon whom he depends; his need to have her shoot herself is the acknowledgment of his impotence as well as his ambivalence.

Alwa Schöning, Lulu's fourth and last husband, is the Wedekind figure in the drama. If this were not obvious from his occupation as playwright and from the oedipal entanglement that has him marrying his father's wife and even claiming responsibility for killing his father, Wedekind made the identification blatant seven years later in *Pandora's Box,* where Alwa is the author of a play called *Earth Spirit.* Once again, however, more is involved here for Wedekind than autobiography and individual psychology. The fictive (as, indeed, the real) competition between father and son is not just the family drama of classical Freudian theory; it is a generational battle over values, and possession of Lulu is both the spoils of victory and the ultimate validation of the ethos of the younger generation. Alwa makes his appearance in the first act as the author of a stage version of Nietzsche's *Thus Spake Zarathustra,* currently in rehearsal, which he describes to the uncomprehending philistine Goll and to the disapproving elder Schöning. The idea for the staging is a comically outrageous bit of self-spoofing on Wedekind's part with a serious edge; it is a ballet in which Zarathustra himself dances and the overman is represented by a well-known contemporary female dancer. Nietzsche, Alwa proclaims in response to Goll's puzzlement, is the greatest dance genius the world has ever seen,[55] an exuberant claim that makes sense in the light not only of the image of dance as sensuous liberation in Nietzsche, but in his own essays. So does the idea of having the overman represented and danced by a woman. If Goll is baffled, however, Schöning is repulsed by the idea of having the crippled Zarathustra hopping about on crutches. For him dancing, to be respectable, must have a veneer of conventional aesthetic values. Schöning's indictment is implicitly from the point of view of the traditional humanist drama of Schiller, beloved by the educated German bourgeoisie, not least by Wedekind's own father. But conventional aesthetic values are also what make plays marketable, a good bourgeois concern—though Alwa himself is apparently not oblivious to financial interest; he has seen to it by engaging a popular dancer for Nietzsche's role.

The implication of the exchanges between Goll, Schöning, and Alwa is that "Nietzschean" art must make its way not only against the crude and decadent sensuality of a Goll; it must also triumph over the more classically refined and credible authority of Schöning. In *Earth Spirit,* Wedekind sharpens the opposition between father and son even further by depriving the father of any cultural standing whatsoever. The editor Schön, Lulu says, doesn't believe in any kind of art; all he believes in is newspapers.[56] In fusing the aesthetic/ethical with the oedipal battles, Wedekind underlined the problem of masculinity for the contemporary young artist who had to struggle not only against the aesthetic taste of the time but against its paternal avatars. Sons come to manhood, Wedekind implied, in part by coming to terms with the authority of their fathers. The task is usually solved by a combination of deference and identification, but that solution is obviated when the son wishes to replace the father's values wholesale rather than

come to terms with and internalize them. In the *Monstertragedy,* the son re-
places the father's values in the most literal and "masculine" way: he provokes his death and takes his woman.

But if Alwa is victorious over his father, he is destroyed in the end by his
relationship with his "mother," or rather, stepmother. For that is of course
what Lulu is, as Alwa himself points out: "Three years younger than me. Even
so she behaved like a mother to me. Of course she *was* my stepmother. My little sister."[57] She is more than that; as his mother/stepmother she is the living
incarnation of *his* overman. Certainly Alwa is no different from the other
men in the play in his desperate lust for Lulu. Invited to a tryst with her, he is
frustrated and petulant when she acts surprised, then insists that they first eat
the elaborate dinner she's prepared. "You said we'd have a Bacchanalian
revel. . . . You offered me a mini-orgy," he whines, and "teases" her with a
threat whose horror can be a joke only because of his timidity. "So, unless you
intend to make a sex murderer of me, I must give immediate expression to
the ecstasy I feel" (107–8). But like his peer Schwarz (and unlike their elders
Goll and Schöning, who will not let themselves understand their psychological dependency on Lulu), Alwa also values her for her ability to bring out
the spiritual in him, however intertwined his admiration for it is with physical desire. "She saw something in me, something better, higher," he explains
to Schigolch in London. "She talked to me about my spiritual problems. It
didn't last.—I made love to her the first time in her bridal dress, the day of her
wedding with Papa, she'd got the two of us mixed up" (178). It is his emotional and sexual, and as a consequence ultimately his financial, dependency
that has brought him to the miserable flat in London where he will meet his
death. "You are my fate," he had told her, prophetically, when he begged her
to take him along in her flight to Paris after she killed Schöning. But when he
sees Schwarz's portrait of Lulu as Pierrot that Geschwitz has salvaged and
brought to London, he believes he understands that fate more clearly than
before. Though Lulu herself now looks haggard and thin, the portrait has
frozen the image of the young woman in her prime. "She had everything that
could make a man happy," Alwa exclaims. "Joy in every joint, that's what this
girl feels. Love-longing underneath—and on top, daybreak. You don't see
lips, you see kisses." This is the vision of the eternal feminine—a vision of total joy, ever-new beginnings, and the promise of infinite love. But that is permanently available only in the portrait, whose ultimate significance at last
becomes clear: only art can capture the eternal feminine. As Schigolch comments looking at the portrait, "It sure is a heavenly boon, this picture. Woman
herself is here today and gone tomorrow" (184–85).

In the two-play version of Lulu, it is not only Alwa's role that is diminished, it is his manhood. In *Earth Spirit,* he is no longer the self-confident,

aggressive oedipal victor. His Nietzsche ballet has turned into *The Dalai Lama,* a celebration of Buddhist ascetic quiescence, and even it is barely mentioned in passing. When he appears at his father's home in the scene in which Schön is killed, it is not for a sexual tryst. He has never had sex with Lulu; indeed she praises him as the only man in the world who's ever protected her without debasing her in her own eyes.[58] And when he finally breaks down and confesses his desire for Lulu, to her great shock, it is with a masochistic boyishness that repels her: "You are as high above me as—as the sun towering over an abyss. . . . Destroy me!—I beg of you, put an end to me" (101). He is not a serious rival to his father.

Yet in *Pandora's Box,* there appears to be something self-chosen about his failure; it looks more like abstinence than incompetence. He is not married to Lulu in the Paris scene; he is dallying with an actress, though he sees her only at long intervals. His answer to Lulu's needling question about how he can stand the deprivation goes to the heart of Wedekind's interpretation of the dilemma of the male artist more clearly than anything in the *Monstertragedy.* "There's a close interplay between my sensuality and my creative impulses," Alwa tells her, "so that where you're concerned, I have the choice of either exploiting you artistically or of loving you."[59] Lulu is still the source of meaning in his life, and hence not only the inspiration but the subject matter of his art. But "life" and "art" are incompatible for him. To love is to be dependent and consumed; love is the death of his independent agency and consequently of his artistic creativity. He is explicit that the price he would pay for loving her would be joining the ranks of the emasculated: "For twenty years literature has produced nothing but half-men," he asserts, "men unable to beget children and women unable to bear them" (119). For Alwa there are only two psychological alternatives: he can be Lulu's object, or he can make her his object. The ultimate paradox he faces is that to be a man, he cannot allow himself to fulfill himself sexually *as* a man. This is the dilemma of the modern artist who has taken the sexually free woman as his muse.

There is some inconsistency between *Earth Spirit* and *Pandora's Box,* written seven years later, as if Wedekind had lost track of all the consequences for the character of Alwa he had to draw in the second play from the revisions he had made in the first. The marital seduction scene in the *Monstertragedy* finds a faint echo in *Pandora's Box;* Alwa boasts to Schigolch that he kissed Lulu for the first time in her bridal dress, and though he acknowledges that she didn't remember it afterward, he is sure she thought of him while lying in his father's arms. The oedipal triumph is now a fantasy rather than a real event, but it is that imagined victory, he admits, that gave Lulu her terrible power over him without his even being aware of it.

63
∎

The power of fantasy in a sense justifies the inconsistency in the portrayal of Alwa over the two plays because it makes plausible Alwa's final surrender to Lulu despite his knowledge that his love for her is the death of his creativity. Mere intellectual awareness of the incompatibility of loving and creating in the end can't protect him. He may have been able to write *Earth Spirit* by keeping psychological distance, but his inability to continue to do so means that he does not survive to write *Pandora's Box*. If, however, Alwa can't act to save himself, Jack the Ripper can, and does. As Alwa's "joke" about being driven to become a sex murderer makes only too clear, Jack the Ripper is Alwa, without the latter's inhibitions of love, conscience, and culture. What is left is the consuming rage that Alwa never allowed himself to feel toward Lulu, and the deification of woman that without the accompanying love for her can mobilize that rage into destroying envy.

Though he may have heard about "Jack the Ripper" in 1893, when he first thought of going to London, it was during his stay there in the winter and spring of the following year that Wedekind learned the full story of the still unidentified figure who had slaughtered his way into undying notoriety throughout Europe and America in 1888.[60] It was in London, appropriately enough, that Wedekind finished the last act of the *Monstertragedy*. With Jack, the whole design of the *Monstertragedy* finally becomes clear. As the play traces the downward descent of Lulu's fortunes, it also traces a double regression, through lower and lower levels of society and through ever-more primitive versions of the fundamental male ambivalence toward women. But each layer is not simply morally and culturally more primitive than the previous one. As the veneer of civilization is increasingly stripped off in the descending layers, what is revealed is the hidden truth of the higher ones, better disguised but no less determinative of behavior. The Paris scene—with its courtesans, stock market speculators, gamblers, swindlers, blackmailers, and white slavers—is both a portrayal of the shady demimonde of the modern big city and an exposé of the moral reality of the more respectable German bourgeoisie represented by Goll, Schwarz, and Schöning. Casti-Piani, the white slaver who is ready without hesitation to sell Lulu to a brothel in Cairo, is just somewhat further along on the same continuum of exploitation occupied by the physician and high governmental official Goll, who kept Lulu in a brothel costume and made her dance for him every night. It is the sinister Schigolch, like Alwa always on the scene, who ties together the sleazy underworld of the cosmopolitan big city and the apparently more staid middle-class German provincial town—not named in the original—where the play begins.[61] He is the brutalized Fagin figure, erroneously taken by many to be Lulu's father, who exploited her economically and abused her sexually when she was a little girl in Germany, and who is quite prepared to blackmail her into sleeping with him again when she needs a favor from him as an adult in Paris. He is also the only one of her original entourage to survive the slaughter of the London flat's inhabitants because he is out getting something to eat when Lulu brings Jack home. Schigolch survives precisely because he doesn't idealize women; to him they are only bodies to be used physically as needed. When Alwa talks about the beauty of a woman as a trap set by Providence that brings beatitude at the cost of misery, Schigolch equably responds, "Late in the evening, when you feel the need, you don't ask questions about physical charms. . . . What do you ask of a girl's eyes? Only that they not be the eyes of a thief."[62]

But Schigolch is the masculine exception, not the rule. Wedekind seems to suggest at one point that only the weary experience of age can rescue a man from a self-destructive idealization of women. In Schigolch's last appearance in the play, before its brutal climax, he comes across the body of Alwa, who has been struck unconscious by one of Lulu's customers. As Schigolch tries to revive him, with an oddly solicitous impatience at the obsession that has brought the playwright to this point, he glances at Lulu's portrait and acknowledges its power for him too. But the power he sees in it is death, the intimation of mortality, from which no woman can save a man. "When a guy's lived as long as yours truly, seen things flare up and then fall flat, he don't jump in the Thames," Schigolch muses. "No, he buys himself some Scotch Whiskey and eats some Christmas pudding" (192). His disillusion saves him, but, as Wedekind implies, for nothing more than a life of petty material comforts. Men who *don't* idealize women are mere animals.

It is Jack the Ripper, not the disabused Schigolch, who represents the logical climax of the masculine psychology of the play, and who in its horrifying conclusion reveals its ultimate rationale. His excision of Lulu's uterus displays, in the very reification of its symbolism, what it is that all the men really want from her. Though he speaks of the money it will be worth, he does not want it for commercial purposes, since he imagines it being auctioned off—with the rest of his collection—only after his death.[63] The uterus is the seat of female productivity, and Jack's appropriation of Lulu's womb is only the material form, the literalization of what all the men want from Lulu—her vital essence, her essential agency, her power of creation. Jack's amazement at Lulu's uterus—"Such a thing happens only once in 200 years"—seems to suggest that there is something special about it, different from all the others in his collection, though there is no hint of what that might be. Wedekind's failure to specify perhaps points to the confusion in the mind of the male characters—and in Wedekind's?—between the physical and the spiritual, between physical sexual possession of a woman and the psychological appropriation of her selfhood. But Wedekind was not the first or only writer of the time to make women's childbearing capacity the symbol of creativity, or to use that biological capacity to dramatize the Modernist male artist's sense of the precariousness of artistic creativity. His dramatic mentor, friend and rival August Strindberg, for one, had done it before him in *The Father*. The Captain's anguished lament in the play that women have children but men don't is true psychologically rather than physically. It is women, mothers in particular, who nurture—or fail to nurture—men's will and self-confidence in early childhood; the ultimate female power is the power to create, or prevent the development of, masculinity itself. Wedekind's notion of female power certainly included the maternal power of fostering the masculine will but went well beyond it. His own mother was the symbol of the energy, the autonomy, and the wholeness of body and spirit that his father, both as husband and as representative cultural ideal, was crushing out of existence. Given the masculine exemplars Wedekind had before him, given his acute consciousness of his own lack of completeness, there seemed to be no alternative but to see the ideal inherent in woman herself.

But that did not mean Wedekind was blind to the actual social situation of women; on the contrary, his mother's fate only served to dramatize it all the more vividly. The play constructs a Lulu quite different from the idealizing and demonizing projections of its male characters. She is not, however, a mere abstraction, let alone an ideal of anarchic sensuality. Her helplessness, her vulnerability, her coquetry, her narcissism, and her manipulativeness are evident from the moment she walks onstage. Her character is virtually summed up in the brief three-way exchange that takes place when she comes out of the dressing room in her Pierrot costume.

> Lulu: "You like me?"
> Schöning: (*Overcome*) Like you!
> Goll: A sight for sore eyes.
> Schöning: You've said it.
> Lulu: And I am fully aware of it.
> Schöning: Then you might be more human.
> Lulu: I do what I must.

The paradox of Lulu's character and situation is most fully epitomized in her killing of Schöning. She does initiate action, indeed she is that most destructively powerful of agents, a killer, but only in self-defense. Virtually everything she does is defensive and reactive. As precarious as her men's identities may be, Lulu's is more so. The mysterious vagueness of her origins, which to her lovers is a sign of her unboundedness—without the defining limitations of place, history, name she is anything and everything—is in fact the emblem and source of her weakness. An orphan abused from early childhood by her dubious protectors, she has no roots, no psychological sustenance, and no center to her being. She can't even throw out the "bitch" of a housekeeper who controls her life in Goll's household because she doesn't know herself well enough to dress herself.[64] Her reaction to Goll's death, after a momentary flash of relief that she'll never have to do tricks for him again, is a fantasy of abandonment, and then panic; he's through with her, what will she do now? (59). But her ultimate dependency is on Schöning; the turning point of the play is when he announces that he wants to end their affair so he can marry someone else. It was he who rescued her from the streets, raised and educated her, and transformed her into a middle-class woman, and this fact has formed her emotional life. "I belong to you," she begs piteously when he tries to break off. "Everything I have comes from you. Take it back. Take me on as your maid or something. . . . Make of me what you wish, why else am I there? Only, don't throw me away" (84). Under the surface flash and insouciance, Lulu loves Schöning with a victim's intense love for her savior, even if, perhaps partly because, he has abused her; it is easy enough for her to confuse his sexual desire for her with love for her.

Her neediness, it is true, has not left her without resources, however much they are misunderstood by men. Though she may be unable to believe in her own value, she is able to read her desirability in the eyes of others, and to manipulate it effectively and even malevolently. It is not through innocent playfulness that she has invited two men to a tryst in her husband's house without telling each of the other. The little displays of narcissism that punctuate the play represent a successful internalization of the admiring male gaze. Flirting with Alwa, she tells him how much she admired herself as she rehearsed her appearance for the ball to which her aspiring lesbian lover Countess Geschwitz has invited her. "It made me feel like slipping between my own legs," she teases salaciously, "oh yes, as I looked in the mirror I understood Geschwitz! I wish I'd been a man at some point—a man focussed on me: think of having ME between the pillows!" (108). But her narcissistic self-presentation, her apparent self-containment, is always in the interests of seduction. Lulu can never get enough love, even from the man she truly desires; her masochistic need for substitutes is even more humiliatingly desperate. She pleads her love to the white slaver who wants to sell her, and as a would-be prostitute she begs her customers to stay the night with her even if they can't pay her.

Undoubtedly the Lulu of *Earth Spirit* is harder, more self-aware, more cruel than the original. But it is not necessary to explain the transformation by assuming an abrupt change in Wedekind's attitude to women or an attempt to evade censorship or pander to public taste. To some extent, the revisions help fill in certain gaps in motivation and action in the original. It might well have seemed necessary to Wedekind to portray Schöning as more obsessed with and dependent on Lulu than he originally seemed to be, in order to make plausible both his marrying her and his murderous rage at her infidelity. Some account of why and how he broke off his engagement would have had to be part of any such modification. Both desiderata are taken care of in the infamous third act of *Earth Spirit,* in which Lulu collapses as she dances in a production of Alwa's attended by Schön, then uses his concern about her to force him with ruthless persistence to admit his need of her. The dramatic requirements of more logical action, of course, do not necessarily account for the sadism that Lulu displays here[65] and elsewhere in *Earth Spirit,* as for example when she tests Alwa's profession of love by telling him that she poisoned his mother. But Lulu's sadism in the revision is only a deepening of her coquetry and heedless manipulation in the *Monstertragedy.* Two motifs converged in the revision. By making Lulu's sadism more prominent, Wedekind rounded out her character, showing more fully the negative effects of victimization; survival in adverse conditions such as hers does not, after all, necessarily breed good character. But Wedekind was not only the playwright who understood his characters; he also identified with them. He shared the ambivalence of his males toward Lulu. The revisions of *Earth Spirit*—perhaps most especially the "Prologue in the Circus" added in 1903, which presents Lulu as a snake created to produce havoc and destruction— only bring out its hostile side of the ambivalence more explicitly.

But in *Earth Spirit,* Lulu is still as needy for love, as much victim, as in its predecessor. Nothing fundamental has changed. She is self-assured only when she is being seductive or when trying to fight off men's negative perceptions. She is "demonic" only when she is fighting for the love that she, as mistaken in this as the men, believes will give her a self. It is in *Earth Spirit* that Wedekind assigns Lulu perhaps the most perceptive observation of the play, the line that most objectively summarizes the mutual tragedy of men and women who distort one another's reality in the hopes of achieving identity in an age of masculine crisis. She senses, she tells Alwa, a higher significance in the excitement that her performance creates in her audience, a sad truth: "No one knows anything about anyone else. Everyone thinks himself the only unhappy victim."[66] Nowhere else in the play did Wedekind strike such a note of balanced empathy.

There is one glaring exception to the generalization that Lulu's cruelty is reactive: when it is directed not against the men who purport to love her but against the woman who genuinely does, the lesbian Countess Geschwitz. The implications of the savage contempt and cruelty with which she rebuffs Geschwitz's advances in the *Monstertragedy* are simply made more explicit in *Pandora's Box*. Lulu repays Geschwitz for the risk she undertook infecting herself with cholera in the plot to free Lulu from prison—an invention of the later play—with literally dehumanizing vituperation. When Geschwitz criticizes the white slaver Casti-Piani, Lulu explodes at her, "Shut up! Say anything bad about that boy and I'll kick you in the stomach! He loves me with an honesty that makes your most extravagant sacrifices seem a beggary. His self-denial makes me see how loathsome you really are. You weren't finished in your mother's womb, and now you're neither man nor woman. You aren't human as the rest of us. There wasn't enough to make a man of you, and you have too many brains for a woman. That's why you're mad."[67]

What accounts for the ugliness of this tirade? And there is an even more elementary question concerning Geschwitz: What function does she serve in a play whose essential concern seems to be the working out of masculine identity through woman? To confuse matters even more, in the foreword added to the third edition of *Pandora's Box* (1906), Wedekind claimed that the main tragic character in the play was not Lulu but Geschwitz. Lulu, he asserted, plays a passive role in all three acts while Geschwitz offers herself in superhuman self-sacrifice in the first act, mobilizes all her energy in the second to overcome the "unnaturalness" that fate has burdened her with, and dies heroically defending her friend in the third.[68] It is not necessary to take the idea of Geschwitz's priority over Lulu at face value; the rest of the foreword makes it clear that it is a ploy to attack the censors, who balked at Lulu's depravity but not at Geschwitz's lesbianism. But Wedekind's insistence on her dramatic significance *should* be taken seriously.

Because of its very accuracy, his description of Geschwitz's behavior seems at first only to sharpen the dilemma of Lulu's response—why so much cruelty in repayment for so much devotion? But Geschwitz's selfless love is of the essence of her ironic function. Geschwitz's love for Lulu can be selfless precisely because it is the love of a woman for a woman; unlike the men, Geschwitz does not need to use Lulu to achieve an identity that as a biological woman she already has. But by the same token, her love is literally fruitless; Lulu cannot respond to it because a woman cannot fulfill her elemental creativity with another woman. It is only the womb that could be impregnated by a man that (in the male view) has creative significance; that is why Jack the Ripper does not cut out Geschwitz's uterus, why the sadistic murderer can dismiss the lesbian as a "monster" and tell her disdainfully that she is safe from him.[69] Geschwitz's second-to-last last speech in the *Monstertragedy* fixes on her childlessness as the sadness of her fate: "One human makes another . . . why am I . . . deformed," she laments. "I'm not gonna get married. There's just one person I want to know: Lulu" (204). Geschwitz is the foil for the idea of the male's necessity for female creativity. Her presence in the play—and Lulu's reaction to her—seem to signal that even if it is the case that man needs woman for his identity, it is equally true that no woman can do for another what a man can do. The sterility of Geschwitz's love in Lulu's eyes is Wedekind's protest against the self-sufficiency of woman's creativity, the symbol of his effort to undermine the very source of her fatal attractiveness to men. Women need men too.

In *Pandora's Box,* Geschwitz's lesbianism takes on new significance through what Wedekind added to and subtracted from the original play. No less unnatural, it becomes a symbol for the outsider status that enables one to see the truth that life's participants cannot see, the truth that Lulu was implausibly given to see, if briefly, in *Earth Spirit.* "People don't know each other—they have no idea what they're like. The only ones who know them are those who aren't human themselves," Geschwitz reflects. "I'm not a human being; my body has nothing in common with human bodies. And yet I have a human soul. . . ."[70]

This new insistence on her soul pushes her to a position she could not have taken in the *Monstertragedy,* where she is all masochistic yearning. "I know," she concludes, "I have nothing to gain by giving away and sacrificing everything." The result is a resolve that tragically comes too late. "This is the last evening I shall spend with these people.—I'll go back to Germany. My mother will send the money.—I'll go to the university. I must fight for women's rights, study law" (166). Wedekind gave the Geschwitz of *Pandora's Box* the autonomy and dignity she does not have in the *Monstertragedy*—a move also just made possible by the admission of women to German universities the previous year. Autonomy and dignity are even translated into a different form of action; instead of helplessly calling for the police as Jack murders Lulu, as she does in the original, she tries to shoot him with a pistol.

But what Wedekind gave with one hand, he took away with the other. By her resolve to become a lawyer and fight for women's rights, Geschwitz has become a New Woman—the kind of feminist Wedekind abhorred. The symbolism of her identity and her fate in this context is doubly baleful. The implication of Geschwitz's decision seems to be that a woman who joins the world of work and profession is unnatural and consequently less than human, or inversely, that only "unnatural" women do so. A woman cannot be both sexual, meaning of course heterosexual, a "real" woman, and active in the world like a man. If Lulu's death at the hands of Jack is the masculine revenge on the feminine woman whose very desirability turns her into a fearsome goddess, Geschwitz's murder is a punishment for women who would unsex themselves and destroy the only possibility men have for salvation. Her murder by Jack suggests also that men have no way to deal with a woman who refuses her salvific role and tries to be one of them. If it is impossible to live with the feminine woman, it is impossible to live without her. The dying curse of Geschwitz's futile love are the last words of the play in its original and its final version.

Despite her real cruelty on occasion, however, Lulu is a "failure" as a demonic woman, not by accident but by authorial design. In a telling vignette, Tilly Wedekind offered a crucial insight into Frank's understanding of his heroine. During a performance in which she and Frank were playing Lulu and Schön, he heard the audience laugh when Tilly, dictating the letter to Schön's fiancée breaking off their engagement, spoke the words, "I write to you at the side of the woman who masters me." Always morbidly terrified of ridicule, Frank, who had been bent over the page and could not see Tilly as she spoke, asked her after the performance what she had done to elicit laughter. She told him that at the word "masters" she had bent her head to one side in a gesture that was both humble and innocent. He declared himself in full agreement with her interpretation; the contradiction between her words and her bearing, which was what had made the audience laugh, were wholly in the spirit of his play.[71] Lulu's power for good and ill comes from the men who need it. Having magnified her into a delivering angel, they must see her as a demon when she exerts that power in any way against them. It is true that without certain obvious qualities—her sexuality, her vitality, the mystery of her origins—Lulu would not furnish the basis in reality that is always required to erect a plausible structure of fantasy. That men can't see the rest of Lulu's reality, however, testifies to the abyss on which their masculinity is so precariously perched. In the Lulu plays Wedekind constructed a broad-ranging social interpretation of the power of women that implicated virtually every level of middle-class masculinity. It represented a diagnosis of the masculine infirmities of his father and his father's generation—as well as his own. Haunted by age, by social, political, and economic insecurity, or by an aesthetic bent that is increasingly marginal in a society dominated by productivity and profit, men find in feminine sexuality, isolated from the forces that have weakened *them,* the fountain of everything they lack. To possess it is to possess themselves, their own masculinity. To need to possess it for that purpose is to declare themselves bankrupt of the very thing they seek.

Chapter One

The Ambiguous Masculinity of the Con Man

> *Why should anyone want to be a useful member of human society? . . . I need no
> justification for my existence! I asked no one for my existence and I deduce from
> that my justification for existing according to my own dictates.*
>
> —Frank Wedekind, *The Marquis of Keith*

Wedekind reworked the Lulu plays for almost twenty years after his first inspiration. But the artist's crisis of masculinity had another dimension that
they had barely touched on—the insecurity of the artist's place in a society
that valued commerce over art and demanded of art that it satisfy the tastes
of those who had money if its creator were to survive. If both the psychological and the social reasons for the precariousness of masculine self-
confidence in Goll, Schwarz, and Schön are made clear in the Lulu plays,
Alwa's problematic masculinity, the masculinity of the artist, is centered almost wholly on the intrafamilial oedipal struggle with his father. Yet that
psychological struggle too had a cultural-ideological dimension, as I have
suggested, and Wedekind's concern with the artist's identity in a commercial society goes back to one of his earliest plays, *The Quick-Sketch Artist*. His
difficulties with the official censorship, however, which banned the production of *Spring's Awakening* and *Earth Spirit* for many years, made him return
to the problem of art and the artist in a modern capitalist economy in a
series of plays dating from the late 1890s, the most famous of which is *The
Marquis of Keith*. These plays can legitimately be considered under the
rubric of "Art versus Mammon."[72] *The Marquis of Keith,* in particular, was
Wedekind's angry but maliciously gleeful reckoning with Munich, with
what he regarded as the truly low-brow philistinism of its vaunted cultural
reputation as a capital of the arts in Germany and Europe. But underlying
the issue of the economic and social precariousness of the artist is the meaning it had for Wedekind in terms of the artist's existence as a man.

The "Marquis of Keith" would seem to be a strange sort of figure to
choose to represent the artist. His only art is that of the con; he is a clever
phony, a man of lower-middle-class origins masquerading as an aristocrat,
who hopes to use the greed and artistic pretentiousness of philistine Munich
businessmen to make a killing and live the high life. He has convinced three
of them to invest in his "Fairyland Palace," a huge cultural complex in which
supposedly "all the arts of the world will find a welcome home," but that is in
reality a vulgarized venue for the indiscriminate mixture of high culture,
commercial space, and Disneyland-type entertainment, complete with food
facilities. "What you see here," he promotes to his backers, showing them the
plans for the building, "is the large concert hall with its sliding ceiling and

skylight, so that in the summer it can serve as an exhibition palace. Next to it here there is a smaller theater which I intended to make popular by means of the most modern of artistic decorations, something, you know, which is a cross between a dance hall and a death chamber. The most modern of styles is always the cheapest and the most effective advertising."[73] Of course there is no Fairyland Palace; Keith has pocketed and spent his investors' money. When they finally demand to see his books, he is destroyed.

But Keith is a rather odd kind of con man, as his insouciance about the mechanics of the con suggests. He is not fundamentally interested in the money, either for its own sake or for what it can buy. He may sound like a cynic; as he tells the rebellious young son of a rich businessman who insists that there must be things of higher value than wealth, "These things are called 'higher' because they are the products of material possessions and are only made possible through material possessions" (239). But his cynicism is not about the existence of higher things, only about the naïvely idealistic notion that one can engage in them and enjoy them without a secure material existence. Keith is himself interested in higher things. Wedekind referred to Keith as a "*Genussmensch,*" a man interested in the enjoyment of life, but Keith's notion of enjoyment is both Nietzschean and Romantic. The swinish Munich businessmen who worry more about toilets and adequate restaurant space than artistic facilities deserve to be swindled precisely because they are utterly incapable of the things of the spirit. "My talent," Keith tells his lover, "is restricted by the unfortunate fact that I'm unable to breathe in a bourgeois atmosphere." Given that he must operate there, however, he will wait for a time when "the crossing of the philosopher with the horse thief will be appreciated at its full value" (241–42).

Keith's self-description as a philosopher, however ironically intended, is in fact fully justified. His philosophy emerges in a crucial exchange with his childhood friend Ernst Scholz, an aristocrat Keith had met when his father was hired as Scholz's tutor. Scholz is Keith's ideological counterplayer. By birth the Baron Trautenau, he gave up his aristocratic way of life because he could not justify it to himself in an era when worth is determined by social usefulness; but in his first useful employment as a railway official, he caused a disaster with great loss of life. Suffused with guilt at the result of his utilitarian ineptness, he has come to his friend to learn how to enjoy life, believing that Keith is the arch-exponent of hedonism, but he cannot give up his moralistic attitude. Now it has become the badge of his superiority over his friend. "Before I came to Munich I was able only to appreciate the spiritual significance of the relationship between men and women, because at the time sensual gratification seemed vulgar to me. I've learned that it's the other way around," he boasts. "But you, in your entire life, have never valued a woman for anything higher than sensual gratification." Keith rejects this characterization. "Things are really quite different," he says, pointedly exposing the unacknowledged material foundation of Scholz's achievement. "I can thank these last two weeks for my *material* freedom, and as a result I am finally able to enjoy my life. And you can thank these last two weeks for your *spiritual* freedom and as a result you are finally able to enjoy life." Scholz replies with some pique, "With the difference that all my pleasures are concerned with becoming a useful member of human society."

> Keith: Why should anyone even want to become a useful member of human society?
> Scholz: Because otherwise one has no justification for his existence!
> Keith: *I need no justification for my existence! I asked no one for my existence and I deduce from that my justification for existing according to my own dictates.* (292; italics added)

74 ■   This is another of Wedekind's highly personalized versions of Nietzsche. It is the absolute rejection of the notion that life needs to be justified by anything higher than itself; the justification, however, is implicitly aimed not at the claims of religion but at the authority claims of a father representing the bourgeois ethic: I did not ask you to be born, and therefore I don't need to be beholden to you by identifying with your values, life-destroying as they are. In the end, Scholz refuses to lend Keith the money that would enable him to rescue his enterprise and invites him to withdraw from the world where they both have failed and join him in entering an asylum. It is an invitation similar in meaning to the one Moritz offered Melchior in *Spring's Awakening*, and Keith, like Melchior, rejects it, this time without the need of a paternal intermediary. Despite adversity, he refuses to renounce his intrinsic worth as a human being.

But this proud autonomy is only the declared side of his philosophy. His lover Anna, the widowed Countess Werdenfels, herself something of a con artist who is working her way up society by trading her voluptuous beauty for advantageous marriage, is well-situated to recognize the other part of Keith—his neediness. Though no great singer, Anna is taking voice lessons; Keith wants her to sing in a concert benefit for the Fairyland Palace, believing that her physical charms will win her the admiration that her singing might not. But Anna is fully aware that Keith's motive is not simply exploitation; she fears that he overvalues both her beauty and her singing because he is infatuated with her. "I no sooner come within your sight," she tells him, "than you hear and see the most fantastic sort of daydreams. You overrate my appearance as much as you overrate my art. . . . Just because you're losing your mind out of love for me, is that any reason why I should heap the scorn of all Munich on my own back?" (282). Without responding directly, Keith confirms her description of him as a dreamer. He is sure their efforts will be rewarded, he tells her, and if not, their children will be. To her no-nonsense rejoinder that he hasn't any children, he responds: "Then you will give them to me, Anna—children with my intelligence, with robust healthy bodies and aristocratic hands. And for that I shall build you a home fit for a queen, such as a woman of your stamp deserves! And I shall place a spouse at your side with the power of fulfilling every desire mirrored in your great black eyes" (283). This is indeed a fantasy; he *has* overidealized his lover. When she realizes that Keith is headed for disaster, she accepts the proposal of Consul Casimir, the powerful and wealthy Munich businessman who refused to invest in Keith's venture and who exploits his failure to take it over. Anna's concert appearance had exactly the effect on him Keith had hoped for, except that Anna, not Keith's venture, is the beneficiary. In his lust Casimir wants to marry her, not caring that she doesn't love him; Anna makes the deal when it appears to be the best she can get. She, not Keith, is the material hedonist, the hard-headed practical schemer who has an eye for the main chance.

Keith is outraged by her betrayal of art. "I know my weaknesses," he tells her, "but these men are domestic animals. . . . [I]f you take refuge from your artist's fate behind a sack of money, then you are worth no more today than the grass that one day will grow on your grave"(304). But the personal betrayal is worse. Keith not only believes in love; it is the ultimate justification of his existence, as he inadvertently revealed when he promised Anna a spouse who would devote his life to fulfilling her wishes. If he always misjudges women, as Anna tells him, adding insult to injury, it is this need that makes him do so. His autonomy is to a great extent nothing but negative freedom, a protest against the restrictive bourgeois ethic. Its positive content is supplied by the service of love.

The one who knows his need best is his other girlfriend Molly, the young girl he has brought with him from the provinces and who serves him selflessly while he carries on his adventures. "You can't live without my love," she tells him in triumphant desperation, knowing that he belongs to her only when he's in misery (246). He is in fact contemptuous of her and what she represents. "She lets herself be eaten up with longing for her petit bourgeois world where, brow to brow, they drudge and humiliate themselves and love one another!" he says trying to justify not loving her. "No free view, no free breath! Nothing but love! As much as possible and of the commonest sort!"(303). But he keeps her with him for the very things for which he castigates her, the steadiness and selflessness, the all-consuming nature of her love; if she is nothing but love, he is its only object. When she disappears, he is at first more concerned about being blamed than he is about her fate because he still has Anna. But after Anna leaves him, his emotional dependency on Molly comes to the surface. He begins searching for her in panic, crawling on hands and knees: "Molly!—Molly! This is the first time in my life that I have whimpered on my knees in front of a woman" (308).

The discovery of her suicide threatens him with total destruction; the angry crowd of local residents who found her body threatens to beat him up or even kill him. But dramatically, the physical threat functions as a deus ex machina, displacing attention from the psychic threat of the loss of love. Consul Casimir steps in to rescue him, using the authority of his wealth and position to chase off the crowd, and gives him money on behalf of Anna to enable him to escape Munich. In a reprise of the ending of *Spring's Awakening,* Keith hesitates between taking the money and using against himself the revolver that he had brandished to protect himself from the crowd, ultimately deciding again for life. But the grin on his face and the jaunty attitude of the words that express his resolve to go on—"Life is one switch back after another"—cannot wipe out the reality that Wedekind dramatized.

Earlier in the play, Keith expresses the hope and belief that his imminent success with the Fairyland Palace will bring an end to the "perilous rope dancing" he has engaged in for ten years. Later he tells Scholz that he needs all the elasticity possible to make his scheme succeed amid all its complexities. In this context, the metaphors of tightrope walking and elasticity have subtly changed their meaning from the original circus essays. Applied to the male artist, they are the essence of precariousness, not graceful balance, the representation of a situation to be ended, not an ethic to be emulated. In the play, they represent the situation of the (male) artist in society, a precarious balancing act of which the almost unavoidable dangers are commercial sellout on the one side and oblivion and penury on the other. Such a life does not give one the masculine solidity necessary to hold a woman. Anna's choice of Casimir is the most humiliatingly direct expression of the artist's questionable masculinity, as Keith's contemptuous dependency on Molly is its most humiliatingly subtle expression. It is the Casimirs of this world who have the power and win the women—though the play gets its masculine revenge on them too. Casimir cannot hold the loyalty and admiration of his own son, who chose Keith over him, and Casimir has Anna but not her love. Despite Keith's insouciance at the end, however, that revenge does not seem to offer much consolation.

The Trials of Marriage

> *"Isn't it a downright superhuman effort for you, my revered master, to risk*
> *your life simultaneously as a playwright and as an actor?"*
> *"And as a lover! That is the most trying!"*
>
> —Frank Wedekind, *Franziska*

The Marquis of Keith, Wedekind's favorite play and the one on which he placed his greatest hopes for winning a reputation as a serious dramatist, was in his own words a "laughable failure"[74] when it was first staged in 1902. Under the circumstances, the judgment uttered by the protagonist of his successful play *The Court Singer (Der Kammersänger,* 1897)—which he regarded as his worst[75]—rings with particularly savage irony. Importuned by the unsuccessful composer Professor Dühring to promote his opera, which he claims has been rejected commercially because it is too musically pure, the court singer Gerardo rejects the would-be artist's self-pity and self-congratulation. "The measure of a man's importance is the world," he says coldly, "and not his own inner conviction. I didn't put myself on the market; I was discovered. *There are no unrecognized geniuses.* We are not even the masters of our destinies. *Man is born to be a slave.*"[76] More precisely, the artist is. Gerardo, whose singing success attracts not only desperate artists but women groupies of all social levels ready to give up everything for him, including their lives, has no illusions about his real power. "We artists are nothing but a luxury item for which the bourgeoisie bid competitively," he admonishes the composer (412). The acknowledgment was not just a lament for the merely ornamental place of art in a utilitarian society; it represented the artist's partial internalization of society's judgment of the worth of the artist, and hence his own judgment of his worth, or worthlessness, as a man. Wedekind was contemptuous of whatever success he had achieved as a cabaret performer, even one who was also the composer of many of the songs he sang. "Put yourself in my place," he had written beseechingly as he struggled to get *Keith* produced. "I have to present myself to the Berlin public as a joker and a clown, while as a serious man I am prevented from saying the best that I have to say, that which is holy to me."[77]

His feelings of impotence and his terrible fear of ridicule found expression in the two plays he wrote after *The Marquis of Keith,* his most directly autobiographical so far. In *King Nicolo, or, That's Life (König Nicolo, oder, So ist das Leben,* 1901), the artist is represented as a king who is deposed because of his self-indulgence and who after many humiliating adventures ends up as the court jester to the man who has replaced him. The speech in which the reigning king appoints him pointedly displays the ambivalent hovering between grandiosity and nothingness that characterized Wedekind's sense of the artistic vocation in the real world, as well as the way he uses irony and wit to mock oversolemnity toward the problem. As itinerant actors, Nicolo and his daughter have impressed the king with their farce about a monarch brought by his conscience to recognize the human costs of the wars he has instigated. Feeling the need for this kind of reminder, King Pietro declares:

> Right beside the throne there is an empty post that I left unfilled up to now because I did not want to make room for stupidity where even the greatest quantity of wisdom was too limited. You, however, will assume that post. You will be without rights and power in relation to the least of my subjects. But your elevated way of thinking will stand between me and my people; it may even thrust itself between me and my child. Just as your spirit stood upright between the ruler and his dark desires there on the stage, so it will rule within me. I appoint you my court fool.[78]

The artist is the moral consciousness of society and its impotent jester. The portrait of the aesthetic moralist in his next play—*Hidalla, or, Karl Hetmann, the Dwarf Giant* (*Hidalla, oder, Karl Hetmann, der Zwergriese*, 1903–4)—was if anything an even more self-mocking caricature. Hetmann, the prophet of a new morality of beauty, has established a League for the Breeding of Thoroughbred Humans to realize his ideal. Its members, recruited for their beauty, have the statutory right and obligation of free sexual access to one another; Hetmann himself, ugly and misshapen, cannot join his own organization but is not the less a zealot for that. Chastened, however, by the exploitative behavior of some of his wealthy supporters (including a publisher who gets him arrested for offenses against decency—a hardly veiled allusion to Wedekind's own recent imprisonment for lèse-majesté[79]), Hetmann recognizes the superficiality of his earlier approach to improving the race. Mere physical beauty can cover spiritual ugliness. It is only where "energy and health are life goals that beauty flourishes all by itself, as the enticingly splendid bloom whose fairest fruits are again energy and health."[80] In that spirit he wants to continue his battle to free humanity from the "feudalism of love," whose barbaric products are the reviled prostitute, the spinster defrauded of a love life, and the virgin whose sexuality must be suppressed as the price of an advantageous marriage. But Hetmann is no more successful with his new approach than with his old. Balked again by the betrayal of supposed allies and the outraged incomprehension of the masses, he becomes an object of ridicule; when a circus master offers him employment as a clown, he commits suicide.

Hetmann was not Wedekind, or not wholly; Wedekind never shared his character's obviously lampooned racial ideas, though he knew and drew upon the literature of the then-flourishing eugenics movement for his play.[81] But Hetmann displays the masculine psychology of the writer-reformer as Wedekind knew it from the inside. Most telling is Hetmann's relationship to Fanny Kettler, the beautiful, spirited, and independent young woman who, though a member of the League, is in love with him for his visionary idealism. Initially, apparent consistency with his own ideals of beauty forces Hetmann to reject her, but even later, when he acknowledges his error of overvaluing mere beauty and insists that he has striven for nothing but enjoyment all his life, he can't allow himself to accept her offer of life and love. Whatever the obstacles to sensual joy presented by an oppressive regime and an uncomprehending society, Hetmann's failure is as much internal as external. A rejected would-be lover vengefully exposes his secret. "Listen to me, Fanny!" she exclaims bitterly. "He is a man who feels the most frightful anguish when he knows he is loved. . . . Mr. Hetmann is horrified by women who love him. He longs for prostitutes who misuse him. His whole philosophy is based on that!"[82] Hetmann implicitly acknowledges the charge and even offers an explanation when he angrily responds to Fanny's unguarded appeal to be his lover, "Should I couple my horrible deformity, which causes people to shudder, to your shining beauty? Should I abandon everything that fills me with knowledge, strength, elasticity and confidence simply to hold you as a woman in my arms?" (656). It is not his crusading idealism that makes the personal fulfillment Fanny offers him impossible to attain. He hides behind his role because he does not trust his own masculine appeal, despite Fanny's obvious testimony to it. Only his work allows him the feeling of power, though this too is an ironic piece of self-delusion, since he has been manipulated and defeated repeatedly by those who understand and control the real world far better than he. The implication of Hetmann's admission of self-doubt was a fateful forecast of Wedekind's marriage and the additional cruel knowledge about the artist's masculinity he would gain from it.

Wedekind had had many liaisons over the years and had fathered two illegitimate children. None of his affairs had lasted very long, however. His friends, who judged him to be authoritarian, moody, and bohemian, did not believe him capable of, or even interested in, a permanent connection. They were wrong about the latter. There was in his psyche an unfinished drama yet to be played out.

It was not simply a bad joke of fate that Wedekind met his future wife Tilly Newes when she played Lulu and he Jack the Ripper in the first performance of *Pandora's Box* produced by Karl Kraus in Vienna in 1905. Life does not imitate art by accident. Wedekind himself blurted out the significance of the scene of encounter, no doubt without fully understanding it. Lulu / Tilly's Pierrot portrait had to be painted again for the play's second performance because the one used in the first had disappeared. Just as she finished changing into the Pierrot costume for the sitting, Wedekind came into the room with the obvious purpose, Tilly noted archly sixty years later, of returning the kiss she had boldly given him backstage at their first performance. But she agilely escaped him and ran teasingly through the studio round chairs and tables with Wedekind in hot pursuit. "Suddenly," she remembered, "he stood stock still, smacked his forehead and exclaimed, 'But this is *Earth Spirit,* act one!'"[83]—the scene in which the artist Schwarz chases a laughing Lulu around his studio. Wedekind was not alone in his realization. When Tilly's father first met Frank on a visit the couple made to her birthplace Graz, where they appeared onstage together in the Lulu plays, he remarked after the performance, "Frank can't be surprised about anything, he has married Lulu, after all." To which Tilly commented with apparent bewilderment, "Strange, that my father and my husband both thought so, and that this made my marriage so difficult."[84]

Whether or not Tilly "was" Lulu, Wedekind made her so, and reacted to her accordingly. It was not just imagination, of course; the facts assisted greatly in the construction, indeed help explain his choice of Tilly. She was nineteen years old when she and Frank met, just under half his age; the difference replicated that of his parents almost exactly—and more or less that of Schön and Lulu. Like Emilie Wedekind, Tilly was a precocious and talented performer, having acted since her early teens; like her, she was independent, vivacious, coquettish. Wedekind was immediately attracted, and their difficulties began just as quickly. Their marriage was bracketed by Tilly's two suicide attempts. The first occasioned Frank's proposal when, pregnant with his child, she jumped into the river in the dead of winter after Frank, in a fit of rage over a fancied slight, tore up all her pictures and stamped on the pieces. The second, more serious, occurred just a few months before Frank's death twelve years later. The core of the marital problem, apart from Tilly's family history of depression, was his pathological jealousy. He saw rivals where there were none, forced Tilly to give up her independent acting contract and appear only with him so that he could monitor her every response, and still attacked her constantly for flirting and worse. The extremes of his behavior might have been comical if they hadn't been so destructive. He gave up a chance at a connection with the archduke of Hesse-Darmstadt, who admired his work, a connection that might have given him the financial security and respectability he craved, because Tilly's first boyfriend was the director of the archduke's theater. Once, when one of Wedekind's sons came to visit, Tilly lent him his father's cravat so that he could go to a formal event. The young man developed a crush on her and wrote a play in which a son falls in love with his father's young wife and makes love to her. It was Alwa Schön come grotesquely to life, with Frank now in the role of the father. "The son had hit his father's deadly wound with unerring instinct," Tilly half understood,[85] but Wedekind never forgave her for "seducing" the boy. When she related the episode to her mother-in-law, who had been cool to her at first, Emilie took her daughter-in-law's side; she had experienced exactly the same kind of thing in her marriage.

Despite Tilly's need for, and demonstrated capacity for, independence, she submitted to Wedekind's every demand. Nothing helped. He would soothe her when his behavior made her cry in despair, then repeat it. Much later, detached enough to look at it more clinically, she suggested that the reason for his constant readiness to suspect the worst was a deep sense of himself as unlovable. If he remained faithful, it was only because she was young and he was afraid of losing her. Though he could be kind, he was reluctant to show it because he was afraid she would exploit it and ride roughshod over him.[86] It was only in retrospect, she said, that she understood that he had almost no personal interest in marital love and sex, though they were the central themes of his work. He was more concerned with the fidelity of her body than with her body itself, more concerned with his art than their conjugal life.

Undoubtedly her psychological observations, though simple, were accurate as far as they went. But in Wedekind's hands they were more than facts of individual psychology. All the plays he wrote after their marriage, exploring new material furnished by the firsthand experience of a permanent relationship with a woman, consolidate, make more explicit, and further develop the theme of the problematic masculinity of the artistic vocation. Under the pressure of marriage, it would become even more problematic, with some surprising results for his work and even for his politics.

Censorship (*Die Zensur*, 1907), the first play Wedekind wrote after his marriage, is ostensibly his dramatic contestation of the allegations of immorality for which his work had so often been suppressed. But the encounter between the playwright Walter Buridan and the censor he hopes to persuade of his moral seriousness is flanked by scenes with Buridan's lover, the actress Kadidja, whom he also wants to convince of the significance of his project. This effort at persuasion is as vital to him as the other, and the crux of the play is the relationship between the two.

Buridan describes his project to Kadidja to justify his request for a two-week leave of absence from their year-and-a-half-long relationship so that he can concentrate on his work. It is the most compact statement of Wedekind's mature moral-aesthetic purpose anywhere in his oeuvre. "I have been working much longer than I have known you," he pleads for her understanding,

> on a project in which I will finally reconcile the contradictions in which I have found myself since childhood. For years I have seen no reason why the esteem in which we hold the eternal laws of the world, and the esteem in which we hold beautiful colors, beautiful bodies, the whole splendor of creation . . . should always be at odds with one another. It was different in earlier times, when devotion to the spirit and esteem for human beauty found themselves together under the same temple roof. The conflict derives only from the fact that we honor the sublime beauty of spiritual lawfulness as little as we grasp the inexorable lawfulness of physical beauty. . . . Joy in the spirit and reverence for the world of appearances are the two things that I would like to reconcile with one another before I die.[87]

Buridan, however, offers this prospectus without real hope that Kadidja will understand the philosophical meaning of his work, even though it is in part a celebration of what she herself represents. She is sensuous, lively, and intelligent, a talented singer and dancer, but the naturalness and practicality that originally attracted him now seem prosaic and earthbound, a hindrance to his aspiration to spiritual heights. Nonetheless he wants her assurance that she will not leave him if he takes time off from her, because he needs her for his very identity. "Ever since you gave me the proof that you are a creature of *unbounded possibilities* I feel with every breath the physical terror of losing you," he confesses (68; italics in original). And the danger seems real enough, if not quite as he fears, for though she loves only him and wants no other man, she would, she says, choose a life of prostitution if she can't have him.

Buridan has greater hopes for convincing the censor Dr. Prantl to approve the production of his play *Pandora,* because he believes that his mission and that of the church are essentially the same. His lifelong goal, he insists to Dr. Prantl, has been nothing but "the reunification of holiness and beauty as the divine idol of pious devotion" (81). Prantl is unpersuaded; every church does that already. The problem is that the two men are using different dictionaries. For Buridan, all of God's creation, not least the human body and its movements, is beautiful; for Prantl, Buridan's notion of beauty is nothing but a rationalization for circus acts and dissoluteness (81). Buridan doesn't simply portray the ugly consequences of human behavior, as the playwright claims; he wallows in them. And after he has played his sinful game with his poor creatures, he sacrifices them on the altar of his so-called beauty. Buridan recoils at these charges. He knows no holier possession, he protests, than the people one loves. As for the charges of blasphemy, he has lived half his life without art but couldn't live for a moment without religion. Prantl is astonished. "But aren't you the one," he retorts, "who came up with the slogan of the reunification of church and brothel in a future socialist state?!" (82). Buridan protests that he has been slandered by his reviewers, and as evidence of the sincerity of his preoccupation with the conflict between spiritual power and worldly pleasure, he shows Prantl his book *A Guide to the Overcoming of the Horror of Death.*

As Prantl reads, he begins to take Buridan seriously for the first time. Suddenly, however, they are interrupted by Kadidja in her skimpy costume rolling into the room atop a drum. "The snake from Paradise!" a startled Prantl calls out, smiling at the sight, but it has destroyed Buridan's seriousness for him. The playwright is crushed. When Kadidja tries to divert him by reminding him about the play opening the next day, he professes the profoundest indifference. Enjoyment for its own sake disgusts him. In that spirit he attacks Kadidja's seductive appearance, and taking on the role of her censor, pronounces the bizarrely puritan dictum that women may wear clothing that endangers others only to the degree that they are engaged in activities that endanger their own lives. The tightrope walker can be virtually nude, but on the street a woman has to wear a long dress. He then attacks his lover directly: "Kadidja, your vanity is a torment to me. Put on sensible clothing, Kadidja, put on sensible clothing. I am dying with thirst . . . for the bottomless depths of the soul where I can hide from everything sensuous. . . . I want ugliness before my eyes! Ugliness! Nothing but ugliness!" (88). In utter despair at his rejection, Kadidja runs to the balcony, saying she will return him to the world of ideas from which she has alienated him. Suddenly aware of the danger, Buridan pleads frantically that he had had a momentary fit of madness and begs her to come in. It is too late; she leaps to her death.

No one even at the time doubted that the play was largely autobiographical. The script for the original performance names the characters "I" and "Tilly" and heads the scenes "1. Tilly against me. 2. I against the priest. 3. I against her."[88] Wedekind raised the question of the propriety of confessionalism in the play itself. "Why," Prantl asks Buridan pointedly, "should anyone trust a man who for the price of a ticket serves up to the whole world what he ought to fight out with himself at home?" (75). That his recent plays were exercises in self-display was a familiar charge to Wedekind, one frequently repeated by later critics. One of the purposes of *Censorship* was to meet it head-on. In later reflections on his work, he acknowledged that the play might more accurately have been called "Exhibitionism" or "Self-Portrait," but insisted that his purpose had been to demonstrate that it was dramatically worth the effort to represent himself onstage.[89] This is the most explicit assertion Wedekind ever made that he understood and meant his own story to be exemplary. But of what?

Buridan tries to blame his interlocutors for his lack of support and success. The priest condemns the body, the actress celebrates it, but neither understands its spirituality. The playwright, however, deconstructs his own effort to externalize the fault, in his admission to Kadidja that he himself has been unable to reconcile body and spirit and in his violent overreaction to her appearance in costume. It looks as if the heart of Buridan's conflict is a residual sexual puritanism that is activated by Prantl's reaction to Kadidja and reinforced by his own bitter disappointment at losing the priest's blessing just when it seemed a possibility. Buridan not only identifies with the censor but outdoes him in moral severity. In this context, some observations of Tilly's suggest that Buridan's reactions were to be taken straight, or at least not simply as ironic. Frank, she wrote, was well aware of her "unbourgeois" inclinations and considered them dangerous. She recalled that he once asked her in all seriousness if she had taught their daughter the Lord's Prayer. Though he belonged to no confession and did not believe in a personal god, he had strong religious feelings.[90] No doubt Buridan is recoiling against his own attraction to Kadidja, which, in the age-old male maneuver, he projects on her seductiveness. Tilly's bohemianism—and its attendant dangers of infidelity—brought out in Wedekind his father's powerful bourgeois moralism. The regression exposes how much male insecurity lay behind nineteenth-century bourgeois sexual morality.

But it is not Kadidja's sensuality, at least not in any simple physical sense, that has kept Buridan emotionally bound to her; it is her infinity. In vehemently reducing her to her exhibitionistic vanity, her body, he is attempting to deny the real source of her hold on him. It was when he realized that she had unbounded possibilities, he had explicitly acknowledged, that he conceived his terror of losing her. Kadidja—the name is a barely modified version of that of a prostitute Wedekind knew in Paris—represents to Buridan not only the flesh but the spirit. She is already that unification of appearance and eternity, sensuousness and spirit, that he only aspires to achieve through his plays and book on the mastery of death. His work, however, is his own creation; through it he could hope to achieve infinity on his own. Buridan's deepest conflict is not between the spirit and the flesh, but between two representations of the spirit, the feminine, on which he is dependent, and the aesthetic, where he can be autonomous. Prantl's refusal to give his work the church's imprimatur and thus recognize his achievement is the more bitter because it is caused by the intervention of the rival source of the spirit. It is this fact that explains the extent of his rage at her. Kadidja's death was not only Wedekind's recognition of the pain he was inflicting on Tilly; it was his revenge on the feminine "rival" to masculine artistic autonomy.

If *Censorship* was Wedekind's reckoning with the sensuously feminine aspect of his partner, *Franziska: A Modern Mystery Play in Five Acts* (*Franziska: Ein modernes Mysterium in fünf Akten*, 1912) was an exploration of his struggle with her independence. It is a mark of the seriousness with which he initially treated that independence that he gave his female protagonist some of his own background, character, and ambition. Soured on marriage by her parents' unhappiness (in the manuscript her mother is sometimes referred to as Mrs. Wedekind), Franziska rejects it as an obstacle to a woman's identity. "But I should very much like to find out who I really am," she responds to a lover's proposal. "If I marry you, I will find out in the next ten years who you are."[91] And when Wedekind's Mephistopheles in the shape of the impresario-writer Veit Kunz offers her anything she wants for two years in return for permanent possession of her afterward, she answers in true Wedekind spirit: "Then I demand—freedom—the enjoyment of life" (449). In this world, however, achieving those to their fullest means becoming a man, and this is what she asks for. Kunz, in an equally authentic Wedekindian note, warns her that that way she will lose her power over men, to which she bluntly responds, "In return I win the competition with men" (450). What was only implicit in the symbolism of Countess Geschwitz's lesbianism is made explicit in Franziska's ambition. When the demon of women's independence was no longer a political or literary abstraction but embodied in a wife, Wedekind saw and expressed his belief about its true meaning more openly.

In this modern *Faust* satire, however, Kunz is neither spirit nor magician. He cannot turn Franziska into a man, only dress her as one. His purpose too is more prosaic than Mephistopheles's: he wants to make Franziska a star. In his role as her servant, he tells her, he procures for her the best opportunities for the most complete, most multifaceted development of all her gifts. "In you," he tells her bluntly, "I wish to get a servitor to whom nothing humanly possible remains alien." When she asks him where he believes her gifts lie, he responds with similar directness: "In your voluptuousness, your love of power, your light-heartedness, your passion for play, your addiction to enjoyment, and, not to forget the most glorious, your infinite vanity" (491). Mephistopheles has become Pygmalion, but this Pygmalion wishes to liberate his goddess in order to use her powers for himself. In an exchange during the bizarre episode in which Kunz marries her off to a woman, presumably to expand her experience, he gives himself away in the consolation he offers Franziska's "wife" for her unconsummated marriage. "In the service of great art," he tells her, "heroic spouses do not suffer in vain. The most sublime works draw their power from the faithful collaboration of suffering women" (471). It is as if Wedekind had become the writer Meier whom he had excoriated in *The Young World*. Woman exists to make the creative man possible.

Kunz, however, is defeated by Franziska's immutable femininity in the other, negative sense of the term. For a moment, she is in love with him, and in her bliss the memory of her parents' terrible marriage is erased; true partnership between male and female finally seems possible. But the moment does not last. With "characteristic" feminine instinctual fickleness and superficiality, she is attracted to a handsome but empty-headed actor. Kunz is devastated. A moment before he was singing the praises of art as the highest human achievement, the mirror that not only passively reflects back the joy of life but actively inspires humanity with its images to even greater enjoyment, working in reciprocity with life to increase human happiness. In the next moment he is lamenting the loss of his love, whom he had erroneously believed he could make his possession through the joy of sacrifice; without his love he has nothing, and is nothing (509, 515–16).

Leaving her new lover in turn, Franziska ends up as the contented mother of a child whose father could be either Kunz or the actor. She rejects them both, however, and prepares to settle down with a mediocre painter whose Panglossian, anti-Wedekind message is that the world isn't as bad as the prophets of unhappiness claim; they are miserable only because they don't know the limits of their talents and the limits of their world. But Franziska had long before foreshadowed her ignominious end. Cautioning her "wife" earlier in the play not to expect too much, she had said, "Woman cannot aspire to a happiness beyond the limits determined by nature. Her happiness remains, however much she contorts herself, limited to what nature has decreed" (465). The "happy" ending is another form of revenge for the artist's inability to control the idealized femininity that functions as his inspiration. Wedekind punished Franziska in the exact opposite of the way he punished Lulu, Kadidja, and many another female protagonist; instead of killing her, he turned her into a cow.

Censorship and *Franziska* dramatize the artist's fateful ambivalence toward femininity; Wedekind's next play—*Samson, or, Modesty and Jealousy* (*Simson, oder, Scham und Eifersucht*, 1914)—presented his most explicit and poignant account of its ultimate cause: the problematic nature of art as an enterprise for the male. *Samson* is Wedekind's own myth of the origins of art. This free adaptation of a biblical story was a radical stylistic departure for him. It enabled him at once to distance himself from his characters and to become even more self-revealing behind the disguise. His self-representation as Samson, given everything that had gone before, was almost too obvious: the flawed strong man brought down by the malevolent scheming woman. The real heart of the play, however, is not in the original plot but in Wedekind's dramatic inventions, which have no biblical source. Reduced to slavery after his blinding, further humiliated when Delilah allows the Philistine princes to observe their lovemaking, Samson becomes a poet and singer to give voice to his pain. Delilah, his betrayer and lover, is enchanted by his song and understands exactly the source of his creativity. When Og of Bassan, the Philistine prince who has become king after Samson's subjugation, wishes to kill Samson, she protects him by convincing Og of the wonder of Samson's singing. The crucial interchanges among the three turn on the meaning of love, poetry, and their relationship to "true" manhood.

Og wishes to kill Samson ostensibly because word of Delilah's immoral behavior with Samson will corrupt the people. As he quickly acknowledges, however, he is really enraged because Delilah's exhibitionistic scene with Samson has humiliated his manhood. Delilah had promised herself to Og in return for Samson's life. When Og came to her, however, she had acted the shy maiden, and he had been "forced" to rape her. It felt good. "I felt mighty, proud, powerful, princely," he tells her, "because you denied my wooing out of modesty. Your bashful resistance gave me the feeling of the highest manly worth. I also owe my masculine power to your modesty; because of it I felt, as your conqueror, immensely strong, stronger than Samson ever was even as a youth."[92] But with one blow, she had smashed his glory to bits. When she embraced Samson while the princes watched, he felt shamed. "You cunningly pretended to be small so that I would seem to myself great. [But] in sensual pleasure so shameless that I was dumbfounded, not knowing whether I was coming or going, you revealed yourself in your true greatness, and I am robbed of all certainty" (562). Delilah's shamelessness *is* her greatness because it means that she does not care how she looks in the eyes of others; she has no need of recognition. Shamelessness makes her self-contained and "infinite" because it removes all barriers to her behavior. Og's gaze has no power over her. Rather, her shamelessness gives *her* the power of the gaze. Now it is Og who has to feel uncertain, because he does care how he appears, what effect he has; his virility is in the eyes and response of the female beholder. Without her shame there is no feminine recoil, no masculine conquest, and hence no masculine self-worth. "Who can guarantee what effect I have on you, what effect I have on others," he says despairingly. "The shame you threw away oppresses me" (562). Now he professes himself envious of Samson's blindness because it makes him superior to Og; Delilah has after all chosen Samson. "If I were blind like Samson, you could exhibit yourself with me every day to your guests. Because of my sight, which robs me of all certainty, which lowers me to the level of a slave to my shame, I am less than this slave dog" (563–64).

But that is not how Samson feels. He experiences his blindness with even greater humiliation than Og felt on perceiving Delilah's lack of shame. Blindness has physically robbed Samson of the power of the gaze, and has thus done more than reverse the power relations between him and Delilah: it has reversed their very genders. As Samson laments to her:

> Because of my blindness, our roles are so completely exchanged that I am the woman and you are the man. Blind, I do not know how I affect others. Because of that I need love, I need security. I am now suffering what millions of women suffer in silence. I am ashamed, Delilah, as only a married woman is ashamed, uncertain of her fortune in the eyes of other men. Of course Adam was ashamed, but only before God, before whom he too was uncertain of his standing. You who can oversee everything for a great distance wallow in that same shameless sensual pleasure with me, that I, seeing my former self in you, once enjoyed with women who were blinder than I am now. (558)

The speech makes it clear that Samson's physical blindness is also metaphorical. "Blindness" represents the status of all those who do not look but who need to be looked at, who depend for their security, for their very sense of being, on the desiring gaze of others. This is, according to Samson, preeminently the status of women, like the ones who doted on him before his blinding but whom he cavalierly enjoyed without emotional connection. Married women are particularly vulnerable to insecurity because they have no claim on the gaze of men other than their husbands—a notion that suggests that "feminine" dependency is insatiable, or can only be satisfied by the infinite other, which in a world of finite beings can only mean the totality of others. Men, however, true men, are the self-contained ones who confer being through their gaze, who do not require the gaze of others. They do not need the security of being loved, though, contradictorily, they need the assurance of the other's desire. The drama fleshes out the response that the youthful Wedekind made years before to Gerhart Hauptmann's praise of his capacity to love, quoted at the head of this chapter. Loving meant weakness to him, rather than strength. It is easy to imagine how great a strain his marital fidelity put on Wedekind; from the standpoint of ultimate self-acceptance, marriage, which limited legitimate love to only one finite person, was a trap, not a fulfillment. His belief in the insatiability of the need for recognition, which he projected on to wives, is another explanation for his unappeasable jealousy of Tilly.

But it is not only the need for love that is "womanly." The most astonishing disclosure of the play is Wedekind's explicit equation of art with passive, suffering femininity. After his blinding and enslavement, out of the depths of his misery, Samson begins to compose poetry and song. Delilah understands the connection perfectly. Trying to protect Samson from Og, she tells the king, "I, Delilah, am a woman. I protect Samson for the sake of his suffering. His song welled up in my house out of his blindness. As he turned the grindstones he sang song after song" (571). When Og persists, threatening never to touch Delilah again if Samson doesn't die, Delilah, unwilling to give up either Samson or Og, her "dearest possession," urges the king to listen to Samson's song, which has, she says, the power to refresh and calm even jealousy. Samson begins a long melancholy song tracing the lives of a warrior and his love from youth to old age. Each verse speaks words of hope— love, joy, beauty, sensuousness, freedom, wisdom, peace—and each ends with the sad refrain "Laughing temptation makes fools of us." Against his will, Og is enchanted; Samson brings his characters to life so vividly that he can see them before his eyes, and he berates himself for doubting Samson.

Despite his enslavement, then, Samson the artist seems to have triumphed, and he gloats over the king's concession. "You fool, you! Dumb as you are, even you feel the superiority of the spirit. Though you are a king, you are not more powerful than the blind man whose song forces you to grasp, in the flesh, really to perceive what the blind man created for his own happiness alone" (578). But Samson's victory cry is premature. To assist him with the effect of his song, Delilah has undressed and returns wrapped only in a veil. Aroused both by her nakedness and the effect of Samson's song, Og goes off with Delilah to enact the love story of the verses, while the unseeing Samson continues on to the end and begins a joyful dance. When he hears no applause, however, he is completely shattered; he realizes he has been mocked and made an utter fool. What Wedekind made Samson face is the ultimate irony of the artist's fate, his ultimate impotence. Out of his suffering and longing for love, the artist can fashion enchanting art. But because the powerful man of action need not merely long impotently for the unattainable, he can exploit the artist's gift to enact in reality what art portrays; aroused by the artist's song, the woman chooses the man of action, not the artist, as her desired object. In the end, however, it is woman who is the true victor. She has seduced the powerful man away from his resolve to kill his rival and she controls the song-maker as well. Og will ultimately kill Delilah—repeating yet again Wedekind's theme of male revenge on the too-powerful woman—and Samson will bring the temple down on his enemies, but it will be a hollow triumph. His final victory, bought only with his own death, is not that of his art but of his superior physical strength, magically returned to him with the growth of his hair. The biblical ending gives only the satisfaction of fictive revenge; and even as a fiction, it ironically confirms the superiority of traditional masculinity over the feminine sensibility of the artist.

89

Thoughts for the Time on War and Death

> *The French believe they have been overwhelmed by the furor teutonicus, by raw*
> *power, by superior numbers. The 42-centimeter cannons haven't the slightest to do*
> *with the furor teutonicus; they are the result of the most rigorous sciences, mathe-*
> *matics, physics and chemistry. They are the loudest heralds in this war of the supe-*
> *riority of German intellectual labor.*

—Frank Wedekind, "Germany Brings Freedom"

It is this dilemma of the artist's masculinity more than anything else in Wedekind's history that explains the turn he took at the outbreak of the war, politically and dramatically. Wedekind's imprisonment for lèse-majesté in 1899 because of a jibe at the kaiser in a poem printed in the satirical period-ical *Simplicissimus* implied virtually nothing about his politics. Indeed his in-volvement with *Simplicissimus* and later with the *Elf Scharfrichter* cabaret, insofar as it had a point other than eking out a living, was an outlet for moral criticism that he himself found superficial by comparison with his plays. His one explicit political stand was in international affairs; he was a declared pacifist. Shortly after the war broke out, however, he gave a public address in which he blamed it on Russia and France, attacked republicanism as alien to the German spirit, and called for a German victory that would once and for all create national unity and self-confident pride in the fatherland.[93]

It is clear from a number of things in the address that it cannot be taken wholly at face value. Above all it is hard to imagine Wedekind—the most censored author of his time—saying with a straight face that German artists more than any other profession could testify to the fact that Germans en-joyed more freedom of action in their monarchy than Americans or Frenchmen in their republic.[94] The address is so puzzling that it has led to quite contradictory explanations. He meant his words to be taken at face value, opportunistically trying to curry favor with conservatives so that per-formance of his plays, banned once again as inimical to the war effort, could be resumed. He meant his words to be seen as ironic, so outrageous that his audience would immediately understand their true antiwar spirit. A more balanced assessment points out that while Wedekind did want the war to end as quickly as possible, he also explicitly insisted that a German victory was the necessary condition of peace.[95] Why that was so is a thornier ques-tion. In letters written during the war, he expressed the belief that a victori-ous Germany would emerge from the war much freer in her domestic politics than before.[96] The Empire was, at least when the war began, a given, and perhaps the only way he could promote the freedom of expression he desired was to take a patriotic line but support it on the grounds that Germany's right to victory rested on its freedom and its social welfare achievements, the most advanced in the world. "If the heroic battle of the young German Empire is crowned with victory," he concluded, "the sons of Germany will develop a pride in their fatherland that, because of its . . . ethical worth is more sublime than shrill hurrah-patriotism, than mean-spirited hereditary enmity."[97]

But Wedekind seemed equally sincere in his argument that unified national pride and strength would be the first fruit of a German victory. The words in which he made this claim are the only ones italicized in the printed version of the talk.[98] "Since its strengthening, a significant majority of the people longed for a war," he wrote in another piece, "through which increased might and intensified enjoyment of life would be transformed into a political power that could no longer be despised or overlooked by other powers." While some interpreted these words not as Wedekind's own but as an Aesopian exposé of Germany's aggressive war aims, it seems much more likely to one commentator at least that Wedekind's talk of might and power must be taken seriously, consistent as it was with his vitalism.[99] Such talk does have to be taken seriously, not, however, because it is consistent with some imagined philosophical vitalism, a dubious characterization of Wedekind's underlying ideal, but because identification with German unity and power through a state that would also recognize the value of Wedekind's work could confer on the artist the masculine credentials he clearly craved.

There is a striking clue in the essay that points in this direction. Among the reasons Wedekind enumerated for the weakness of German unity and pride even after Bismarck's unification of the Empire was its illiberal spirit. "Whoever fought for Germany's unity in 1848 and later perhaps suffered for it through imprisonment or banishment," he pointed out, "could not hail the achievements of the great war with an unburdened and free heart. Above all because his holy youthful feelings had been humiliated."[100] The bow here to the ideals of his father and maternal grandfather is unmistakable. Wedekind could not commit himself wholeheartedly to the Empire in its present form and remain loyal to the liberalism he had adopted from his father, but unlike his father he wanted to identify himself with a powerful Empire that would incorporate more of his father's ideals. It was in the spirit of just such a compromise that he congratulated Heinrich Mann on the publication of his wartime essay on Émile Zola, which praised the French enemy's great contemporary culture hero. He did not laud it as a courageous expression of Mann's universalist ideals in the face of wartime chauvinism. Mann's essay, he wrote him, was a sign of the "superiority of the German spirit not just to other peoples but to the whole world."[101]

91

But the inner meaning of Wedekind's desire for a moralized German national strength and pride most clearly expressed itself in his wartime play *Bismarck*. It was for him a very odd play, the least characteristic of his works. For one thing, it is his only historical play, and with a vengeance; every word in it is taken from the actual historical record, in which Wedekind did an enormous amount of research. Most strikingly, it has apparently nothing whatsoever to do with his usual themes of love and sex; the very few female characters, such as Bismarck's wife, play quite minor roles. The play presents in meticulous detail Bismarck's diplomatic maneuvering between 1863, when he drew Austria into an alliance against Denmark over the duchies of Schleswig and Holstein, and 1866, when he turned the issue against Austria and defeated her in a war that set up the last stage of German unification. Throughout the play the emphasis is on the mixture of shrewdness, lack of sentimentality, perseverance, and iron sense of duty with which Bismarck outmaneuvered everyone—the Austrians, the German states, France, his own king—to achieve his aims.

As with Wedekind's wartime address, but even more so because of the apparent objectivity of his authorial method, critics in Wedekind's time and ours have differed sharply over the assessment of Wedekind's attitude toward Bismarck. Arthur Kutscher, Wedekind's friend and first biographer, saw it as unequivocally positive. Disgusted at the political dilettantism that was wrecking the German war effort, Wedekind looked enviously to the days when a strong man was at the helm of the ship of state. "*Bismarck*," Kutscher claimed, "was the expression of his longing for a savior." Wedekind had openly praised Bismarck's political skill, his virtuosity in managing the great affairs of the time, and the magical effects of his personality to other acquaintances.

> The author was moved to an idealistic embodiment of this almost superhumanly great energy. Here we have the central theme of this historical play, but also the one that ties this work to the earlier ones and constitutes the red thread through all of Wedekind's creativity. For as a result of the fact that, instinctively and inevitably, qualities that Wedekind was drawn to by elective affinity were made the main theme—with the exception of the erotic—he once again found himself to a certain extent portraying himself. Bismarck was for him the very type of the man of action.[102]

Heinrich Mann, unlike Kutscher an opponent of the regime that Bismarck created, was less sure. Wedekind, he claimed, wrote the play to locate the roots of Germany's current disaster. Bismarck was an "unloved hero. Or did he love him, but nonetheless see through the consequences of such a hero?"[103] And the general editor of the modern critical edition of

Wedekind's works, without venturing his own interpretation, reminds readers of Friedrich Wilhelm Wedekind's flight from the Bismarckian Reich and labels all interpretations of Bismarck as a positive hero "from a literary critical point of view historical falsifications."[104]

With an admixture of Mann's ambivalence, Kutscher is closer to the truth, but not for the political reasons he attributes to Wedekind. At crucial points Wedekind chose quotes from Bismarck that reveal attitudes he seemed to identify with, even if in his own utterances he shrank back from their brutality of expression. Pressed by a French journalist about why the German national spirit is concerned only with the German fatherland and not with the universal rights of man, Bismarck replies sarcastically, "You mean, why aren't we concerned with making the world happy? You might just as well ask me, why we Germans don't make as big a fuss about women as you French. For the present, Germany has to keep working, and our women work alongside us, as far as their strength allows. In Germany's politics, as you see, women have no place. . . . But we don't presume to make people or even women happy to any greater degree than we for our part expect them to make us happy."[105] Toward the end of the play, when the Bavarian representative accuses him of hypocrisy with regard to his supposed nationalist sentiment, Bismarck responds: "You too have taken me for a Junker, for a reactionary. Appearances are deceiving. Around the king I was suspected on all sides of being a secret democrat. I was only able to win his trust by showing him that I wasn't too afraid of the chamber to push through the army reorganization, without which we couldn't have waged war and the very security of the state would have been endangered. This battle cost me my nerves, my life force. But I defeated all of them—all!" (179). Not however, for his own selfish purposes, or even ultimately for that of the state as such. "The war was waged as protection against war," he claims. "The world does not exist for your sake, or for mine, or for any other individual existence. The purpose of existence is the increase of strength, for whose maintenance the battle with evil is indispensable" (180).

But if Wedekind admired these attitudes and goals, he could not see the practices that translate them into reality as his own. A very curious section of the play deals with an encounter between Bismarck and a number of artists, among them the writer Konrad Deubler and the composers Johann Strauss and Johannes Brahms. The point of including the encounter in the play is to reflect on the relationship between art and worldly power. Of the group, only Brahms correctly assesses Bismarck's strength; the others appear buffoonish in their comments. Recognizing in Bismarck the self-confident man who represents the only chance of freeing the German fatherland from impotence and degradation, he wants to stay and meet him, because it is unlikely that they will ever see such a man again. Strauss responds that Bismarck could say the same about them, but he doesn't even look at the artists (145, 148). There is a double implication here. Except for Brahms, the artists are represented as vain and envious of the movers and shakers of the world. They pretend to equality; Brahms can at least acknowledge the statesmen's worth, even their superiority. But the cost of being one of those movers, in morally ambiguous action as well as in the anxiety of risk taking and in psychological exhaustion, is not one that artists are capable of paying. Bismarck represented the manly ideal for Wedekind, but it was not one that he as an artist could ever think to aspire to—for what to him were both good reasons and bad. The man of action is inevitably morally compromised. But at least he is a man—the artist, by implication, is not.

If not in this world, though, perhaps in the next. Wedekind's last drama, *Hercules* (*Herakles*, 1917), offers a rather more grandiose image of the artist than *Samson*. It depicts the Greek hero, half-god and half-human, as a tragic figure who achieves manly fulfillment only in the afterlife. He has fought persistently for the cause of human happiness yet has been unable to win either the love of humanity or personal fulfillment because he has been unable to conquer himself. Though mightier than Samson, he is even less controlled, lustful, easily enraged, ready to kill when his sexual desires are balked. When King Eurytos, defeated by Hercules in an archery contest, reneges on his promise to give the victor his daughter Iole, she accedes to her father's betrayal and refuses the hero; in revenge, Hercules kills her brother. Later, he rejects his adoring wife Dejaneira, his prize for defeating the god menacing her father's kingdom, because he blames her for his murder of a young man who aroused his jealousy by flirting with her. When she will not leave, he tolerates her remaining, but his attention shifts to elsewhere. Still unable to forget Iole's rejection, he attacks Eurytos's castle, killing the king and his three remaining sons. At last, horrified by what he has done, he feels that only Iole's love can bring him the inner freedom and peace he seeks, but it is too late; he has destroyed any love she had for him. In despair, he undertakes the greatest of his adventures, the liberation of Prometheus from the punishment of the gods. Prometheus, it becomes clear, is the other side of Hercules; he is the culture hero who has used his art only to benefit humanity, to his own great cost. Both have fought for human happiness, both have suffered, but Prometheus is autonomous and selfless, while Hercules is consumed by the struggle for love and by the destructive jealousy that is for him its apparently unavoidable accompaniment. Returning from his triumph, he prides himself on the fact that his greatest victory is the fidelity of his wife, Dejaneira, but his enjoyment is short-lived. Jealous of Iole, Dejaneira gives him a cloak dipped in a substance that she has been told will assure her husband's love, but that is really a deadly poison. As he faces death, Hercules humbly bends himself to the will of the gods. Only after he dies does the goddess Hera reveal that she has been behind all his woes, trying to destroy him because he was her husband's bastard son. His lack of self-control is apparently not his fault. As compensation, she gives him Hebe, the goddess of youth, as his wife. Hercules hesitates at first, fearful that the moment of his highest joy will be shattered by jealousy, but Hebe reassures him that the heavenly host is there to help her consecrate him with pleasure and love.

There could hardly be a more apt climactic statement of the writer's masculine dilemma as Wedekind saw and experienced it in his own marriage. A fighter dedicated to the sensual liberation of humanity, he undermined his own mission by the masculine insecurity that both drove him to seek the love of woman as the source of identity and created the insurmountable jealousy that made it impossible for him to believe in its reality. The very project of writing for Wedekind came from the European's lack of the body and lack of self-trust, which made him a slave of repressive morality. As long as he could see sensual repression as a social problem, he could attack its external sources in crass materialism, sexual hypocrisy, and the prevailing authoritarian miseducation that alienated young people, and especially women, from their most intimate selves. More regularly, however, he half perceived the problem as one internal to men. Half perceived, for increasingly unable to look at it steadily and unflinchingly as a problem about masculine identity, he as often saw it as a problem of difficult women, who held the power of masculinity in their hands and wielded it with frightening arbitrariness.

Wedekind had been ill for some time when he wrote his last play. Shortly afterward, just before the onset of the stage that would lead to his death, his wife, barely recovering from a serious suicide attempt, was insisting that they be divorced. She could no longer live with the constant jealousy that was undermining her self-confidence with its bitter accusations and rejections. After long, anguished conversations with her husband, still in his sickbed, she decided not to leave. Wedekind died before her resolve could be tested again.

CHAPTER TWO

Thomas Mann and the Feminine Passion for Transcendence

> *What is, after all, the origin and purpose of writing if it is not an intellectual-moral effort in behalf of a problematic ego?*
>
> *Art is the mastered, liberated and liberating knowledge of life through form.*
>
> —Thomas Mann, *Reflections of a Nonpolitical Man*

> *We artists cannot tread the path of Beauty without Eros keeping company with us and appointing himself as our guide; yes, though we may be heroes in our fashion and disciplined warriors, yet we are like women, for it is passion that exalts us, and the longing of our soul must remain the longing of a lover—that is our joy and our shame.*
>
> —Thomas Mann, *Death in Venice*

Is Thomas Mann a "Modernist"? Though critics of German literature have usually considered him one, the question arises out of a legitimate understanding of Modernism. The earliest paradigm defined it as an aesthetic revolution, a rejection of representation in painting, literature, and music in favor of the formal self-containment of the work of art.[1] When that definition was abandoned as inadequate for its omission of Modernism's spiritual and sociopolitical agenda, formalist innovation still remained a central descriptive hallmark.[2] But Mann, certainly in his work before World War I, and arguably right through to *Doctor Faustus,* was no formal innovator. If the term Modernism inevitably calls up the radical aesthetic experimentalism of Picasso and Kandinsky, Schönberg and Stravinsky, Strindberg and Pirandello, Kafka and Joyce—even, as we have seen, that of Mann's fellow townsman and sometime friend Frank Wedekind—Mann hardly seems of their company. His stories and novels preserve a formal realism that their incorporation of mythic elements, their symbolism, and their irony do not substantially undermine. Early in his career Mann, protesting against the view that *Buddenbrooks* was overly concerned with the aesthetic at the expense of the human, explicitly eschewed the notion that formal "inventiveness" was the hallmark of the great artist. "I say that very great writers did not invent anything in their whole lives," he wrote his friend Kurt Martens, "but merely poured their souls into traditional materials and reshaped them."[3] It is his formal traditionalism that seems to justify one critic's perhaps too clever double entendre: "Whether Mann was himself a 'practicing' modernist is by no means as obvious as some critics seem to think; his whole relationship with aesthetic modernity is extremely complex."[4] The particular irony of that relationship is that the quasi-autobiographical protagonist of the novel Mann intended as his summa is the arch-formal experimentalist, the inventor of serialism in music, while the novel that describes his invention and his fate is structurally and stylistically conventional, even deliberately old-fashioned.[5]

Yet the more perspicuous of Mann's contemporaries recognized from the beginning that even his most apparently "Realist" works were not conventionally so, unconcerned as they were with the usual social issues of literary Realism. One of the first among them was Thomas's own brother, Heinrich, himself a "social" novelist. When, during the bitterest stage of the quarrel between the brothers, Thomas reproached Heinrich for repudiating his point of view as an author, Heinrich responded with an ostensible conciliatoriness that did not blunt its sting: "Your own ethos, who tells you that I have mistaken it? I have always been aware, have always respected it as subjective, as you, and when I have met its representation in a work of art, I have not burdened it overlong with my doubts as to its value for humanity."[6] Just shortly before, Mann had protested the social usefulness of his writing precisely because he was so acutely sensitive to Heinrich's charge of solipsism: all his works were, he had explicitly acknowledged, "an intellectual-moral effort in behalf of a problematic ego."[7] No other formula could more succinctly epitomize Mann's "substantive" Modernism. Whatever its structural affinities with them, Mann's work broke with the assumptions and concerns of both the bourgeois *Bildungsroman* and the literature of social conflict and identity because he could not take for granted the unified, socially-anchored personality ideal that was their foundation. The "problematic ego" is Mann's Modernist bridge—as it is that of Proust and the early Gide—to the more dramatic formal experimentalism of Joyce and Kafka.[8]

But Mann's formal conservatism is not a simple matter either. "Art," Mann also wrote, "is the mastered, liberated and liberating knowledge of life through form."[9] Mann was interested in form as a thing in itself, if not quite as an end in itself. If the subject matter of his work was the problematic ego, the "solution"—the ego's mastery and liberation—was not existential but aesthetic, to be found not in life but in the constructs of art. In his own way, Mann made aesthetic form autonomous, lending a paradoxical support to the formalist definition of Modernism. In fact, Mann's prewar work seems to furnish one of the stumbling blocks to the political interpretation of early Modernism, despite his own blatant—and perverse—effort to politicize its bearing during World War I. Mann's prewar writing had no social-political program, not even a conservative one by default. He was accurate about himself at least when he argued for the artist's lack of interest in public affairs at the beginning of *Reflections of a Nonpolitical Man*. "[The artist's] life element is a public loneliness," he asserted, "a lonely public life that is of an intellectual nature, and whose feeling and concept of dignity differ completely from civic, material-social public life. . . ."[10] Mann's turn to politics was a belated and logically inconsistent development of his initial aesthetic solution to his "problematic ego," though it is both psychologically and historically quite intelligible.

The Love That Would Not Speak Its Name

> *To long for love to the point of dying and yet to despise anyone who loves you. Happiness is not: to be loved, that is a satisfaction, mixed with disgust, for one's vanity. Happiness is: to love . . .*
>
> —Thomas Mann, *Notebooks*

Mann criticism, directed by the author himself, has of course always interpreted his work in terms of the problematic self. It is only since the publication of his diaries, however, that the true nature of the self's problem seems to have been revealed. The diary disclosures—and the change in cultural climate that helped make them publicly available—have finally made it possible to give the issue of homosexuality in Mann's life and work its due. Previously largely invisible or suppressed, treated as incidental when not, Mann's homosexuality has been increasingly seen as the not-so-hidden subtext of his famous opposition of suspect artist and respectable bourgeois, epitomized in his most famous novellas *Tonio Kröger* and *Death in Venice* but at work everywhere in his writing. The older equation artist = marginal man = criminal has been amended to artist = marginal man = criminal = homosexual. The most consequent analysis of Mann's work along these lines argues bluntly, though with exhaustively detailed demonstration, that "the close psychodynamic connection between homosexual desire and a socially motivated compulsion to self-suppression is *the* constitutive and dynamic factor of Thomas Mann's life and work."[11]

Assuredly Mann's writing can't be adequately understood without considering both his sexual desire and his fear of living it. But the critical zeal to rectify previous neglect has tended to stop analysis with the new equation of artist and homosexual, and to miss or oversimplify what for Mann himself was most problematic about homosexuality. As concerned as he was with bourgeois respectability, moral decency, and literary fame, he did not simply bow to external pressure from prevailing social and sexual mores, nor simply even, in a more psychologically sophisticated understanding of how such pressure works, internalize the stigma attached to homosexuality in Germany, and the West, at the time.

Karl Böhm comes somewhat closer to the heart of the matter when he points out that Mann's homosexuality was identical for him with the lifelong feeling that his masculinity was problematic.[12] That anxiety did have to do in part with the ways in which homosexuality was socially stigmatized in the late nineteenth century. The traditional religious condemnation of homosexuality as sin and abomination and its long-standing criminalization by the Prussian and later the Imperial penal code were reinforced at that time by the new constructions of contemporary medical sexology, which defined homosexuality as both biologically degenerate and sexually effeminate. Ironically it was the first advocate of homosexual rights in Germany, Karl Heinrich Ulrichs, who in 1867 advanced the theory which a homophobic society would quickly turn against gays, the theory that the male homosexual was a type of androgyne, a female soul confined in a male body, a "manwoman."[13] Though Ulrichs was not himself widely read, his ideas were picked up by physicians and psychiatrists like Carl von Westphal and Richard von Krafft-Ebing and made current especially by the wildly popular success of the latter's *Psychopathia Sexualis,* which first appeared in 1886 and was republished twelve times during its author's lifetime in continually expanded editions. Intended as a technical work in forensic psychiatry, *Psychopathia Sexualis* almost instantly furnished the terms of sexual pathology for popular discourse. Krafft-Ebing's views were more nuanced than he is often given credit for. Though he arranged his classification of those who manifested "antipathic sexual instinct" according to degrees of effeminacy, he insisted that in "homosexual individuals," defined as people who felt sexual desire exclusively for their own sex, "character and occupation correspond with the sex which the individual represents"[14]—in other words, homosexual males were psychologically and socially masculine. But in his summary remarks on diagnosis, he asserted that in general persons with homosexual impulses are not only tainted hereditarily but are as a rule "also abnormal so far as character is concerned. They are neither man nor woman, a mixture of both, with secondary psychical and physical characteristics of the one as well as the other sex, which grow out of the interfering influences of a bisexual disposition and disturb the development of a well-defined and complete being."[15] By the end of the 1880s, it was not necessary to have actually read Krafft-Ebing to "know" that homosexuality was effeminate, though there is evidence that Heinrich Mann had in fact read him around 1891, and it is almost certain that Thomas too knew his work directly or indirectly.[16]

The medicalization of homosexuality was the most important source of its characterization as effeminate during the fin de siècle, but effeminacy was not the only discourse of homosexuality culturally available at the time. In fact a "hypermasculine" conception was being simultaneously advanced by a number of homosexual critics of contemporary cultural decline such as John Addington Symonds, Benedict Friedländer, and most notably Stefan George. Citing the case of classical Greek culture, they argued that homosexuality was the expression of a creatively superior masculinity and therefore, in the form of an aesthetically sublimated all-male brotherhood of artists, the necessary foundation of any modern cultural renewal. But so widespread was the influence of the sexologists' feminizing model that even the early-twentieth-century leader of the German homosexual liberation movement, Magnus Hirschfeld (who Mann for a long time abominated), accepted its terms. The relative triumph of the medical model was a symptom of the enormously increased public awareness of and anxiety over homosexuality in the last decades of the nineteenth century. It was this new public visibility and concern that made it possible, even unavoidable, for a whole generation of European writers—Wilde, Gide, Mann, Proust—to reflect on the place of their homosexuality in their identities and to attempt to integrate it, however obliquely, into their art.

The ambiguous new prominence of homosexuality in the later nineteenth century resulted from the convergence of opposing pressures. It was not simply, *pace* Foucault, the negative product of a new kind or increased intensity of social surveillance and control. The growth of urbanization as continental Europe, particularly Germany, industrialized at an accelerated pace in the later nineteenth century made possible the emergence of gay subcultures in the relative anonymity of big towns and cities.[17] As one of the numerous readers who contributed their own case histories to the later editions of *Psychopathia Sexualis* testified, "Almost every large city has some meeting-place, as well as a so-called promenade. In smaller cities there are relatively few 'aunts' [as he labeled himself], though in a small town of 2,300 inhabitants I found 8, and in one of 7,000 18 of whom I am absolutely sure—to say nothing of those whom I suspected. In my own town of 30,000 inhabitants I personally know about 120 'aunts.' The greater number of them, and I especially, possess the capability of judging another immediately as to whether they are alike or not. . . ."[18] But urbanization was only one feature of a wide-scale transformation of the European middle classes in the last third of the nineteenth century. The years after 1870 in particular saw an increased democratization of politics despite the continuing power of the old elites; a great expansion of the middle class as new layers of white-collar workers joined it; the growth of leisure and consumerism brought about by industrialization, which led to a relaxation of the links between the bourgeoisie and the more rigid puritan values of the earlier nineteenth century; and a loosening of the structure of the bourgeois family.[19] One result of these changes was the increasing spread of liberal ideas of rights to individual freedom and self-expression and an intensifying demand for their realization, despite the continuing force of the equally bourgeois ideas of discipline and propriety. Homosexuals were more emboldened to live according to their sexual desires and a small minority even to organize publicly to press through education and petition for the decriminalization of homosexuality and the social acceptance of its legitimacy.

Not surprisingly the same economic, political, and social developments that helped foster the growth and determination of homosexual subcultures greatly exacerbated public anxiety about homosexuality, which in any case seems endemic in postclassical Western societies. In the late nineteenth century, however, there were quite specific historical reasons for concern. The growing material comfort and consumerist appetites of urban culture were felt to breed a softening of character that was increasingly dangerous in an age of intensifying nationalist and imperialist rivalries. Aristocratic conceptions of manliness as warrior virtues had hardly disappeared from Europe in general and Germany in particular, where the army occupied the highest institutional status rank and even bourgeois honor was still defended by the duel.[20] Military manliness seemed indispensable to national greatness and even national survival in the light of international developments around the turn of the century just as they were being dangerously eroded by an increasingly materialist civilization. But the partial recasting of aristocratic militarist notions of action, valor, and service into the bourgeois virtues of energetic, disciplined, and rational productivity created its own anxieties about manliness in those circumstances. Economic and social problems such as France's declining birth rate, Britain's loss of industrial supremacy, and Germany's labor unrest, all of them threats to national greatness, were necessarily seen as symptoms and effects of a waning virility.[21]

102

Because of its contemporary identification with effeminacy and its increasing visibility, homosexuality could become a highly charged symbol of all these anxieties about manliness and an easy scapegoat for attack. It is hardly coincidence that what amounted to the show trials of Oscar Wilde in England and the public scandal of the Eulenberg affair in Germany took place in the same period as the rise of Magnus Hirschfeld's homosexual emancipation organization, the *Wissenschaftlich-Humanitäres Komitee.*

Yet despite the weight of hostility that threatened homosexuals not only with exclusion from decent society but with public humiliation and actual imprisonment, Thomas Mann never mentioned such dangers even in the privacy of the diaries in which he revealed his homosexual desires. The omission may seem without significance given the self-evidence of the dangers to those who lived amidst them, and there can be little doubt of their impact on a writer who thirsted for universal acclaim, let alone bourgeois respectability. But Mann did in fact talk openly about other kinds of dangers, profoundly, movingly, and sometimes at length, in all his writings—not only in the published work, where the disguises might be expected to be the most elaborate, but in his letters to intimates, where he could let down his guard to some extent, in the notebooks in which he compiled story ideas and that included much barely veiled autobiographical material, and finally in the diaries themselves. One of the greatest ironies in the work of the supreme ironist, and one of its most striking paradoxes, is that while even the private references to homosexuality are often indirect or oblique, Mann's fictional analysis of its enormous promise and its grave dangers are completely out in the open and available to any reader.

In his discussion of homosexuality, Krafft-Ebing made an observation that, though very different from Mann's sensibility on the subject, leads nonetheless into the heart of the Mann paradox. "The vita sexualis of these urnings ['Uranians'—the name Ulrichs coined for homosexuals]," he claimed, "is entirely like that in normal heterosexual love; but, since it is the opposite of the natural feeling, it becomes a caricature, and the more so as these individuals, at the same time, and as a rule, are subject to sexual hypersensitivity; for which reason, their love of their own sex is emotional and passionate."[22] There is no difference between the ways in which homosexuals and heterosexuals feel about the objects of their love: "The urning loves and deifies the male object of his affections, just as the normal man idealizes the woman he loves. He is capable of the greatest sacrifice for him, and experiences the pangs of unhappy, often unrequited love; he suffers from the disloyalty of the beloved object, and is subject to jealousy, etc." But the implication of Krafft-Ebing's observation about the homosexual's hypersensitivity is that homosexual love is like heterosexual love only more so. The

103

"deification" of the homosexual's beloved, it is implied, is more emotional and passionate, more consuming, than the heterosexual male's idealization of his—as the difference between the words "deification" and "idealization" itself might seem to suggest.

Mann sometimes even agreed, at least in his more pitiless or masochistic moments, with Krafft-Ebing's description of homosexual passion as caricature—one need think only of the grotesque transformation of Aschenbach as he tarts himself up in his pursuit of Tadzio. Unquestionably, however, Mann shared Krafft-Ebing's belief that homosexual love was more passionate than heterosexual love—at least male heterosexual love. It had much more in common for Mann with traditional female love. In an odd review essay of 1903 significantly titled "The Eternal Feminine," he praised a trifling novel by a woman—whose literary merits even he questioned—for its rendering of the female protagonist's understanding of love as the yearning for union and eternity with another person rather than as sensuality in the service of nature's (procreative) purposes. "What is expressed here is the complete superiority of a woman with experience of the soul over the theoretical intellectual sophistication of the young man of the same age," he bluntly asserted.[23] The most beautiful passages in the book were those in which "feeling raised and intensified itself to the level of the transcendent, where longing brushed the mystery of love itself with trembling wings." And he concluded:

> What I wanted to say is this: we poor plebeians and outcasts who honor a feminine cultural and artistic ideal despite the contemptuous laughter of the Renaissance-men; we who as artists believe in pain, experience, depth, and suffering love, and who oppose a superficial beauty with a little irony: to us it must seem likely that we can expect from woman as artist the most remarkable and interesting things, that indeed at some point she can even reach a position of artistic leadership amongst us. . . . The final line of *Faust* and the song the violins sing at the end of the *Götterdämmerung* say one and the same thing, and it is the truth. The eternal feminine draws us onwards.[24]

What Mann found to praise in the novel is of course up to a point simply the traditional Western discourse of femininity and feminine love, elevated, spiritual, not grossly physical or animal. But talk of a discourse of femininity in Mann can be as reductive as talk of a discourse of homosexuality. What Mann appreciated about the "eternal feminine," that is, about feminine desire, was its character as ontological or religious quest. True passion, as he noted in the essay, is a passion for the transcendent, for what is greater than human, and therefore for that to which the human willingly submits. In one of the notes written during the height of his passion for Paul Ehrenberg, he made open avowal of love's submissive essence: "To long for love to the point of dying and yet to despise anyone who loves you. Happiness is *not:* to be loved, that is a satisfaction, mixed with disgust, for one's vanity. Happiness is: to love and to find subtle approaches to the object of one's love. . . ."[25] Fifty years later, in love again at the age of seventy-five, he wrote in his diary, "That the adoration of 'godlike youths' surpasses that for everything feminine and arouses a desire comparable to *nothing* in the world is my axiom."[26] What is perhaps most striking in this entry is not the avowal of homosexual desire but the terms in which it is stated—its object "godlike," desire itself unearthly. Love was a search for an object of ultimate concern, for that which one could worship, and one could not hope, should not hope to be the object of such an object, for then it would not be worthy of adoration. Mann's fundamental understanding of love was Nietzschean, Dionysian: it was the quest for fusion with the ground of being itself, which pursued to its end led either to failure or disaster because ultimately it meant de-individuation, complete loss of self. The human being desired totality, and individuality was a precarious good because it was an ambiguous good. As he put it in one of his notes, "Individual existence: consequence of an act of will and resolve on concentration. But precisely in the strong individual, always homesickness for the whole: perhaps nothing but [the yearning for] rest. . . . For the I is a *task.* The coexistence of obsession for self and obsession for world [*Ichsucht und Weltsucht*], of egoism and expansive passion."[27]

105
∎

And to the extent that love aimed at such self-transcendence, Mann could not have believed and in fact did not believe what he said about the future of writing belonging to women. Women were not, in Mann's ironic view, adequate to the most "womanly" of experiences. Feminine submissiveness was naïve rather than sentimental, not intellectually self-aware, and therefore not really capable of grasping as idea the infinite character of the beauty to which it surrendered in the transports of love. Furthermore, woman's *whole* being was identified with longing and passive suffering rather than with activity; fidelity and patience were her essence and greatest virtues.[28] Since female desire did not arise in the opposing context of "masculine" need for the self's autonomy and power, women were neither aware of the immense dangers of surrender, nor driven to master them by translating them into art. Only men, or rather certain men, could both appreciate what women instinctively knew about passion and yet not be absorbed and destroyed by it.

It was both the glory and the pain of the homosexual for Mann that he could do both. The socially forbidden nature of the object of homosexual desire converged with Mann's need to experience transcendental emotion without going under. The social situation of homosexual desire made it the perfect symbol for the inherent unreachability of the transcendent. It was because of his understanding of the Dionysian that Mann actively embraced the impossibility of open homosexual fulfillment that contemporary society imposed as a condition of its acceptance. He deliberately put himself between desire and gratification, a metaphysical-erotic purgatory analogous to the *Zwischenstufe,* the intermediate level between the sexes, occupied by the homosexual in contemporary discourse. Only from that place could he hope to preserve both pure transcendence and himself.

Sadistic Women, Masochistic Men

> *If a woman falls today for love, she will fall tomorrow for money.*
> —Thomas Mann, "Fallen"

106
■

The ultimate nature of desire is the true subject of the novel that brought Mann his early fame. It was preceded by a series of short stories whose appearance marked him at the time as a promising writer, but whose strangeness has only recently been appreciated. Nor has their relationship to *Buddenbrooks* seemed very clear, and the two points are related. The stories are miniatures portraying the intimate feelings of private life, with nothing like the apparent social focus and sweep of the novel, and they are almost astoundingly cruel, bitterly misogynistic, and often grotesque.

The first story Mann wrote, "Fallen" (*Gefallen*), is explicitly pointed as a refutation of the idea of women's emancipation. And though the broader ideological context is absent from succeeding stories, the antifeminist Dr. Selten is only one of a string of Mann protagonists, most of them physically or psychologically deformed outsiders, hopelessly in love with women who are at best indifferent and at worst sadistic toward them, and who in the extreme case drive them to their death.[29] Selten's disillusion began with his discovery that his "innocent" young lover was a prostitute who, moreover, had failed to reveal that while she had been enjoying a love idyll with him, she continued to see her paying customers. The political lesson this experience has taught him—he tells his tale to disabuse a naïve supporter of the contemporary women's movement—is the fundamental corruptibility of women: "If a woman falls today for love, she will fall tomorrow for money."[30] Perhaps Mann's best known early story, "Little Herr Friedemann"—the very title is a cruel taunt—is the story of a thirty-year-old man, made a hunchback through a fall in infancy caused by a drunken nurse, who allows his protective shell of self-denial and outward equanimity to be shattered by an infatuation with a coolly elegant married woman, Gerda von Rinnlingen. Their first encounter is a portent of the inversion of conventional gender relations. At the opera, they both stoop to pick up a handkerchief she has dropped at his feet; she reaches it first, however, and mockingly smiles a thank-you. "How she had looked at him!" he agonizes afterward in bewildered rage. "How? She had forced him to cast down his eyes? She had humiliated him with her glance? But was she not a woman and he a man? And those strange brown eyes of hers—had they not positively glittered with joy?"[31] Despite his initial emasculation, however, Friedemann persists, and to his surprise, Gerda seems receptive. They discover a mutual interest in music, and she not only invites him to her soirées but confides in him, sharing feelings of nervousness and unhappiness and drawing him out in a way that makes him feel understood for the first time in his life. But when in a transport of gratitude he throws himself at her feet, she rebuffs him with a shockingly unexpected callousness whose emotional impact is the greater for the minimalism of Mann's description: "She did not repulse him, nor did she bend her face towards him. She sat erect, leaning a little away. . . . Then she gave him an abrupt push and uttered a short, scornful laugh. She tore her hands from his burning fingers, clutched his arm, and threw him sideways to the ground. Then she jumped up and vanished down the wooded avenue."[32] Overcome with "insane" rage at her for treating him "like a dog" and with violent disgust at himself "which filled him with a thirst to destroy himself, to tear himself to pieces, to blot himself utterly out," Friedemann drags himself to the nearby river and drowns himself.

Undoubtedly the most grotesque of the early stories is another one with a sardonically cruel title, "Little Lizzy" (*Luischen*). "Little Lizzy" is in fact a man, the fat, hapless older husband of a young and sensuous wife—"her organic, indolent voluptuousness suggested the harem"—with whom he is slavishly infatuated. Amra Jacoby, however, has only disdain for her husband. When he humbly comes to her bedroom literally to beg for sex, she fends him off with "a look of malice and sensuality combined," and as he dissolves in tears at her coldness, she strokes him and repeats "in the soothing, mocking singsong one uses with a dog who comes to lick one's feet: 'Yes, yes, good doggy.'"[33] The narrator asserts that her reason for marrying him is unfathomable, a profession of ignorance that suggests the mystery of women, but he clearly has no doubt that a central purpose in her life is to humiliate her husband. She engages more or less openly in a long-term affair with a young musician, and with him concocts an event that will destroy her husband in the most publicly embarrassing way. The lovers plan a party in which the guests will supply the entertainment. The mystery finale is to be a song and dance performed by the husband in a red satin baby dress. Despite his distress, Jacoby can refuse his wife nothing. At the climax of the program, he makes his appearance in the grotesque costume, a wide shape-less dress "cut out above to make a repulsive display of the fat neck, stippled with white powder" and a high blond wig with a green feather, and hops clumsily from one foot to the other singing an absurd little verse that pre-sents him as "Little Lizzy" the femme fatale. The music, described in some detail, has been composed by Amra's lover; music here makes its debut in Mann's work as an embodiment of, and code for, sexuality, ecstasy, and shame. Beginning as a pretty but banal tune, the composition takes an orig-inal turn, becoming more and more dissonant and then suddenly modulat-ing into a new key whose unexpectedness "was a miracle, a revelation . . . like a curtain suddenly torn away to reveal something nude." It is at that mo-ment that Jacoby, as if emerging from a trance, becomes aware of the eyes of the audience on him, and in the sudden knowledge of his abjection, col-lapses and dies.

The sadism of the women in these stories is unmitigated, without nu-ance, and with no apparent motive other than gratuitous malevolence against men—more exactly, a certain kind of man. Reading backward from a knowledge of Mann's homosexual preference, the prominence of the trope of the yearning man and the coldly rejecting woman can seem puzzling, unless in the interests of disguising that preference the female fig-ures are stand-ins for men, the more traditionally feminine ones for Mann himself, the more "masculine" ones (like Gerda von Rinnlingen) for the unavailable homosexual object.[34] But while this is certainly true in impor-tant instances throughout Mann's work, such an explanation hardly does justice to the antifeminist animus of "Fallen" or the fear and hatred of women that is so obviously the motor of the other early stories. The sadistic female characters look more like exemplars of the "demonic woman" whose power purportedly haunted the fin de siècle male imagination than male stand-ins.[35] But even the zeitgeist seems insufficient as an explanation. However melodramatic the situations Mann created for them, his women are too vivid to be simply stock figures or literary conventions.

In fact, Gerda von Rinnlingen and Amra Jacoby share striking traits with Mann's mother, Julia, and along with other of his female portraits raise the suspicion that she—or a fantasy-distorted version of her—may have been their model. Julia Mann, Brazilian-born and exotic in the starchy milieu of the Lübeck upper bourgeoisie, was, according to the accounts of both her older sons, musical and sensuous yet aloof and imperious. Even the specific detail of Amra Jacoby's affair had a biographical referent in Julia's flirtations with a lieutenant in the local Prussian garrison and the violinist-conductor of the Lübeck opera orchestra, with whom she played duets on the piano.[36] Mann claimed to be his mother's favorite, and most of his recorded memories of childhood are happy ones, but his fiction, buttressed by at least one of the very few direct comments he made about her, suggests a different emotional reality. In a letter written years later to his American friend and patron Agnes Meyer, he noted his mother's "sensuous, pre-artistic nature" and her "inclination to the Bohemian," but also her characteristic coldness, and the vanity that had made her suffer greatly as she aged; he had memorialized those sufferings, he added, in the portrait of Grand Duchess Dorothea, mother of the autobiographical Prince Klaus Heinrich, in his novel *Royal Highness*.[37] The actual description of Dorothea in the novel is even harsher than the letter indicates: "Her face was soft, but its beauty made it stern, and it was easy to see that her heart was stern and absorbed in her beauty. . . . Did she love anyone—himself, Klaus Heinrich, for instance, for all his likeness to her? Why, of course she did, when she had time to. . . . But it seemed as if she reserved any expression or sign of her tender feelings for occasions when lookers-on were present who were likely to be edified by them."[38] The ironic portrait is a more distanced but still bitter version of the narcissistic women in the early stories (and for that matter of Gerda Buddenbrook) whose tenderness for display only might well have been felt by a yearning young child as sadistic cruelty. And the letter to Agnes Meyer makes it clear that even well into middle age Mann remained powerfully ambivalent about his mother's sensuality.

But the idea of a biographical origin for the attraction to and fear of narcissistic women evident in Mann's early work, however plausible, must remain speculative, and even more so any insinuation of its relevance for his homosexuality. What in any case is most significant about the representation of women and of men's feelings toward them in the stories is not that it might supply a possible explanation for the sexual preference of their author, but that it renders a particular image of desire; it is a heterosexual counterpart to the passive homosexual longing Mann later described and admitted to. Passive longing is in fact far too mild a term. The masochism of the men in the stories is as blatant and shocking as the sadism of the women. Their abjection is almost boundless, limited only by a murderous rage that is impotent against their victimizers but deadly against the self. Mann had an affinity for dogs as pets and metaphors. In both "Little Herr Friedemann" and "Little Lizzy," men are degraded into dogs, to be condescendingly petted or contemptuously kicked aside; and in the first story, the metaphor is the victim's rather than the perpetrator's. A dog figures even more prominently in another of the early stories, "Tobias Mindernickel," which, perhaps just because of the absence of women, presents the least melodramatic and most chillingly acute portrayal of sadomasochism in the early work.

Tobias Mindernickel—his name advertises his insignificance—is an eccentric recluse, a figure of fun to the neighborhood children, who torment him whenever he walks the street. One day one of the boys chasing him trips and smashes his face. Mindernickel consoles the weeping boy, verbally caressing his pain, and ties his handkerchief around the boy's head to stanch the bleeding. Suddenly his eyes regard the world with a new sense of self-confidence and pride and his face wears a look of pained happiness.[39] A few days later he buys a pet dog whom he names Esau—the biblical rejected brother, denied his mother's favor and his father's blessing. Mindernickel affectionately feeds and pampers the dog, but when the animal tires of obeying his incessantly repeated order to come, he becomes infuriated and beats Esau savagely with his walking stick. Only when the dog is reduced to whimpering supplication does Mindernickel take pity on him and hug him, in tears himself. The cycle is repeated whenever the dog, in animal high spirits, does not do his master's bidding. One day Mindernickel accidentally stabs the frisky pet while cutting him pieces of bread. He finds deep pleasure in caring for Esau's wound and feels sad disappointment when it heals and the dog's good spirits return. Mindernickel cannot stand Esau's happiness and independence. In the terrible climax, he grabs the playful dog with raging fury and plunges a knife into him, cutting him deeply from shoulder to chest. The next instant he is once again trying to take care of him: "My poor animal! My poor animal! How sad everything is! How sad we both are! Do you suffer? Yes, yes, I know, you suffer,—how pathetically you lie there before me! But I, I am with you! I will console you! My best handkerchief, I will . . ."[40] This time, however, Mindernickel has gone too far; Esau is dead.

That Mindernickel's psychology may seem transparent to readers schooled by a hundred years of psychoanalysis does nothing even now to lessen the impact of the story. Mann chose his subject well; it is impossible not to feel horror at the savage treatment of the innocent pet. But the author has manipulated his reader's emotions even more astutely, for it is obvious that Esau is also Mindernickel himself. It is thus equally impossible not to feel pity for the man, for his total exclusion and loneliness, for the absence of love and self-respect that make him identify so wholly with Esau and rely so completely on a poor animal for both. Another psychological twist further undercuts the possibility of simple emotion and univocal judgment in reading the story. Mann showed that the presumably legitimate needs for love and respect could have highly ambiguous moral consequences. Mindernickel wants not just a companion but unconditional love and absolute power. The humble need that makes him tender and caring of his alter ego is paired with a savage imperiousness that demands total control, and is willing to destroy if he can't have it. And this paradox points to a deeper one, perhaps the most profound of Mann's realizations. The sense of nothingness that depends on unconditional love for a feeling of self-value is only the other side of the omnipotence that wants to reduce everything else to dependency; and while one seems deferential and the other can be destructive, both aim at the same sense of totality, the same domination. In the shabby, enclosed little world of Tobias Mindernickel, matters of wide import are already in play.

The Privatization of Transcendence

> *The success of* Buddenbrooks *is based ultimately on a misunderstanding.*
> —Thomas to Heinrich Mann

> *Art is honored when it is understood to be related to religion and sexual love.*
> —Thomas Mann, "Thoughts in War"

The move Mann made from the early stories to *Buddenbrooks* was twofold: he translated the purely personal psychology of the stories into metaphysical-aesthetic motives—into religion, philosophy, and music—and he historicized the crisis of personality that they portray, in a profoundly original and revealing way. The figure of the reclusive outsider in desperate need of love and meaning is still central to the dynamic of the novel; it is in fact embodied in two characters, representing two stages of its evolution, Thomas Buddenbrook, the last owner of the grain firm bearing his family name, and his son Hanno, who dies at sixteen of typhus. Thomas is more or less satisfactorily married—his wife Gerda's aloofness and mystery are not the melodramatic sadism of her predecessors, though she engages in an "affair" and is clearly their descendant—and Hanno has a close, obviously homoerotic friendship with a boy his own age; neither relationship, however, answers their needs and yearnings. Thomas finds his fulfillment, if only for a fleeting moment, in the philosophy of Schopenhauer, or Mann's version of it, and Hanno finds his in a more self-integrated way in the music of Wagner. The temptation to read these impersonal sources of gratification as nothing but displacements or disguises for the all-too-human objects of the short stories, or even of homosexual objects, is a serious error of reductionism. What Mann revealed in the transfiguration of desire from the interpersonal in the stories to the metaphysical in *Buddenbrooks* is desire's deepest structure. He would revert to the interpersonal again, transfigured by the accomplishments of the novel, in his work after *Buddenbrooks,* above all in *Death in Venice.*

The novel tells the story of the Buddenbrook family through four generations, covering a span of forty years between 1835 and 1875. Though the time frame is foreshortened and shifted backward, the novel is in good part thinly veiled family history and autobiography, as even contemporaries knew. Mann did extensive research on many aspects of life in Lübeck, his hometown until age nineteen and the model for the story's setting, quizzed relatives closely about their lives, and even had them fill out detailed questionnaires. The Buddenbrooks own a family grain business, as did the Manns, that passes from the self-assured patriarch Johann the elder to his son, Consul Johann, a successful but somewhat less confident businessman, and then in turn to the Consul's oldest son, Thomas, a man whose inchoate cultural yearnings and psychological sensitivities ill equip him for the ruthlessness of business life. The longest portion of the more than seven hundred pages is devoted to this third generation, the last to run the firm. Thomas's sister Tony, good-spirited and natural but feckless and snobbish, makes a series of disastrous marriages that eat up family money in lost dowries; his brother Christian, a hypochondriac with literally no stomach for business, lives the life of a bon vivant and raconteur, frequenting nightclubs and theaters. Thomas's only son, Hanno, is a sickly child interested only in music and daydreaming, and despite Thomas's efforts to make him a more "manly" boy, it is painfully clear to him that Hanno will never be a businessman. Exhausted and prematurely old in middle age, Thomas dies of complications from a botched tooth extraction; his son Hanno follows him soon afterward. The fate of the Buddenbrook firm more or less paralleled that of the Manns. Heinrich Mann, Thomas's father, had realized that his two older sons, both of whom had literary ambitions, were neither desirous nor capable of running the business, and ordered it to be liquidated upon his death, which occurred prematurely shortly after the celebration of the firm's hundredth anniversary in 1891.

As the Buddenbrook family declines in energy, wealth, and status through the novel, other families, notably the Hagenströms, prosper. Mann made a point of the sharp difference between the two families' business practices and ethics. The Buddenbrooks are patrician businessmen whose ethos harks back to an earlier merchant capitalism that tempered acquisitiveness with morality; the family motto, inscribed by an ancestor in the family Bible as an exhortation to his son, reads: "My son, show zeal for each day's affairs of business, but only for such that make for a peaceful night's sleep."[41] By contrast, "the easy, flamboyant way [Hagenström] earned and spent his money was very different from the dogged, patient labor based on strict traditional principles that characterized his fellow merchants. This man stood on his own feet, unencumbered by the chain of custom and reverence for the past" (401). This sharply pointed difference between a traditional business ethos and the untrammeled pursuit of profit seems to explain the decline of one family and the ascent of another, and is the basis for the sociohistorical interpretation of the novel, whose virtually canonical formulation is that of Georg Lukács. In his view, *Buddenbrooks* is *the* document of the transformation of the patrician burgher, and the genteel merchant capitalism he represented, into the late-nineteenth-century bourgeois avatar of freewheeling free-market industrial and financial capitalism who has shucked off the constraints of the older religious and moral universe for an ethic of pure acquisition.[42]

Mann—who was to have a complicated relationship with Lukács—repudiated this view even before it was expressed. "If I contrasted the rising burgher, the newcomer, the speculative buyer and successor, with the declining burgher," he wrote years later in the *Reflections of a Nonpolitical Man,* "it was only in passing, without my in any way being particularly interested in the opposing type. The burning problem for me that stimulated me to write was not a political one, but a biological, psychological one. . . . [T]he psychological one was my main interest; I included the sociopolitical one only half subconsciously; it did not preoccupy me much."[43] Despite the polemical intention of the *Reflections* to present his newfound conservative politics as nonpolitics, this is entirely believable—as far as it goes. Mann was not at all interested in the social or political implications of the economic change he described in *Buddenbrooks,* but rather in the "transformation of the burgher into the artist" that supposedly took place simply as a parallel to the economic transformation. But Mann also missed something about his own novel, an important truth that lies halfway between his account and Lukács's interpretation. Lukács rightly rejected Mann's tendentiously self-deprecating claim to have "slept a little through the metamorphosis of the German burgher into the bourgeois,"[44] nor was it accurate that Mann simply noted it "in passing" and without particular interest. The transformation plays a pivotal role in the novel, though not the one Lukács assigned it. In documenting the replacement of the burgher by the bourgeois, Mann was in fact offering a historical explanation for his main theme, the "emergence" of "the artist"—*his* kind of artist, the artist of weakness, of a state of crisis. Viewed this way, the question of the objective historical accuracy of Mann's account of the transformation of German (or Lübeck) capitalism, which has been much debated, is somewhat beside the point. Perceived or constructed, the transformation is *Mann's* interpretation of a causal nexus. That interpretation is thus itself a historical datum, a symptom of its time even more than it is the "naturalistic" record of an objective historical event. It is also, by the same token, a biographical datum, a fact about his own self-understanding.

The earlier generations of Buddenbrooks live within forms of culture that, however different from one another, have in common that the transcendent, the ethical, and the aesthetic dimensions of life are fully and seamlessly integrated into the fabric of everyday life. The evolution of nineteenth-century capitalism, as Mann saw it, pushed the transcendent further and further out of public life, leading ultimately to its complete privatization. As commerce became more single-mindedly profit-oriented, the self increasingly had to turn in on itself for the spiritual nourishment no longer to be found in the public sphere.

Significant change is already apparent in the differences between old Johann Buddenbrook and his son, the Consul. Johann is an uncompromising man of the Enlightenment; guided by the secular ideal of rational autonomy, he has no need or tolerance for religion, which to him is nothing but superstition and obscurantism. Freedom and reason go hand in hand in his moral universe, the internalized but objective and transcendent norms of the second controlling and limiting the personal claims of the first. The family motto codifies the proper equilibrium in the sphere of economic activity: self-interest is automatically subject to the constraints of moral reason. A quite specific aesthetic-moral culture is also an integral part of this Enlightenment ethos, a Neoclassicism that understands the purpose of literature and art to be moral edification sweetened by pleasure. Poetry is a public function in this culture. The town poet's job is to compose verse to celebrate major events in the life of the city and its most eminent citizens; he is an important guest at the Buddenbrook banquet that takes up the whole of part 1 of the novel. As Johann rejects religion, however, he also has no patience with a certain kind of art, the art of free-floating imagination, which dreams up idle and irrational fantasies. Though a practical businessman, he values traditional classical education and is distressed by the encroachment of "practical ideals" into contemporary schooling. "Practical ideals. Nope, set no store by 'em," he grumps. "Trade schools and technical schools and commercial schools are popping up like mushrooms, and grammar schools and classical education are suddenly all foolishness, and the whole world has nothing in its head but coal mines and factories and making money. Fine, fine, it's all very fine. But on the other hand a bit *stupide,* over the long term—is it not?"[45]

It is to his son that he makes this complaint; Consul Johann has just praised the July Monarchy in France for its useful combination of constitutionalism in politics with practical ideals and interests in economics. The Consul represents the modernity of the 1830s. He admires the political and economic liberalism of the "Bourgeois Monarchy," whose eponymous head dressed like a banker to herald the respectability of moneymaking. To the consternation of his father's more traditional guests, Consul Johann is strongly in favor of joining the *Zollverein,* the newly created, Prussian-inspired German customs union; it would open up new duty-free markets in states that had been surrounded by tariff walls and create prospects of unlimited expansion for the Buddenbrook firm. But the other side of Consul Johann's more adventurous sense of enterprise is a pious religiosity, in the new Romantic edition that worships infinite nature as an incarnation of the divine. The shift from Enlightenment Neoclassicism to Romanticism is much more than aesthetic. As transcendence recedes from its immanence within the business ethos, the Absolute must be looked for outside daily life, outside this world. Johann no longer has the easy commerce with transcendence that his father's fully internalized sense of moral absolutes allowed him to enjoy, that easy commerce that also afforded the elder Buddenbrook a more relaxed sense of autonomy. The greater latitude that the new business ethic permits to self-interest requires as a moral counterweight the projection of a more stringent source of authority outside the self, as well as a new will to obedience. The end of moral sociability as the governing principle of social relationships also means the excision of emotion and the sense of affective communal bonds from those relationships. Mann brilliantly brought out the enormous consequences of these economic-ideological changes in an apparently tiny detail, the differences in the feelings of father and son toward a large overgrown piece of land the family owns. Old Johann expresses regret that he didn't tidy it up and make a rational French garden out of it, "the trees nicely trimmed in little spheres and cubes." The Consul prefers a wild Romantic garden; all would have been spoiled, he protests, "if a piece of free and beautiful nature were to be piteously snipped and shorn." The exchange that follows foreshadows the transformation that the rest of the novel will chart from assertive individualism to dependent longing, from Enlightenment manliness to the fin de siècle crisis of masculinity. "If that piece of free nature belongs to me," father Johann insists, "I'll be hanged if I don't have the right to tidy the place up just as I please." "Oh father," the Consul protests, "when I'm lying there in the tall grass under some luxuriant bush, it's more as if I belonged to nature and hadn't any rights at all over it" (26). In the Romantic trope, nature is not only a figure for the divine, it is the maternal Absolute, which holds and empowers. The Consul's vision of lying in tall grass beneath a luxuriant bush is of a child cradled in the bosom of the maternal infinite, over which he of course has no right except the "right" of belonging, which however allows him to participate in the infinite itself.[46]

Johann the Elder does not understand the logic of his son's conjoining religion and business. For him it spells nothing but hypocrisy. His estranged older son Gotthold, Johann's half-brother, has demanded his fair share of inheritance "with all the sense of justice I can muster as a *Christian* and as a *man of business,*" and threatens that if it is not forthcoming, he will no longer be able to respect his father "either as *Christian* or as . . . a *man of business.*""Un-Christian!" old Johann explodes in Voltairean sarcasm and rage. "Very tasteful, I must say—pious and money-hungry"(43). But Consul Johann is no hypocrite. His Romantic reverence is quite real, though sharply separated off from the sphere of autonomous, self-interested business activity, where he feels himself master and has no difficulty asserting himself. The rigid compartmentalization is in fact precisely what makes *his* autonomy possible. Emotion and the need for worship can be satisfied in ways that do not inhibit the new demands of business.

Johann's son Thomas, however, is no longer able to find this compartmentalizing solution possible. "Dogmatic faith in a fanatical biblical Christianity, which his father had been able to couple with a very practical eye for business . . . had always been alien to him," the narrator informs us. "All his life he had approached these first and last things with his grandfather's worldly skepticism; but his needs were too profound and too metaphysical for him to find genuine satisfaction in old Johann Buddenbrook's comfortable superficialities, and he had looked to history to answer the questions of eternity and immortality" (631).[47] The novel gives no direct clue to the reason for this loss of faith between the generations. On one level, Mann was dramatizing the increasing secularization of the nineteenth century; Thomas is the unwitting product of the process that Max Weber, whose insights Mann later claimed to have duplicated without having read him, described as the "disenchantment of the world." On another he was projecting the facts of autobiography onto Thomas, who, he once explicitly said, represented the threefold image of father, offspring, and double.[48] In Thomas Buddenbrook, emotion and the need to worship have nothing in which to be invested, nowhere to go. Though he is for a time more or less successful in business, his achievements come only with strenuous effort and at great emotional cost, constantly distracted as he is by a restlessness and self-concern he cannot fathom and by his continual efforts to suppress them. And suppression is all the more necessary because of the ever-increasing need to concentrate energy on new business opportunities and methods as capitalism continues to evolve in the direction of entrepreneurial initiative and ruthlessness. This development offers another explanation for Thomas's inability to believe; the disparity between religion and the world has become too great for the easy compartmentalization his father practiced.

Thomas is caught between two demands, neither of which he can fulfill. He must maintain the family firm and standing, but his ethical-spiritual patrimony and his own native emotions will not allow him to use the new business methods that are necessary to do so. When Tony first suggests to him that he can recoup the firm's recent financial reverses by buying out the grain harvest of an aristocrat in desperate need of immediate cash at half its potential value, Thomas is outraged at the idea that he undertake a "highly unrespectable, shabby operation [and] brutally exploit a . . . poor defenseless fellow" so that he can "make a profit that is nothing but usury" (447). Thinking back a few years to his first serious financial setback, he is still pained at his reaction: "For the first time in his life he had been forced to experience personally and completely just how cruel and brutal business can be, had watched as all his better, gentler and kinder sentiments had slunk away before the raw, naked, absolute instinct of self-preservation" (461). When having allowed himself to indulge his own instinct for self-preservation and accept Tony's proposed speculative venture, he sees it collapse with great loss to the firm and is more relieved than distraught (483).

But the demands of his burgher identity also thwart his equally pressing needs for emotional expression and his yearning for transcendence. He can barely allow himself to recognize these needs because without socially sanctioned objects or structures such as his father and grandfather had, they both seem unjustifiable and preoccupy him to the point of distraction, undermining action and independence. In one telling instance, he is almost overwhelmed by his son-in-law's violent emotional outburst at Thomas's refusal to bail him out of bankruptcy: "like any man of his generation, he felt a fanatical reverence for all human emotions that stood at odds with his sober and practical outlook as a man of business" (222). More troublesome for family harmony is his chronic disdain for his brother Christian's constant self-indulgence; it is a measure of his watchful need to guard against his own. In a bitter confrontation with Christian, Thomas acknowledges his revulsion at Christian's hypochondria, indolence, and self-scrutiny and defends himself against Christian's angry rejection of his ideals of balance, poise, and dignity, which are nothing but masks for his coldness. "I have become what I am," he confesses, "because I did not want to become like you. If I have inwardly shrunk away from you, it was because I had to protect myself from you, because your nature and character are a danger to me" (563). He had put it to himself earlier, when he had been so agitated by the cruelty of business, that he was a mixture of the practical man and the "tenderhearted dreamer" (462). But the real nature of the emotions he has tried to suppress revealed itself when his mother impulsively embraced him on the occasion of the celebration of the firm's hundredth anniversary. "The senator felt himself go weak in her embrace. It was as if something deep within him had worked itself free and left him. His lips trembled. He felt an enervating urge to remain there in his mother's arms, at her breast, where the gentle scent of perfume lingered on the soft silk of her dress, to close his eyes and never to have to see or say anything more" (472). He is tempted by surrender to the ultimate source of the child's security. What for his father had been represented by the Romantic garden, a culturally sanctioned vision of all-embracing maternal nature, has returned for his son to its first, its most private incarnation. In this form it is a frighteningly regressive, passive infantile desire.

Thus the deepest meaning of the danger that he fears from his emotions emerges only in the even more displaced form of anxiety over his son. Hanno is a sickly, unassertive, and shy young boy, an unlikely prospect to head the Buddenbrook firm, but Thomas's greatest anxiety about him is always couched in terms of his questionable virility. When during the celebration of the firm's hundredth anniversary Hanno stumbles painfully through the recitation of a poem, Thomas jibes at him cruelly in front of everyone, aware of what he is doing but feeling that it is necessary because Hanno "had to learn to be strong and manly." And when Hanno inevitably breaks down in tears, unable to continue, Thomas berates him with humiliating directness: "What are you crying about? . . . Are you a little girl? What's to become of you if you keep up like this? Do you think you can still break into tears when you grow up and have to give a speech to people?" (476–77). Matters get worse as Hanno begins to evince the musical talents of his mother and to be consumed with her passion for music. "Thomas," the narrator notes, "regarded music as a hostile force that had come between him and his child—after all, he had hoped to make a genuine Buddenbrook of him, a strong and practical man with a powerful drive to master and take control of the world outside him" (497). But the influence of his mother, as well as all the other women who dominate the household, Thomas reflects, "was not likely to stimulate and develop manliness in the boy" (508). The deleterious effect of women on the growing boy's manliness is a constant theme. A hundred pages later Thomas is still worried about it, resolving this time that he must do something: "But the time had now come for a father to exert his own influence on his son, to draw him to his side and offer manly impressions to neutralize previous feminine influences" (601–2). Mann's awareness of the possibility and power of a boy's feminine identification had obvious autobiographical roots. He always attributed the polarity of his own character, artist and bourgeois, to his dual heritage from his exotic, sensuous, and artistic Latin-born mother and his sober, rational north German father, but by vocation it was his mother with whom he was fully identified. Not only was passion feminine then; art itself, the very essence of Mann's being, was too.

Under these circumstances, it is hardly surprising that Thomas repudiates

118
■

emotion and culture, to which, however, he is magnetically drawn. He has been able to indulge them legitimately only by indulging them vicariously, by loving and marrying a woman who, as a woman, is allowed to embody them. Gerda Buddenbrook is deeply, passionately musical, but since Thomas must keep away from the very thing in himself that drew him to her, he is unable to fathom her passion or join with her in a genuine and full emotional partnership. She appears throughout the novel withheld and utterly mysterious, as she is to Thomas—and it would seem to Mann himself; she is the one character in the novel, male or female, whose interior is never plumbed and whose exterior never gives it away. What she does clearly represent is Thomas's final and complete unmanning. When she starts playing duets with an officer stationed in town, who shows up without any advance notice to Thomas, it is of little moment whether the trysts are sexual or "just" musical; Thomas has been effectively cuckolded, even if he feels that "'cheating' and 'adultery' were not the right words for the melodious and abysmally silent events happening above him" (627). He cannot release the emotionality that might enable him to share his wife's world and so he has to give her over to another man. But the more serious problem is that even if he could release it, emotion as he experienced it when his mother embraced him makes it doubtful that he could share his wife's world as an equal partner. It is not just that he is not musical enough or not expressive enough; he is, even in his own eyes, not man enough.

Only once, in the celebrated "Schopenhauer episode," is Thomas able to let himself go, and then only because through the philosopher he finds, if just for a moment, a way of reconciling passion and control, submission and mastery, and above all feminine surrender with masculine self-assertion. Serendipitously picking up "the second half of a famous metaphysical system," Thomas has an epiphany. It is a momentary ecstatic sublimation of the essential Romantic contradiction between the dissolution of flawed, finite individuality in an infinite totality and the ultimate affirmation of individuality as itself infinite; but Mann gives it a uniquely concrete autobiographical twist, homosexual and narcissistic. "Individuality! Oh, what a man is, can do, and has seems to him so poor, gray, inadequate and boring," Thomas reflects, on reading Schopenhauer's chapter on death. But the death of individuality is meaningless, the philosopher shows him, because the individual is nothing but a fleeting manifestation of the cosmic will. "Nothing began and nothing ceased," Thomas muses. "There was only the endless present, and the energy within him, which loved life with such a painfully sweet, urgent, yearning love, and of which his own person was no more than an abortive expression—that energy would now know how to find access to the endless present." Thomas's true consolation, however, lies not in being part of the undifferentiated eternal cosmic will, but in the thought of being reincarnated in, and one with, an idealized self, a finite-infinite being. The affirmation of individual will is contradictory, more Nietzsche than Schopenhauer, but it is an eccentric, highly personalized version of Nietzsche, which subverts that philosopher as well as Schopenhauer by its metaphysical idealization of the other:

> Where will I be once I am dead? . . . I will be a part of all those who say, who have ever said, or will say "I": and, most especially, *a part of those who say it more forcibly, joyfully, powerfully.*
>
> A boy is growing up somewhere in the world, and he is well equipped and well formed, capable of developing his talents, tall and straight and untroubled, pure and fierce and vigorous—just to look at him increases the joy of the joyful and drives the unhappy to despair. That boy is my son. *He is me*— or will be soon, soon, as soon as death frees me from this wretched delusion that I am not him and me. (634–37)

Mann fuses the quest for transcendence with longing for homosexual merger and makes it indisputably clear that in this instance at least homosexual desire is, in the classical Freudian definition, narcissistic identification with an idealized self. Submission to the cosmic All is not self-dissolution but union for the sake of self-perfection; that fusion makes possible in Thomas's imagination his own self-affirmation as the ideal male according to the previous century's definition of masculinity—and presumably also that of Mann's father: physically imposing, emotionally integrated, energetic, and tough.

If Thomas is unable to sustain this vision, it is not only because the practical businessman is too embarrassed to be a philosopher. It is because the philosophical vision is itself logically unsustainable, based as it is on the most elementary logical contradiction. Only the ecstasy of fantasy, the fantasy of gratified desire in a climactic fusion with the healthy young boy—the passage tellingly shifts to the present tense in the actual moment of vision—has occluded the contradiction that is entailed in a simultaneous effacement and affirmation of self. Almost immediately, however, reflection forces grammar back to the future—a sign that Thomas realizes the unattainability of the vision in this world.

It is because of its unattainability that in the final stage of the individualized self's quest for transcendence, represented by Thomas's son Hanno, the scene shifts from the philosophical to aesthetic, that is, from the conceptual to the experiential. Transcendence is an emotional event, a feeling of merger, not a concept, a merger that for Mann was possible only in music and sex, where thought would not undermine the experience by exposing it to reality and logic. But Hanno does not simply represent the full-blown surrender to the needs of transcendence that in his father still had to be suppressed. In keeping with the interpretive line of the novel that posits the increasing privatization of the search for transcendence taking place against a background of radical historical change, Mann sees in the political and social environment of Hanno's generation the final stage in the disenchantment of the German world.

Hanno is born sickly, introverted, and musical; in a vestigial Naturalism, Mann insisted on biologizing the cause of familial decline. But Hanno's innate character makes him even more out of phase with his world than his father was, for his childhood is virtually congruent with the era of Bismarck's military unification of Germany and his adolescent schooling with the first years of the new militarized empire. What had begun with the transformation of the economy, the expulsion of spirit from the mundane, is completed by the creation of a brutal and spiritless polity. Mann's ironic, even contemptuous attitude toward the new patriotism of the *Bismarckzeit* is consistent with his theme and particularly striking in the retrospect of the nationalistic *Reflections of a Nonpolitical Man* some fifteen years later. Describing the new era, Mann, in keeping with the other major theme we have been tracing, explicitly yokes together politics and masculinity. "Having grown up in the atmosphere of a bellicose, triumphant, and rejuvenated Fatherland," Mann writes of Hanno's schoolmates, "they had embraced the habits of crude virility. They spoke in a jargon that was both slipshod and dashing and was replete with terms from technology. High on their list of virtues were physical strength, gymnastic skill, and prowess at drinking and smoking; the most despicable vices were effeminacy and dandyism" (694–95). The disappearance of moral culture from education, which old Johann Buddenbrook had long ago bemoaned, is now complete in the coarse utilitarianism of a schooling whose task was to prepare the upper classes for material rewards, financial and political. "Where previously classical learning had been considered a joyful end in itself, and was pursued with a calm, leisurely, cheerful idealism," the author virtually editorializes, "now the concepts of authority, duty, power, service and career were held in highest honor. . . . The schools have become a state within a state, where the Prussian notion of rigorous service held such sway that not only the teachers but also the students thought of themselves as civil servants, interested only in advancing their careers and therefore always concerned to be well regarded by those in power" (697). In this fully coordinated *Machtstaat,* there is no place for the idealist universals of the great-grandfather's confident Enlightenment morality, the grandfather's reverential Romantic Christian piety, or even the father's consoling post–Romantic philosophical pessimism. Kant, discoverer of the categorical imperative, that quintessence of Enlighten-

121

ment moral universality, has been eviscerated and put to work as the philosophical patron of Prussia's chauvinistic power interests; the categorical imperative now means duty to the fatherland.

What is left for the soul aspiring to the eternal in such a world is the private ecstasy of musical improvisation. "I know what you're thinking when you improvise," says Hanno's one friend, the young Count Kai, turning beet red; their relationship has long been suspected by their teachers of having "something foul and hostile behind it." The language in which Mann describes the improvisation, as has been often noted, describes an act of masturbation. The privatization of transcendence charted in the novel reaches its ultimate form in solipsistic sex. Equally significant, the structure of Hanno's music is a dialectic of submission and aggression, femininity and masculinity, parallel to but more psychologically primitive than his father's vision of oneness with an idealized young boy.

The music alternates at first between assertion and supplication, imperious announcements in the bass giving way to "yearning, painful" modulations in the treble, agitated runs and syncopations yielding to melodies "like a child's prayer." It builds to a kind of hunting song, daring and stormy, a masculine adventurousness that feels to Hanno like "overcoming great obstacles . . . slaying dragons, scaling mountains, swimming great rivers, walking through fire." Then however begins the "long slide down into lust" and climax: "And it came, it could not be held back any longer, the convulsions of desire could not be prolonged; it came—like curtains ripping open, doors flinging wide, thorny hedges sundering, walls of flame collapsing." The words that follow seem to interpret the structure of the climax, musical and autoerotic: "Resolution, dissolution, fulfillment, perfect contentment." But the music does not end with fulfillment and contentment. The climax is followed by a return of the first theme, modified into "a celebration, a triumph, an unrestrained orgy . . . marching victorious and laden with all the bluster, tinkling chimes and churning pomp of a great orchestra." This musical passage has about it, Mann writes,

> something brutal and doltish . . . and something ascetic and religious at the same time, something like faith and self-renunciation; but there was also something insatiable and depraved beyond measure in the way it savored and exploited. *It sucked hungrily at its last sweet drops with almost cynical despair, with a deliberate willing of bliss and doom and fell away in exhaustion, revulsion and surfeit, and finally, in the languor that followed, all its excess trickled off in a long, soft arpeggio, hesitated and died a wistful death.* (720–21; italics added)

This is less the image of postclimax triumph than it is the description of an infant oscillating between the worshipful adoration and the sadistic plundering of the breast, sucking nourishment with envious violence until it is sated to the point of stupor. There is no celebration of independence here, rather a desperate, brutalized dependency that feels it can get the nurture it needs only by force and is enraged by the very externality of the source. Though more sublimated, the emotional tonality of the metaphor is not unlike the sadomasochism of the first stories. Mann understood the rage of the supplicant; the desire for devotion, worship, and submission does not breed one-sided submissiveness. This savagery will appear again in other works, most openly and powerfully in the dream sequences in *Death in Venice* and *The Magic Mountain*. Hanno's climax is not a triumph of assertive creativity, of masculinity, but its defeat; it ends, as Mann says, in "wistful death"; though momentarily sated, the hunger, and the desperate struggle to satisfy it, will return. Hanno's physical death from typhus, following immediately after the musical episode, is the material expression of spiritual surrender. Though not subject to contradiction in the way his father's effort at philosophical consolation is, the musical/sexual experience also ends in defeat. After the moment of fulfillment through union and self-loss, there is left only the empty self of yearning.

Writing and Masculinity

> *Art is the holy torch which turns its light upon all the frightful depths, all the shameful and woeful abysses of life.*
> —Thomas Mann, "Gladius Dei"

> *The power of intellect and words [is] a power that sits smilingly enthroned above mere inarticulate, unconscious life.*
> —Thomas Mann, *Tonio Kröger*

Buddenbrooks would seem to be a definitive statement of triumphant defeat that does not point beyond itself. And indeed, with the exception of the aberrant *Royal Highness,* a failed effort at an alternative masculinity, Mann did not write another novel for almost a quarter of a century, when his original metaphysical and psychological problem had become complicated by the problem of politics. The epiphany of *Buddenbrooks,* however, is a purely solipsistic one, the epiphany of narcissistic adolescent fantasy, related not to a real object but to an internal state. In one sense, the whole of Mann's erotics is already contained there, but it had yet to be developed in the direction of object relatedness. Mann's exploration of sexual passion became more explicit after *Buddenbrooks.* Simultaneously, and not coincidentally, a new theme appears in his work: the problem of the meaning of art and the nature of the artist. Both developments were driven by events in his life, literary and nonliterary, intertwined with one another. While finishing the novel, he had met and fallen in love with Paul Ehrenberg, his first adult passion—there had been two boyhood infatuations—and, as it would turn out, the most profound love of his life. The ecstatic, frightening revelations of this consuming event came just at the moment when the success of *Buddenbrooks* was consolidating his identity as a writer, strengthening his powers to domesticate aesthetically what "life" was teaching him. But his new self-assurance as a writer also brought his early rivalry with his brother Heinrich into new focus. Heinrich was a very different kind of writer, and was for the moment enjoying even greater success than Thomas. His art seemed a challenge not only to Thomas's hopes of fame, not only to a conception of art that he believed was so much truer than Heinrich's, but to one that meant salvation from "feminine" self-loss.

124
▪

If we can trust the implications of one of Mann's reports of conversations with Paul, the love affair was never consummated. Bantering about sexuality, one of them had asserted that from a medical point of view a love affair with a married woman was the safest. Mann, always on the lookout to turn their conversation to their relationship, added that his friendship with Paul was good for him also from a psychiatric point of view, because it served him as tranquilizer, purification, and release from sexuality. This was, Mann admitted in his notebook, a lie,[49] though hardly one he could have told Paul if they had been sexual. But it was a lie in another way that Paul was probably quite well aware of, or so at least Mann feared. Mann was never at peace in their relationship, one of the numerous things about him that he felt kept Paul at a distance; the notebook entries of this period are a continuous lament for a one-sided and desperate passion. They are not, however, simply an autobiographical record. Mann did keep diaries for these years, which he later destroyed, but these were entries in literary notebooks, meant to be mined for his work; some would appear in contemporary published writings, more were intended for a project called "The Loved Ones," which was never written, but were incorporated much later in the Joseph novels and *Doctor Faustus*. For Mann himself, these outpourings of yearning and despair were not just subjective; they were an anatomy of passion as such.

Mann was exultantly grateful for his feelings for Paul; they proved to him, so concerned about his writerly dispassion and irony, that he was human after all.[50] Emotion, however, was a highly ambiguous good. In the discourse of masculinity, emotion was suspect in any case, and most especially in a writer who considered himself more a lyric poet than a novelist because his work was the expression of his own interior.[51] "Many people," Mann noted, "are ashamed of enthusiasm as a 'poetic' and weak thing. They will not let their admiration go beyond a 'quite nice' or 'very nice.'"[52] This comment appears just a few entries before his effusive poem of thanks to Paul, his "savior" and "happiness," for the days of "lively feeling" he was enjoying because of him.[53] But Mann's kind of passion was especially troubling. "There are two kinds of people," he wrote in reflection on his affair of the heart, "those who are called to love, and those who are called to be loved."[54] There was no question about which group Mann fell into, and which Paul. Mann experienced the dependency of those whose calling was to love with the masochistic pleasure of a willing martyr. Writing to Paul about a painting exhibit he had attended, he described his "favorite painting in the whole show," *The Heart* by Martin Brandenburg: "In a forest rendered in a strange moody way, a girl stands leaning against a tree trunk and holding in her hand a heart, with which she is playing pertly and gracefully; while at her feet kneels a young man, a knife in hand, a great gash in his chest, his eyes—fanatic, ecstatic, and suffering—directed upwards. The picture made a great impression on me," Mann affirmed, adding with wry self-knowledge, "from which it probably follows that it is not worth two cents as a painting."[55] Except for the pro forma aesthetic qualification, however—Mann's taste in painting was resolutely conservative and he had no interest in, if indeed he had any knowledge of, the Modernist developments in that sphere taking place in his own Munich—he expressed absolutely no irony at Brandenburg's Gothic literalization of the clichéd idiom of love. But of its dangerous femininity he had no doubt.

"The Loved Ones" was planned as the story of a married woman's hopeless love for a dashing young violinist. The violinist Rudolf was Paul, Adelaide was Mann himself, and her husband Albrecht was a version of Heinrich. Writing about a heterosexual love affair was not just a way to disguise homosexuality; Mann's identification with the female protagonist was the objective correlative of his "female" passion, as his notes and letters make clear. "*Loyalty* as the highest *feminine* virtue," he had noted of the theme of the novel. "Then patience. Concerning the viewpoint of 'The Loved Ones' as apotheosis of the eternal feminine."[56] At about the same time he had written to Heinrich about the satisfactions the affair with Paul afforded him: "My sentimental need, my need for enthusiasm, devotion, trust . . . loyalty, which for so long had to fast to the point of wasting away and atrophying, is now feasting."[57] And sometime later in "The Loved Ones" notebook, he quoted a verse from his favorite German poet, the homosexual writer Platen, which ended with the line "Patience is our whole virtue."[58]

If the identifications are obvious, the notes for the novel suggest that the

125
∎

need that was now "feasting" was also painfully, but inevitably, frustrated. In an entry that might have referred equally to his feelings about Paul and Adelaide's about Rudolf, and that he did use to describe those of Baroness Anna's about her husband in the story "A Gleam," Mann wrote, "Jealousy over pretty girls, with whom he spends time, not because they make him especially happy but because his vanity demands that he . . . show himself as a fortunate soul who . . . *does not know the meaning of longing.*"⁵⁹ "Occasionally she decides, as if to punish him for her love, not to see him at all for a time, not to worry herself about him at all," runs another note. "But she soon realizes again that *he* has no need of *her* at all, that he, in the richness of his life, can well await the continuation of the novel, that he bears these times only too easily,—while she sits idle and neither can nor wants to be free of his image. *She* is the one who can't hold out."⁶⁰ One of the most poignant entries, explicitly labeled for "The Loved Ones," clearly points to a real-life event: "'The Loved Ones'. . . . Fever-night of love after an unhappy meeting: A series of utterly explicit dreams in which He is always there. Acts cold and suspicious, or, in order to clear the air, tells her to her anguish about his involvement with others. In between constant waking up, sitting upright and turning on the light. 'My God, my God, how is it possible! How is so much suffering possible . . .'"⁶¹ But a fourth, equally moving, is more psychologically and philosophically analytic in its characterization of yearning:

> The pain of longing for oneness on days she doesn't see him. Not to be beside him, with him, in him! To know that the "other" lives, laughs, speaks, works, busies himself, and one has no part in it—and also that on his side he must live for himself. . . . Must? One guards oneself against that. One does not want to live "alone," "individually." One does not want to stir, every action seems directly *as a betrayal of love*—and he to, oh he too must feel the same. One only wants to sit still and love.⁶²

The difference between one who loves and one who is loved for Mann was that the latter was like the God of medieval scholasticism, *a se,* complete unto himself, self-sufficiently in need of nothing. But that was also Mann's definition of masculinity—masculinity knows no yearning, no neediness. Ultimately, Adelaide/Mann's most basic feeling toward her/his lover is "envy over the completeness of his *manly* existence, while she only feels and lives."⁶³ Transcendent self-sufficiency and manliness are one.

In the same letter in which Mann had expressed his relief to Heinrich that Paul had made him feel alive and human, he had cursed writing as death because, treating everything with irony, it blasted and corroded feeling. But as the notes implied, "life" was a kind of death too, for the life of feeling was a desperate, needy thing that wanted nothing more than to obliterate itself in the other—even if for the purpose of obtaining (a vicarious) self-sufficiency. Apparently caught between Scylla and Charybdis, however, Mann felt that there might be a way out, through the paradox of writing itself. Though literature was death, and he would "never understand how anyone could be dominated by it *without* bitterly hating it," Mann wrote, "its ultimate and best lesson is this: to see death as a way of achieving its antithesis, *life*."[64] Writing was the only way that "life" could be indulged without succumbing, the way in which both the desired surrender and the desired autonomy could be achieved. Evoked fictively, surrender could be imaginatively lived, and paid for, while language mastered oblivion by constructing it, making it the writer's object. If this seemed, in transcendental terms, merely the hollow triumph of one form of death over another, there was yet a prize to be won: what might be rescued from the temptations of desire by writing was masculinity.

That writing was a battle for masculinity whose outcome was in doubt emerges in one of Mann's greatest novellas in a surprisingly conventional way, especially surprising in view of Mann's homosexuality. *Tristan* is the site of the most explicit confrontation in Mann's early work between the artistic and the bourgeois ethos, and it is represented there as a contest between two men, an artist and a bourgeois Everyman, for possession of a woman. On this point the novella makes a striking companion piece to the even more famous one published at the same time, the autobiographically inspired *Tonio Kröger*, the story of the making of a writer.

As if Tonio's early literary sensitivity and boyhood homosexual yearnings were not sufficient to mark his effeminacy, Mann made it comically blatant in the dancing class episode, where, infatuated with one of the girls, Tonio mistakenly joins in the women's part of the dance. "Kröger has got mixed up with the ladies," the dancing master gleefully announces. "Miss Kröger, get back . . . !"[65] This humiliation of adolescent masculinity, however, is only a prelude to the emasculation of the adult writer by Tonio himself. "Can we even say that an artist *is* a man?" he rails self-deprecatingly at his friend—a woman painter, whose exclusion from the species "artist" by the very form of the question posits the dilemma of the artist implicitly as a crisis of masculinity. "Let Woman answer that! I think we artists are all in rather the same situation as those artificial papal sopranos. . . . Our voices are quite beautiful. But—" (155). The thought is left unfinished; the implied "we are impotent" sounds silently. The writer is a castrato because he cannot have experience; he can only observe and analyze it. "You may not live, you must create," as Detlef, the protagonist of "The Hungry," written at the same time, puts it; "you may not love, you must know."[66] But this lament about the artist's nonparticipation in life is incomplete and, by itself, misleading. After all, the other theme of *Tonio Kröger* is that the artist is also a criminal, which suggests that he is deeply involved in highly suspect experience. The hint at the literal criminality of homosexuality is unmistakable. But behind the complaint about the incompatibility of life and art, about the artist's impotence, lay another issue, the problematic "femininity" of Mannian "experience," the passivity of self-dissolution in desire that makes (male) creative agency impossible. It is exactly the same disjunction between loving and creating asserted by Alwa in *Pandora's Box,* and for the same reason. To love (whether homosexually or heterosexually) is to unman oneself.

In one passage in the story Mann does suggest that writing confers its own kind of potency. When Tonio left the oppressive philistine normality of his hometown, he

128

surrendered himself utterly to that power which he felt to be the sublimest power on earth . . . the power of intellect and words, a power that sits smilingly enthroned above mere inarticulate, unconscious life. . . . It sharpened his perceptions and enabled him to see through the high-sounding phrases that swell the human breast, it unlocked for him the mysteries of the human mind and of his own. . . . With the torment and the pride of such insight came loneliness. . . . But at the same time he savored ever more sweetly the delight of words and of form, for he would often remark . . . that mere knowledge of human psychology would in itself infallibly make us despondent if we were not cheered and kept alert by the satisfaction of expressing it.[67]

The power of words is first of all the power to rise above the feminine passivity of passion in general, which, whatever its aim, is a natural force driving us prior to self-consciousness, assent, and control. Implied in this conception of desire was the prevailing German, and European, cultural distinction between *Geist* and *Natur,* spirit and nature, conventionally seen as respectively male and female. The power of language, however, is in addition the power to exert a measure of mastery over the psyche's most fundamental passion, not named here but implied as a source of despair; if the artist can't tame the need to love, he can at least name it. But finally, language is a weapon that can also be used against other people, above all against the smug ones who enjoy life unselfconsciously, in blissful ignorance of their blindness and self-deception. Again it is Detlef in "The Hungry" who expresses this aggressive resentment most succinctly. As he jealously watches the woman he loves dancing gaily at a ball, he reflects darkly on the revelers,

"I am above you. Can I not see through your simple souls with a smile? . . . The sight of your artless activities arouses in me the forces of the Word, the power of irony. It makes my heart beat with desire and the lustful knowledge that I can reshape you as I will and by my art expose your foolish joys for the world to gape at."[68] The power of language is the power of *ressentiment*.

In *Tristan* this theory of the artist's superiority is put to the test. The artist's silent *ressentiment* turns into aggressive open competition with one of these rival "simple souls." Detlev Spinell, a writer of dubious talent taking the cure at a sanatorium, is mesmerized by a new arrival, Gabriele Klöterjahn, a young wife and mother of ethereal appearance who has come for treatment for a supposedly minor ailment. When he discovers that she plays piano exquisitely, he is shaken but not surprised, for he has already seen her as spirit personified. Though she has been forbidden to play for reasons of health, Spinell prevails upon her, egging her on through increasing exhaustion until the climactic scene in which she plays for him the prelude, love duet, and *Liebestod* from Wagner's *Tristan and Isolde*. Following that epiphany, he writes to her husband, a bluff, hearty, uncultivated businessman, telling him in effect that his wife doesn't belong to him and that he, Detlev, has taken her away from him. Herr Klöterjahn is a primitive who has almost destroyed beauty incarnate by "harnessing it to the service of everyday triviality and of that mindless, gross, and contemptible idol which is called 'nature.'" Spinell, however, knows that Klöterjahn's wife is something more than nature; by resuming her music, she has reappropriated the sublime in her even at the cost of her health: "She has risen from her degradation and perishes proudly and joyfully under the deadly kiss of beauty." And, he boasts, "it is I who have made it my business to bring it about." He has been able to win her for beauty and away from her husband because he has insight and the language to express it; "it is my ineluctable vocation on this earth to call things by their names," he writes in explanation of the letter, "to make them articulate, and to illuminate whatever is unconscious." Though Herr Klöterjahn may be stronger, Spinell will be able to shake the husband's robust equanimity not only through his wife but directly, with his letter, for he has "the sublime avenging weapon of the weak: intellect and the power of words."[69]

With inevitable Mannian irony however, Spinell has predictably set himself up for defeat. In the face-to-face confrontation with Klöterjahn that follows, he backs down before the husband's furious assault on his deviousness and lack of manliness "like a great pathetic gray-haired scolded schoolboy." But the story's irony is unrelenting. Klöterjahn acknowledges that Gabriele's behavior toward him has changed—a hint that Spinell has successfully disrupted their sex life—and the confrontation itself is interrupted by the news that Gabriele is dying, the fulfillment of Spinell's boast and the awful proof of his apparently ultimate victory. In a final ironic twist, however, Spinell is driven from the field of battle by the sight, and even more the sound, of the happily shrieking, disgustingly healthy Klöterjahn infant. In the end, though irony seems to have cut down every position, "life"—procreative masculinity—triumphs over the power of the word.

Spinell, of course, is a second-rate or failed writer, more Heinrich than Thomas, according to Mann's mythology of sibling rivalry, in his pretentiousness and lack of accomplishment. But the sensibility that understands the meaning of the music was Thomas's. And given Mann's masculine dilemma, the defeat of language, though rendered by language, was inevitable. Despite the proud assertions of both Detlev Spinell and Tonio Kröger, Mann did not believe that language's capacity to name experience was its most salient characteristic. Tonio himself offers a rather different conception of literature later in his story, one that brings us closer to Mann's particular preoccupation with style and offers an apparently more profound argument for its superiority to experience. *What* one says, Tonio argues, is not the artist's main concern; content is only the raw material out of which the work of art is made, and the act of making it must be a game, aloof and detached, performed in tranquillity.[70] The reason he gives for this claim is that "warm, heartfelt emotion is invariably commonplace," and if the artist is too invested in the emotions he describes, he will produce art that is solemn, sentimental, and insipid. Here, ostensibly, is the thrust of Mann's idea of irony; irony supposedly deflates the grandiose pretensions of commonplace sentiment. An example in *Tonio Kröger* itself—one that contributes to Tonio's sentimental education—is the waning of his youthful passion for Ingeborg Holm, despite his vows of eternal fidelity: "He hovered watchfully round the sacrificial altar on which his love burned like a pure, chaste, flame; he knelt before it and did all he could to fan it and feed it and remain faithful. And he found that after a time, imperceptibly, silently and without fuss, the flame had nevertheless gone out" (149). Art here confers power because it frees us from the false idols of merely sentimental worship. But an adolescent crush is rather too easy a target for irony. Music offered a much better test case for understanding the workings of Mann's irony. And as *Tristan* shows, the argument that art can't be about content because of the banality of the emotions it deals with is an inversion of Mann's real problem. It was not at bottom the banality of the emotions that Mann feared; it was their awful potential sublimity. In the face of sublime emotions, writing can't win—and it doesn't.

There is nothing trivial about the emotions the *Tristan* music evokes in that novella; like Hanno's improvisation at the piano, Gabriele's playing, and Spinell's response to it, is a true epiphany. In the face of such sublime feeling, *language* might perhaps run the danger of banality, for how can the differentiated and finite express the undifferentiated and infinite? But that did not seem to be the problem worrying Mann. The narrative offers an unabashed description of the movement of feeling in the music, from the yearning "for the sacred night which is eternal and true, and which unifies all that has been separated" to the ecstasy of the moment of union, where "thought and the vanity of thinking have vanished," and "I myself, oh wonder of wishes granted! then *I myself* am the world"[71]—perhaps the most explicit evocation of Romantic consummation anywhere in Mann's early writing. As David Luke points out, Mann's usual irony is here almost completely suspended.[72] In fact, it isn't clear just whose experience the description of the music is meant to capture; the voice in these passages, the identity of the "I," hovers ambiguously between a paraphrase of the libretto, of the feelings of Spinell, those of the narrator, and perhaps of the author himself.

Irony is almost completely suspended here—but not quite. At two points the description of Gabriele's playing is interrupted by notice of other patients, one a vapid woman who leaves the room in utter boredom, the other, demented, shuffling through it in an unseeing haze. Mann did ironize the music scene by undercutting the description of visionary experience, though not from the inside, from within the consciousness of its participants, but from the outside, from the narrator's—and reader's— viewpoint. He does this by briefly shifting the focus to figures whose nature disqualifies them from appreciating the music. The shift does disrupt the epiphany, but it is a different tactical move from Tonio's philosophical deflation of the claims of inevitably ephemeral human passion to eternity. Mann's irony is not Schlegel's Romantic irony, which Mann applauded, but which insisted on maintaining the breathtaking contradiction that the experience of the Absolute is simultaneously complete and incomplete, true and false. Mann was more wishful than Schlegel, and so less ironic; in the musical epiphany, oneness *is* unambiguously achieved. To be possible at all, therefore, writing had to get away from "content," for in the experience of union with the All, individuality, and with it language, is obliterated. That inevitability is the implication of Gabriele Klöterjahn's death: she who alone is able to create the experience of unity through her playing must suffer its inevitable consequence, the end of selfhood. It is why Mann, in the story's most important idea, had Spinell tell her, when she asks him why he can't play the music if he understands it so well: "The two seldom go together."[73] Mann undercut the contradictoriness of Romantic irony by splitting the experience of the Absolute and its demystification between two different types of consciousness, and two different forms of artistic expression, music and literature. Literary "style" allowed Mann the masculine power to create by abstracting from the overpoweringly "feminine" reality of music, from the ultimate experience of fusion and loss of self. Description enabled him to pull out of the fatal vortex of feeling created by music and freeze the movement downward toward death into a static verbal sculpture. Mann's style can be said to be "Modernist" in its paradoxical semi-rupture with representation; it both represents passion's fulfillment and simultaneously empties it out, chilling it in the icy fetishism of linguistic precision or moving outside it to describe those incapable of it. "Our stylistic and formal talent, our gift of expression," Tonio asserts, "itself presupposes this cold-blooded, fastidious attitude to mankind, indeed it presupposes a certain human impoverishment and stagnation."[74] Better this impoverishment, however, than total self-dissolution. In the contemporary essay "Bilse and I," Mann insisted that there was no greater aesthetic mistake than supposing that coldness and passion were mutually exclusive. But at the same time he acknowledged that "cold, remorseless precision of description" is the "sublime revenge" of the writer on the pain that inevitably accompanies "experience"— pain that comes from the ultimate need to refuse the dangers of its gratification.[75] Writing may confer masculine power, but it can never replace feminine passion. The writer will be drawn back to it again and again because his very writing is parasitical on it.

It is just the "fastidiousness" Tonio half boasts and half complains of that separated Thomas from his brother Heinrich, whose literary practice had come to seem to him the negation of his own. In fact we can get a full understanding of the meaning of Mann's stylistic "cold-bloodedness" only by the contrast he drew with his brother's work. The unabashed expressiveness of the *Tristan* music episode is deceptive, for that expressiveness turns out to be a clever façade, or sublimation—or both. For Mann musical consummation always stood for sexual consummation—and it was sexual passion that Mann felt had to be drained of its content in writing. I have already suggested the basic reason; it goes far beyond mere prudishness or prudence, though prudishness and prudence there doubtless were.

Though a number of Mann's works from around this time, notably the story "Gladius Dei" and the closely related play *Fiorenza,* were barely veiled confrontations with Heinrich's aesthetic, Mann made his most direct challenge to it in an extraordinary letter to Heinrich violently attacking his most recent novel and the career direction it represented. In effect, without using the word, he called Heinrich's *Chasing After Love* pornographic, a book written solely for erotic effect. It had neither beauty nor historical interest. Mann wrote:

> What's left is the erotic, that is to say: the sexual. For sexualism is not eroticism. Eroticism is poetry, is that which speaks from the depths, is the unsuspected, all of which lends it its thrill, its sweet charm, and its secrecy. Sexualism is the naked, the unspiritualized, that which is simply called by its name. . . . The utter moral nonchalance with which your people, once they've just touched hands, fall down with each other and make *l'amore* cannot speak to the better sort of people. This flabby lust without end, this perpetual smell of the flesh are tiresome, disgusting. It's too much, too much "thigh," "breasts," "loins," "calf," "flesh," and one fails to understand how you would want to start it all up again every morning when there was already a normal, a lesbian, and a pederastic sex act the day before.

The disgust with the flesh evident here sheds a good deal of light on the puzzle of how the secular Thomas could figure himself in his work as the fanatically ascetic monk Savonarola.

133
∎

But his puritanism wasn't quite what it seemed. It wasn't the literary handling of sexuality that revolted Mann, as he made clear in his comparison of Heinrich with Thomas's fellow Munich writer Frank Wedekind. "Wedekind, probably the boldest sexualist in modern German literature, comes off sympathetically in comparison to this book," Mann lectured his brother. "Why? Because he is more demonic. One feels the uncanny, the depths, the permanently questionable nature of sexuality, feels the suffering caused by the sexual; in a word, one feels the passion."[76] Thomas's objection could be summarized uncharitably as the accusation that Heinrich was not sufficiently conflicted about sex. In fact, Thomas said something like that quite explicitly, presumptuously attributing Heinrich's intention in writing the novel to a resolve to overcome his previously neurotic attitude to sex and become "wholly sensuous, wholly physical." But Mann's need to view sexuality as demonic was the same as Wedekind's, and Wedekind was decidedly not a prude—or a conflicted homosexual. Sexuality for both men was more than the superficial rubbing of flesh or something to be exploited for the effect produced by broaching the scandalous in print. It was the uncanny; its true depths were plumbed not by physical penetration but by awareness of the vulnerability one opened oneself to in passion, which could therefore also turn one into a monster. A few years later Mann, then a member of the Munich board of censors, wrote a memo in support of a permit for a production of Wedekind's *Lulu* in which he also expressed agreement with the board's opinion of Wedekind's "problematic human character [*Menschlichkeit*]." His comment was neither a sincere reservation about Wedekind's personality nor a simple political ploy to aid his lobbying efforts. "Stupidity is right, the state—the censorship—is right (at base), and not the refined people who call for culture," Mann had written ruefully in one of his notebook entries. "Culture, art—decadence. A people that is ripe for Wedekind is lost." But these comments about Wedekind had a self-referential irony only Mann could have appreciated. "As history teaches us," he suggested slyly in his memo to the censorship board, "problematic characters can be the bearers of an important cultural mission."[77]

Certainly Mann's Savonarola, the historical alter ego he chose to dramatize his artistic credo in the battle with his brother, is a man of highly problematic *Menschlichkeit,* a fanatic of dubious motivation. Mann, however, showed no equivalent ambivalence about Savonarola's target. Inherent in Mann's disdain for his brother's sexualized literary display was contempt for the wider *Weltanschauung* that he believed lay behind it, the contemporary idol of expressive individualism, which he identified, under the influence of Jacob Burckhardt, with Renaissance Humanism. The static and talky qualities that make *Fiorenza* a failure as drama—though Frank Wedekind thought extremely well of it and criticized its neglect[78]—make it intellectually gripping as a sharply polemical exposition of Mann's ideas about modernity and the self, and the art adequate to them.

In Mann's version, Savonarola's crusade against the vanities is an attack not on luxury or hedonism, but finally on the shallow optimism about modern selfhood that is Renaissance Florence's (and modern Munich's) official philosophy and that inspires the art that flourishes under the patronage of Lorenzo the Magnificent. "The individual is enlightened and set free to rejoice in his own personality,"[79] claims Poliziano, friend and adviser to Cardinal Giovanni de' Medici, who will assume the leadership of Florence after the death of his ailing father. The sleazy aesthetic entailed by this philosophy is epitomized in the declaration of the painter Ghino, one of the claque surrounding Lorenzo: "I am an artist. A free artist. I have no opinions. I adorn with my art what is given me to adorn, and I would as soon illustrate Boccaccio as our holy Thomas Aquinas" (226).

But even many of those against whom Savonarola preaches are skeptical of such license, and see merit in the monk's moral strictures against the culture of Florence. The great humanist Pico della Mirandola is disgusted with a worldview in which "everything is permissible; at least nothing is disgraceful" (212), and Lorenzo himself is closer to the monk's views than Savonarola wants to see. Both of them oppose the permissive spirit of the times, which Lorenzo characterizes as "subtle, skeptical, tolerant, inquisitive, vacillating, manifold, without clear limits" (268). Lorenzo has sought to overcome the "democratic" leveling of standards through the ideals of artistic beauty. For Savonarola, however, *all* art is tainted with the indiscriminate sensuousness that modern expressiveness permits; for him there *is* no difference between illustrating Aquinas and Boccaccio. (In "Gladius Dei" it is a painting of the Madonna in the window of a Munich gallery, a work of "entirely modern feeling" portraying the Holy Mother as a feminine, sensuous woman, that excites the Savonarola figure's disgust.) Beauty is too easy psychologically, no matter how high its standards. Beauty and spirit, he claims, are morally antithetical. His objection is at bottom epistemological more than ethical. Spirit, Savonarola admits, yearns for beauty, and even allows itself in moments of weakness to succumb to it, but only at its own peril, for in the temptation to realize the beautiful, "blithe and lovely and strong," spirit is seduced into forgetting what it knows that is not beautiful. By beauty Savonarola clearly means Nietzsche's concept of the Apollonian, the classical ideal of equipoise and harmony that denies the lawless frenzy and self-loss of the Dionysian urge. It is Apollonian beauty that is a lie because it excludes the ugly.

135

Savonarola, however, does not want to acknowledge that beauty can know the Dionysian and sublimate it. To suppress all knowledge of the Dionysian within himself, he has displaced the source of his own mission and made it one against art as such, represented by "corrupt" Florence, rather than against merely shallow or sensationalist art. Lorenzo knows that Savonarola is self-deceived; when Savonarola claims that God has summoned him to greatness and to pain, Lorenzo answers knowingly, "God—or passion." His mistress Fiore has told him the monk's secret: when he was younger, Savonarola was obsessed with her and, one day in a fit of uncontrollable passion, abjectly confessed his love. In a reprise of the scene in "Little Herr Friedemann," she brutally rejected him; it was only then that he embarked on his crusade against beauty and art.

Lorenzo sees through his *ressentiment*. If for Lorenzo art is the expression of a will to power, he forces Savonarola to admit his own will. "A torrential love, a hate all-embracingly sweet—I am this complex," Savonarola finally thunders, "and this complex wills that I be lord in Florence" (271). The two men are alter egos; Mann once said explicitly that he was as much the Magnifico as the monk. Both, as Lorenzo insists to a vehemently resisting Savonarola, are artists of a sort, both disdain the masses. And both derive their will to art and power from sexual passion. But Lorenzo desires them through the sublimation of sexuality, and Savonarola through its denial and through self-elevation disguised as moral superiority. Sexuality is a source of weakness for both, though in quite different ways. Lorenzo is fully aware that his patronage of art derives in part from his lust and the physical ugliness that is the visible stigma of its grossness. "People call me the lord of beauty? But I myself am ugly. . . . Is that only my body? . . . My soul," Lorenzo admits, "was a smoldering torment of desire and a flame of lust. . . . *Without my longing I should be but a satyr.* . . . [N]ot one [of my court poets] dreams of the long, stern, discipline which went to bridle my wild nature. Had I been born beautiful, I had never made myself the lord of beauty" (268; italics added). "Without my longing"—it is his knowledge of the transcendent, and his desire for it, that saves him; his longing transfigures his lust. In a moment of feverish exaltation near the point of death, he hallucinates the figure of his inspiration, the goddess of love herself: "Oh my dreams! My power and art! Florence was my lyre. . . . Am I chosen to look upon you, Venus Genetrix, you who are life. . . . Creative beauty, mighty impulse of art! Venus Fiorenza! Do you know what I would like? The perpetual feast— that was my sovereign will!" (270). Venus is erotic love—but she is a goddess, a higher being who sublimates sex into beauty.

But if Lorenzo understands himself as a sinner saved, a transfigured prisoner of lust, Savonarola is the envious and unaware prisoner of unappeased longing. He cannot sublimate what he has never been able to enjoy, and his pain, the pain of yearning, is too great to allow him Lorenzo's self-knowledge. It is Fiore who tells him to his face what he really is: Nietzsche's nihilist, who would rather have nothingness for a purpose than have no purpose, having given up on passion. "Cease to will, instead of willing nothingness," Fiore cruelly admonishes her former would-be lover. "Void the power! Renounce! Be a monk!" He cannot; "I love the fire," he says in the final words of the play (272). In the end, Savonarola is a power-mad nihilist: he represents the pure negativity of the ironist who, while seeing truly into the shallowness of contemporary art, wants to destroy everything in his fury at being rejected, even that genuine art that comes from suffering knowledge. In the figure of Savonarola, Mann saw through the extremes of his critique of his brother, saw its all too-easy perversion. Savonarola was the enraged, narcissistically injured dimension of Mann's masculine ambivalence, the bid for a perverse masculinity that wanted potency through the moralistic denial of sexuality. At the end of the play, Lorenzo is dead, and Savonarola rules, but the last stage instructions tell us that Savonarola also walks away "to his destiny"—to be burned at the stake. If sexuality leads to obliteration, self-denial and irony lead to sterile self-assertion. The dilemma of masculinity was only sharpened for Mann by his condemnation of its too-easy modern version of sexual liberation.

Confession

> *The magisterial poise of our style is a lie and a farce.*
>
> —Thomas Mann, *Death in Venice*

It was, paradoxically, marriage and the attempt at "normal" masculinity that freed Mann to explore most fully the depths and consequences of homosexual passion. Not that he intended it that way. Marriage certainly provided an outward show of normality, but it originally also promised more: the inward sense of traditional male success at having won a—socially highly desirable—woman whom, with part of him, he evidently needed. There is no reason to believe that the professions of love and of the desire to achieve real "happiness" in his courtship letters to Katia Pringsheim were meant for effect. The daughter of an extremely wealthy and cultivated assimilated Jewish family, she was a formidable young woman in her own right, mathematically gifted, spirited, ironic, and independent-minded; her maternal grandmother Hedwig Dohm, a pioneering German feminist, was bitterly disappointed that her granddaughter married instead of pursuing a career. She was a prize, in social and personal terms, for whom Mann was willing to try to suspend or bracket his most authentic sexual desires. "You know what a cold, impoverished existence mine had been, organized purely to display art, to represent life," he wrote her early in their courtship, "you know that for many years, *important years,* I regarded myself as nothing, humanly speaking, and wished to be considered only as an artist. . . . Only one thing can cure me of the disease of representation and art that clings to me, of my lack of trust in my personal and human side. Only happiness can cure me; only *you.*"[80] A flattering sentiment from a nationally famous young writer, but in its self-description severely honest. Up to the time he met her, he wrote two months later, "where I had loved I had always at the same time despised. The mingling of longing and contempt, ironic love, had been my most characteristic emotion. Tonio Kröger loved 'life,' blue-eyed commonness, nostalgically, mockingly, and hopelessly. And now? . . . This love, the strongest there can be, is from this point of view—whatever may happen—my first and only *happy* love."[81] Mann was not necessarily deceiving Katia or himself. This was a possible love for him, one that, unlike all the homosexual passions of his life before—and after—could be allowed to come to fruition. Yet he might have known, perhaps knew, from the very self-confidence it inspired, that it was not passion as he understood it. "A primitive and vital instinct tells me, in a kind of colloquial and unsophisticated language," he wrote with masculine bravado, "that emotions of the sort I have for you cannot be in vain."[82] He could never have expressed, let alone

137

felt, this certainty of success with a homosexual love. It was of the essence of true passion that its object be out of reach, loved but not requiting. Less was at stake emotionally where the temperature of love was lower and the extent of idealization consequently less.

Royal Highness, the only novel Mann wrote in the quarter century between *Buddenbrooks* and *The Magic Mountain,* is a self-conscious testament to the will to traditional masculinity that motivated his marriage. It tells the story of a prince's transformation from a mere representative figurehead, who puts the ceremonial seal on the work of others but does nothing real himself, into a useful and productive ruler. The transformation is accomplished through his love for a tough, practical, and unromantic American heiress, whose disdain for his empty life leads him to start following the news and studying economics in order to become concerned with the lives of his people and the affairs of state that affect them, an active policy-maker instead of the mouthpiece of his ministers. Marrying her, the prince finally becomes a "real" person, that is, a man who lives up to the contemporary ideal of bourgeois masculinity, socially productive and ultimately sexually reproductive. Mann was explicit about the fact that the novel was an allegory of the writer, who was a "representative" person in both senses of the word: his writing accurately articulated the experience of others, but he himself could only re-present experience, not live it. The description of the emptiness of Prince Klaus Heinrich's life when he takes over official ceremonial appearances from his older brother, the titular but chronically ill head of state—another version of his rivalry with Heinrich—is an eloquent displacement of Mann's complaint about the uselessness of the writer's life: "A strange unreality and speciousness prevailed in places where he exercised his calling; a symmetrical, transitory window-dressing, an artificial and inspiring disguising of the reality by pasteboard and gilded wood."[83] It was such speciousness and unreality, the unreality of "style," that Mann himself hoped to escape through immersion in the bourgeois identity of husband and father.

However much Mann later argued that the novel's allegorical style was a developmental step to his later work, it was and is a failure, not so much because it is a Ruritanian fairy tale with little relevance to anyone except a self-identified prince, but because it is tonally unpersuasive. It was driven not by Mann's usual dialectic but by a one-dimensional wishfulness, even propagandizing, that he himself did not believe, as in the following passage:

> He read about the State expenditure and what it always consisted of, about the receipts and whence they flowed in when things were going well; he ploughed through the whole subject of taxation in all its branches; he buried

himself in the doctrine of the budget, of the balance, of the surplus, and particularly of the deficit; he lingered longest over, and went deepest into, the public debt and its varieties, into loans, and relation between interest and capital and liquidation, and from time to time he raised his head from the book and dreamed with a smile about what he read, as if it had been the gayest poetry. (301)

Not the claim to comedy, nor even irony, can save this passage. Mann was simply not interested at this time in the economic and social problems of material betterment to which Prince Klaus Heinrich learns to devote himself in his conversion to the ideal of public usefulness (Joseph would come much later). "My entire interest has always been captured by decay," he wrote his brother a few years later, "and that is probably what prevents me from developing an interest in progress."[84]

Mann not only did not achieve, he did not wholly want the self-confident masculine normality the novel celebrated. A note proposing an idea for a short story, obviously referring to his courtship of Katia, makes it plain that the same psychological contradiction between dependency and self-sufficient masculinity that governed his passion for Paul Ehrenberg was at work in his heterosexual relationship with Katia Pringsheim as well: "Detail for a love story: As his own infatuated loving [*Verliebtheit*] wanes, the ability to conquer, to make himself loved, grows. For days he had suffered terribly over her, longing, weak, lost, crushed, sick. Then, after seeing her again in a big hat which did not flatter her, he suddenly felt healthier, refreshed, freer, more in charge, less filled with yearning, stronger, more 'egoistic,' able now to challenge, score points, pay court, make an impression."[85] As with Paul, his sometime idealization of Katia could unman him, and only by lowering her to his level could he feel even the possibility of winning her. Yet even with a heterosexual love, Mann had to imagine nonfulfillment as the condition of his continuing creativity, the theme of which was always the quest for the unreachable transcendent, with its inevitable masochistic yearning. Another idea for a story around this time brings this fact into the sharpest relief: "A little novella. A pessimistic poet falls in love, gets engaged, marries ('Life.') Is so happy that he can't work any more, becomes completely desperate. Then he observes that his wife deceives him. Works again."[86]

Mann never had reason, however, to doubt Katia's fidelity. And while marital stability may have created the condition for the possibility of further creativity for Mann—the writer did not need to be an adventurer in his life, he once said acidly of Heinrich, as a writer a man was always enough of an adventurer internally[87]—stability was only a necessary, not a sufficient condition, and by itself even an inhibitor. It was in good part his internally misconceived striving for normative masculinity that accounts for the relative paucity of Mann's literary output in the ten years between *Tonio Kröger* and *Death in Venice* and the weakness of the one large work on which he had spent so much of that time. In *Death in Venice,* however, Mann achieved the perfectly crafted emblem of the struggle between the desire for traditional manliness and the desire for transcendence through passion. Rather than editorialize about it, as *Tonio Kröger,* for all its excellence, did, *Death in Venice* brilliantly dramatizes as well as analyzes it. And the novella offers Mann's most explicit presentation of what was problematic about passion before he became aware of and began exploring passion's political dimension.

That homosexuality as such was not the essence of the story is suggested by the fact that its germ was the episode of Goethe's infatuation at the age of seventy-four with a seventeen-year-old girl, the great man so heedless of his dignity that he made her a proposal of marriage. There is no logically necessary connection between the two master themes of *Death in Venice,* homosexual desire and the Dionysian nature of passion. But it is impossible to imagine Mann writing so movingly about passion other than the only kind he had ever experienced with genuine power. And it is unlikely that any but a homosexual passion, understood from the medical-psychiatric perspective of the times as well as from the depths of Mann's need for worship, could have driven home what he had long known but had never before been so ready to articulate so clearly: the "femininity" of passion itself.

Mann's sense of the fatality of love emerges most sharply through Aschenbach's musings toward the end of the novella, when, grotesquely made up like a woman, totally given over to the humiliating but shameless pursuit of the boy Tadzio through the streets of Venice, he awaits his fate in the plague-ridden city with the awful clarity of one whom insight can no longer save. His thoughts at that point are the ultimate negation of everything he has tried to stand for as a writer. All his life he had striven to live up to the manly ethic of his ancestors: military officers, judges, government administrators, "men who had spent their disciplined, decently austere life in the service of king and state."[88] This had sometimes felt like an impossible task for an artist whose very vocation seemed to be the opposite of the virile Aristotelian civic virtue he so admired, which demanded political participation and the military defense of the state. But he had consoled himself with the thought that he had also served, "he too had been a soldier and a warrior, like many of them: for art was war, an exhausting struggle" (246). Even his critics, at least his most perceptive ones, had understood that. The new kind of hero favored by Aschenbach, one of them had written, displayed "an intellectual and boyish manly virtue, that of a youth who clenches his teeth in proud shame and stands calmly on as the swords and spears pass through him" (202). But Aschenbach's erotic adventure in Venice had revealed to him the irony hidden in the masochistic symbolism of Saint Sebastian. "For you must know," he addresses Phaedrus in the ironic guise of the wise Socrates of the *Dialogues*, "that we poets cannot tread the path of beauty without Eros keeping company with us and appointing himself as our guide; yes, though we may be heroes in our fashion and disciplined warriors, yet we are like women, for it is passion that exalts us, and the longing of our soul must remain the longing of a lover—that is our joy and our shame"(261).[89] A century of Kantian aesthetics—and two millennia of Platonism—are dismissed with a word; there is no disinterested pursuit of beauty—there is only sexuality hardly concealed by the threadbare disguise of aesthetic sublimation. But most shameful of all—for a man—that sexuality itself is feminine, for passion is desire, and desire yearns for total surrender to the lover. "*Finally,*" says one of the early working notes for *Death in Venice,* summarizing the climax of the novel, "State of effeminacy, enervation, demoralization."[90] If poets are also heroes and warriors, it is because they must engage in deadly battle against the most powerful and destructive of enemies, their own temptation to feminine surrender. In the service of that weakness, men may indeed be capable of the most highly prized masculine virtues, defiant independence, fearless courage, but those virtues collapse before the beloved. "Doesn't this testify to divine enthusiasm," runs another of the working notes for the story,

> that the lover, who practically disdains everything else, not only his friends and relatives, but also laws, authorities and kings, who fears nothing, admires or flatters no one, is even capable himself of "opposing the crashing bolt of lightning" (Pindar), (doesn't it further testify) that this same one, nevertheless, as soon as he views the object of his love, "is thunderstruck, like the rooster who fearfully drops his wings in a fight," that his courage is broken and his proud bearing completely pushed to the ground?[91]

Pindar's metaphor of the fighting cock with drooping wings was vividly appropriate to Mann's meaning. Before the object of his love, the toughest male is rendered abject and impotent.

Nor is there any escape from the abjection of surrender in linguistic mastery, whether by way of knowledge or art. These last musings of Aschenbach are full of acute perception and astute judgment, the form of mental activity Freud called "secondary process," controlled by reason, the ego; but they have been preceded by Aschenbach's dream of a Dionysian orgy, the original "primary process" unleashed by instinct uninhibited. "Knowledge . . . sympathizes with the abyss, it *is* the abyss," continues Aschenbach, consciously reflecting on the unconscious knowledge of the dream. "And so we reject it resolutely, and henceforth our pursuit is of Beauty alone, of Beauty which is . . . a second naiveté, of Beauty which is Form. But form and naiveté . . . lead to intoxication and lust"—as they had in what Aschenbach initially tried to believe was a purely aesthetic appreciation of Tadzio—"they may lead a noble mind into terrible criminal emotions . . . they too lead to the abyss." Aschenbach's conclusion about literature is inevitable: "The magisterial poise of our style is a lie and a farce" (261).

It is worth dwelling for a moment on Aschenbach's dream because it is so out of keeping with what is usually implied by the idea of feminine passivity or surrender. Conventional "feminine masochism" is certainly encapsulated in some of Mann's descriptions of Aschenbach's obsessive behavior toward Tadzio: "So it was that in his state of distraction he could no longer think of anything or want anything except this ceaseless pursuit of the object that so inflamed him: nothing but to follow him, to dream of him when he was not there, and after the fashion of lovers to address tender words to his mere shadow" (245). But this passage describes Aschenbach's waking state. His dream reveals an entirely different mode of being, a human frenzy of orgiastic eating, screaming, moving, dancing, men swinging torches and brandishing daggers, women lewdly offering their breasts with both hands, and all raging around a gigantic wooden phallus, foaming at the mouth, thrusting prods into each other's flesh and licking the bloody wounds, tearing sacrificial animals with bare hands and devouring the live flesh, and coupling shamelessly everywhere. This too, Mann writes, is uttermost surrender (256). Little wonder that Aschenbach earlier muses that "to passion, as to crime, the assured everyday order and stability of things is not opportune" (243). Passion embodies the primal unity of antithetical feelings and desires, love and hate, fusion and destruction, the complete loss of control that turns the self into an elemental natural force, but with human intention. If passion is self-obliteration, it is not the undifferentiated static unity of Parmenides' "All things are one," but the whirling energy of Heraclitus' "All things flow." The dream realizes the full frenzy of hate that is apparent in Mann's earliest stories, the hate that is the other side of dependent love and would destroy its object as it fuses with it.

We are faced of course with the irony, which Mann himself noted years later, that the story "displays in its manner and style that very stance of dignity and mastery which is denounced in it as spurious and foolish."[92] Mann, a contemporary reader hardly needs to be warned, was not Aschenbach. But this does not mean that Mann wholly rejected Aschenbach's wisdom about the falsity of "magisterial poise" either. If Mann made his life out of the very renunciation of which Aschenbach was incapable, he did not believe that style alone made the man, or rather a *man,* in the honorific sense. The magisterial poise, the "classicism" of Mann's style in *Death in Venice,* was not a lie in the sense that Aschenbach's was, for Mann never tried to deny, as his protagonist did, that his writing always flirted with the abyss. Precisely for that reason, however, he was also constantly aware that his style was necessarily parasitical on the "feminine" temptation of loss of control. Such awareness could not give him a sense of masculine power. The most it could do was give him the feeling of *durchhalten,* of holding out, enduring rather than submitting, the cardinal virtue Mann ascribed to such heroes of Aschenbach's early work as Frederick the Great. For all the extraordinary psychological and stylistic mastery the story displays, it does not resolve but highlights the continuing tension between the threat of going under in passion and the desire for traditional masculinity. Building a bulwark of form and style against addiction and surrender was at best a defensive maneuver. "I should never have been allowed to become a writer," he wrote gloomily to Heinrich in November 1913. "*Buddenbrooks* was a novel of the bourgeoisie and means nothing to the twentieth century. 'Tonio Kröger' was merely *larmoyante, Royal Highness* vain, *Death in Venice* only half-cultivated and false. There you have my latest realizations, consolations for the little hour of one's death."[93]

Masculinity through Politics

> *The patriot . . . is moved by reason and current events to demand the identity of people and state, the politicization of minds and hearts, so that Germany can live, so that she can live powerfully and masterfully.*
>
> —Thomas Mann, *Reflections of a Nonpolitical Man*

The unresolved precariousness of masculinity helps to explain not just the direction but the very fact of Mann's extraordinary political writings of the war years. As late as 1913 he acknowledged in a letter to Heinrich his "inability to find a proper intellectual and political orientation." The reason was not only, as he said there, that his interest in decay precluded an interest in the whole issue of political and social progress. Mann's exclusive concern with the problematic ego made him an inexorably individualistic and psychological rather than a social and political thinker. The antidemocratic undertone of *Fiorenza* was a purely aesthetic rejection of contemporary mass cultural taste. Perhaps nothing in the prewar years showed his radical psychological individualism more crudely than the ending of one of his frankest stories about the voracious yearning for love, "The Hungry." The writer

Detlef, miserably observing the object of his love dancing gaily at a festive ball from which he feels completely alienated, flees from the hall only to encounter another form of misery in the streets. A tattered, obviously impoverished and hungry man stares at Detlef with undisguised envy and hatred. The writer is suddenly aware of how he must look to the other, with his air of prosperity and well-being, but he immediately wishes to correct the man's misapprehension. "You thought to show me a horrifying warning out of a strange and frightful world, to arouse my remorse," Detlef addresses him in his mind. "But we are *brothers*. . . . Nothing is strange to me of all the sorrow that moves you. . . . We are both at home in the land of the betrayed, the hungering, the lamenting, the denying."[94] In his solipsism, Detlef completely elides any difference between social-economic marginality and psychological (and sexual) marginality—more accurately, he lacks the first category altogether. The Christian ending of the story—Detlef feels moved to utter "those gentle words: 'Little children, love one another'"—is ironic in more than the sense intended by a writer so ambivalent about love. But if a Marxist might argue that Mann was offering a quintessential bourgeois response to poverty by psychologizing it rather than seeing it in social context, Mann's "ideology" was surely prepolitical rather than political.

What then could have moved him to the vitriolic nationalist, antidemocratic, and militaristic outburst—if six hundred pages torturously written over four years can be called an outburst—of the *Reflections of a Nonpolitical Man*? There was arguably nothing extraordinary about Mann's patriotic reaction to the war; the vast majority of Germany's most distinguished thinkers, academics, and writers, many of them previously also ostensibly "apolitical," responded in much the same way.[95] But the obsessional animus of the *Reflections* is personal. Certainly the book is on one level a bitter running feud with Heinrich, never explicitly named but constantly demonized as the pro-French, antipatriotic *Zivilizatsionsliterat* ("civilization's literary man") who had stung Thomas badly with his 1915 antiwar essay on Zola. On the other hand, Mann's first pro-war essays preceded Heinrich's attack, and he had begun the *Reflections* themselves some months before reading the Zola essay. Nor is it a sufficient explanation that the outbreak of war cast the *Kulturkampf* Mann had long been waging against Enlightenment humanism into a national-political form. Despite a tradition of German polemics that went back to the French Revolution, which in its late-nineteenth-century version pitched German spiritual "culture" against British and French material "civilization," no easy identification of political Germany with culture was possible for Mann. In the description of Hanno's school day, the longest and most overtly polemical chapter of *Buddenbrooks,* he had shown art and the ethos of the Prussianized Second Reich to be rad-

144
■

ically incompatible. Yet there is something to the idea that Mann had long since felt himself engaged in a war. His first political essay, "Thoughts in War," written immediately after the outbreak of World War I, picked up directly on the image of the artist as warrior from *Death in Venice*.

Art, Mann wrote, is an elemental human force closely related to religion and sex. But for the same reason, it is also related to that other fundamental human force, war. The artist recognizes himself in the soldier: the principle of any victorious war, organization, is the essence of art; and like the soldier, the artist must have the qualities of precision, bravery, perseverance in the face of hardship and defeat, disdain for bourgeois security.[96] So Mann had indicated in *Death in Venice*. But there it was clear that the artist's most dangerous foe was himself and that his most important struggle, as it was in the case of Mann's model Nietzsche, was to achieve self-overcoming. That inner war, however, as the novella also showed, could never be conclusively won; at best, the battle was always a defensive one, a perpetual struggle to stave off the ever-lowering threat of defeat. Suddenly, the outbreak of war gave Mann a means of resolving the persistent inner tension by turning the battle outward against an external enemy, and identifying wholly with soldiers—literal, rather than literary, warriors. Turning the battle outward, he could also split off and project his internally threatening femininity outward onto the enemy France, becoming at last wholly masculine.

However self-contradictory Mann's identification of "art" with Imperial Germany, there was at least a certain internal consistency in the way in which he identified the Entente powers as the cultural enemy. At last, in the war years, under the impress of necessity, the implicit sociohistorical villain of *Buddenbrooks* could crystallize into a consciously analyzable object, augmented by Mann's disgust for the sensual art-culture he had found in Munich. It was the modern "wolf-like mercantile" ethos, "without compass and belief," that had driven the spiritual from public life, caused it to turn so self-threateningly inward, and replaced it with a mass-marketable sensuality. Though rapacious capitalism was originally a domestic villain for Mann, he now identified it with Western Europe and most especially with the "plutocratic Bourgeois-Republic" France, which even more than England was the marked enemy, the original home of shallow Enlightenment and revolutionary values, the cultural home of his brother Heinrich. But Mann added his own unique form of vilification, whose origins also went back to his earliest work: France was behaving disgustingly like a woman. "Your behavior reminds one strikingly of the certainly not stupid but not very honorable tactics of the suffragettes who throw bombs and then when put in prison cry out, 'They're torturing women!'" he apostrophized France contemptuously, returning to the explicit antifeminism of his early story "Fallen."

145

"France has a way of putting its opponent in the wrong—feminine to such an extent that one lowers one's arms. . . . This nation makes claims for the rights of women, there is no doubt. Delicate and charming as she is, the unqualifiedly most enchanting of peoples allows herself to dare anything. But if one so much as touches her, tears come from her beautiful eyes and all of Europe trembles in chivalric rage. What is there to do? They won't let us live, but when we insist with some vigor on our right to exist, we open ourselves to the charge of lack of gallantry" (202). The paranoia about French and European hatred for Germany that Mann shared with many other Germans mixes here with personal visceral hatred for coquettish ultra-femininity that trades on charming helplessness but in reality wants to dominate and destroy the male. Whatever the actual source of this hatred, Mann was excoriating more than just the feminine in himself in this antifeminist diatribe.

For all its antifeminism, however, "Thoughts in War" was only a warm-up for the misogyny of Mann's next pro-war essay, surely one of the oddest of that genre ever written. "Germany is today Frederick the Great," Mann had written in the first essay. "It is his battle that we have to wage to a conclusion, that we have to wage once again." Frederick's battle against the coalition of France, Austria, and Russia during the Seven Years' War was for Mann in 1914 a doubly determined symbol. It was the historical precedent for Germany's current sense that she was fighting for her life against an entire world that had ganged up to destroy her. But Mann had long since planned a work on the man who was for him the epitome of *durchhalten,* the man who had held out above all against his own weakness, the temptation to give in to overwhelmingly superior forces. He had attributed just such a work to the heroic period of Aschenbach's writing in *Death in Venice.* The peculiarity of "Frederick and the Great Coalition" as a historical and patriotic essay was its central focus on the issue of femininity. Before he became king, Mann noted pointedly, Frederick was "thoroughly unmilitaristic . . . civilian, lax, even feminine."[97] No one expected the transformation to the strange, hard, fanatic warrior that he became on ascending to the throne. But that transformation was obviously connected, according to Mann, with Frederick's misogyny.

An autobiographical undertone is unmistakable in Mann's descriptions and analyses of Frederick. "A good part of his wicked and sinister nature certainly has to do with his relationship to women," Mann asserted, "which was really no relationship and not easily intelligible even in a time which could be quite capricious about these things. . . . Profound misogyny is inseparable from his character. . . . The other sex did not only leave him cold, he hated it, he was contemptuous of it, he didn't tolerate it around him" (224–25). Except to battle with. He attacked Maria Theresa in the War of

the Austrian Succession without qualm, contemptuous of the gallant pro-
tectiveness she excited in other European rulers. "Frederick had no feeling
for the majesty of weakness," Mann wrote, "even the pallid motherhood of
the woman against whom he fought excited in his kind of manliness disgust
rather than honor." According to Mann, Frederick saw the coalition of
powers arrayed against him during the Seven Years' War as a coalition of
women—though he had to make Madame Pompadour, Louis XV's mistress, into the real ruler of France in order to sustain the fantasy—and since
Mann acknowledged, even insisted, that Frederick was waging an offensive
war under the guise of a defensive one, he even seemed to be suggesting that
Frederick actually provoked the war in order to battle "the three whores of
Europe." In any case, Mann explicitly raised the question of the connection
between Frederick's policy of aggression and his misogyny, hinting that the
question had more general implications. "The mysteries of sex are profound," he wrote, "and will never be fully illuminated. Could this king not
abide women because he was such a bad man, or was he such a bad man because he could not abide women? The knot can't be unraveled. But that his
wickedness was somehow connected with his enmity to women seems to us
certain" (228).

The constant references to Frederick's "wickedness" should not mislead;
Mann was, after all, ambivalent about all his artist figures, who, like Tonio
Kröger, were from the point of view of bourgeois respectability, criminals;
in any case, some of the occasions of the word with reference to Frederick
are heavily ironic. Frederick was unmistakably Mann's hero. The war "was
without exaggeration the most terrible test that any soul on earth ever had
to withstand," Mann exaggeratedly claimed. "To withstand it demanded
passive and active qualities . . . which no man before or after had ever revealed or had the opportunity to reveal" (263–64). Mere endurance was not
however the whole essence of Frederick's heroic manliness. Though Frederick was not in the right according to conventional majority standards of
morality, Mann conceded, he forged his own right, the right of the ascen-
dant world power. And though that right was still problematic, still illegitimate while he was fighting for it, he *was* in the right and retroactively had
always been in the right when success proved him to be the agent of destiny
(256). This surprisingly crass version of might makes right was Mann's boldest reach for an active aggressive masculinity, crudely Machiavellian even by
contemporary standards, though perhaps less obviously extreme in time
of war. The model of masculinity Frederick presented, however, was in
Mann's representation hardly conventional—an effeminate, very likely homosexually inclined prince who achieved warrior toughness not only by
the ruthless exorcism of his own effeminacy but by phobic hatred of

147

women, who might taint him with their femininity. The truly manly homosexual was furthermore not only a misogynistic soldier but an authoritarian ruler who despised the "rabble" beneath him and labored mightily on his subjects' behalf only out of a sense of duty to a higher will. Through wartime militarism and identification with Frederick the Great, Mann had found a way of achieving a masculinity that was less ambiguous than the always-precarious version of it that the mastery of form and style provided the writer. One could be both a homosexual and a *man* in the most honorific contemporary sense, a successful military leader and forger of nations.

Reflections of a Nonpolitical Man was Mann's full-scale attempt to justify this version of masculinity, not only against his brother Heinrich, but against his own instincts. The strain shows both in the obsessive length of the argument and in the many contradictions that mar it, contradictions of which he was well aware. "The motifs of the following reflections . . . are the detailed product of an ambivalence," he acknowledged, "the presentation of an inner-personal discord and conflict."[98]

Contradictions begin with the major concession of the prologue, written in 1918 after the bulk of the book was finished. "[The artist's] life element is a public loneliness," he declared, "a lonely public life that is of an intellectual nature, and whose feeling and concept of dignity differ completely from civic, material-social public life, although in practice both can, as it were, coincide. Their unity consists in the literary public life that is both intellectual and social at the same time (as in the theater) and in which the emotion of loneliness becomes socially acceptable, civically possible, and even civically meritorious" (6). What Mann was saying here was entirely consistent with the implications of his prewar writing. The artist's loneliness stemmed in part from the fact that he plumbed the depth of the most personal of emotions; "what is, after all, the origin and purpose of writing," he claimed, "if it is not an intellectual-moral effort on behalf of a problematic ego?" (9). But these same personal emotions were essentially nonsocial emotions, aimed at transcendence, though in their fanaticism to achieve it through sexuality they could become destructively antisocial, as *Death in Venice* had inexorably demonstrated. The artist's dignity lay in his heroic inner conquest of such emotions, and thus precisely in *nonaction* in the public sphere, other than that of communicating his art. If his loneliness was socially acceptable, even meritorious, it was because it could be understood not as antisocial withdrawal but as his sacrifice on behalf of society, his bearing the sin of knowledge of the dark depths of the heart for the rest of humanity by baring his soul in his work. As Mann put it later, "Personal examples teach that an art that never liked to assume a social attitude, a parasitic, nonpolitical art of personal ethics, can still *help* the human being to *live*" (228).

The artist's pessimism then, born of the knowledge of the "Dionysian" human heart, had nothing to do with politics in the usual sense. It was wholly inconsistent with this fundamental position for Mann to translate it into conservative nationalism. What might have given the political translation of Mann's pessimism in the *Reflections* a certain superficial plausibility was the optimistic psychology and metaphysics of liberal and radical ideology in the nineteenth century. Its conservative counterideology since the French Revolution did after all rest on Christian pessimism about fallen human nature. From this premise it drew the political conclusion that hierarchical authority, both earthly and divine, was necessary to keep human evil in check. Hierarchical theory had always had to wrestle with the fact that rulers were no less tainted with original sin than the ruled. The conservative justification for authoritarian hierarchy thus rested additionally on organic metaphors of the hierarchically ordered "body politic" and the "natural" hierarchical family structure ordained by God, as well as the notion that earthly rulers were only the agents of God, subject to His ultimate authority and punishable by Him (though by Him alone) for violations of their mandates to secure social order and justice.

Mann, however, neither a religious believer nor for that matter a particular partisan of authoritarian politics, was not in the slightest interested in this religious-political argument for authority, nor in its secular Hobbesian equivalent. Instead he identified his pessimism with what he called the political realism of the nineteenth century, whose spirit he contrasted with the self-deluded utopianism of the eighteenth. "More bestial and ugly, yes, more vulgar, and precisely for this reason, 'better,' 'more honest,' than the former, the nineteenth century was *truer, more subservient to reality of every kind,*" Mann claimed. "The eighteenth century sought to forget *what one knew of the human being* in order to adapt him to its utopia. Superficial, soft, humane, enthusiastic for the 'human being,' it advocated, with the use of art, *reforms of a social and political nature*" (11; italics in original). Specifically, he identified nineteenth-century political realism with the *Realpolitik* of Bismarck. The language in which he praised it, however, gives Mann's real game away. "And how much of [the nineteenth century's] brutal and honest pessimism, of its particularly stern, masculine and 'unpretentious' ethos still holds sway in Bismarck's *Realpolitik* and anti-ideology," he argued (12). Stern and masculine ethos—that was what he was after and what identification with wartime Germany gave him.

This quest for masculinity made him try to rewrite both German history and his own previous work, though his faithfulness to his fundamental aes-

149
■

thetic/spiritual commitment made consistency in that effort impossible. He had excoriated Bismarck's Germany in *Buddenbrooks* for its soulless materialism and power-hunger, for the very spiritual emptiness that drove Hanno out of the everyday world and into music. Now he found himself not only supporting Germany's power-political aims, but attempting to rationalize them with specious history and metaphysics. When the war broke out, Mann wrote, his exaltation carried him to the belief that Germany had a great right to rule, a valid claim to participation in the government of the earth, and that it was justified in gaining the recognition of these natural rights through war. If he had doubts about the "national catechism," it was only about Germany's resolve to be a commanding nation, not about its right to do so, and even those doubts, he claimed, bothered him only sometimes. "Let Europe's peace rest on the fact that the best educated, the most just, most sincerely freedom loving nation is also the most powerful, the ruling one—on the power of the German Reich," he exclaimed in one especially chauvinistic outburst (149).

In the light of this new valuation of the Reich that Bismarck created, the character of Hanno was subtly rewritten in a description that was not inaccurate but that managed to exactly reverse the previous valences of Hanno's spirit and of his social environment. "The resistance, the highly sensitive-moral revolt against 'life as it is,' against what is given, reality, 'power,'—this resistance is a sign of *decay*, of biological insufficiency," he wrote of Hanno; "intellect itself (and art!) is understood and presented as a symbol of this, as the product of degeneration: this is the nineteenth century; this is the relationship of intellect to life that this century sees" (13). The exquisite balancing act between life and art of, for example, *Tonio Kröger* has completely disappeared here; Bismarck's Reich is identified favorably and unambivalently with "life" and Hanno's spirituality negatively and one-sidedly with decay. There is also a curious reevaluation of the new bourgeoisie whose birth he traced in *Buddenbrooks*. The new burgher who evolved through the nineteenth century is no longer the speculative buyer, the soulless capitalist amorally and effortlessly piling up his fortune, or even the cheerful, decent philistine materialist of *Tristan*; he was now abruptly identified with the true artist, with Frederick the Great, with Mann himself. "If I have understood anything at all of my times sympathetically," he claimed, "it is its type of heroism, the modern-heroic life and attitude of the overburdened, overdisciplined *moralist of accomplishment* 'working at the edge of exhaustion,' and here is my psychological contact with the character of the new burgher" (103). This redescription enabled him to claim that he had discovered Weber's Protestant ethic on his own, but in fact it had nothing to do with the bourgeois types he had described in his work to that point, the Hagenströms, the Klöterjahns; indeed it was their complete effacement.

Along these lines, one of his most significant rewritings in the *Reflections* was his assessment of Munich. From *Buddenbrooks* on, most centrally in "Gladius Dei" and *Fiorenza,* Munich had been representative of the unholy confusion of superficial, titillating sensuality and art that he despised. It was the deceptively seductive environment that in its very bohemian hospitableness toward art had in fact undermined the very possibility of true art. Now Munich, with its premodern, old-fashioned, artisan-based economy was to be contrasted favorably with Berlin, that "Prussian-American" metropolis where pure acquisitive capitalism reigned. Again, Mann's rewriting was not so much a blatant falsification of his past attitudes as it was a shift of accent. Munich also had participated in the Americanization of the German lifestyle to a degree, he acknowledged. But he had found that "the atmosphere of Munich had and retained something congenial and suitable for me, that the old German mixture of art and burgherly nature is still very much alive and current here. This city is completely unliterary; literature has no footing here"—a criticism he had always made. "But all the more does the Munich burgher know what an artist is. . . ." On this point Mann even invoked, with at least a semi-straight face, the support of Wedekind, benignly transmuting the latter's biting irony that once would have been his own into amused affection. "Frank Wedekind said once that the Munich burgher was himself an artist, because he wanted his peace and quiet, and because he wanted to amuse himself. . . . But the most important thing is that here in an old, genuine way artistic genius really arises from burgherdom and remains intertwined with it, that old, established Munich burgherdom and craftsmanship are artistically combined. . . . What I saw growing out of the burgherly character was again not the hard bourgeois, but the artist, and this time without the slightest hint of degeneration" (100–1). Even when he invoked a past model of a healthier integration of morality, art, and business, Mann had never celebrated the premodern craft economy or the easy *Gemütlichkeit* of Munich's mores. Lübeck was never Munich. When Tony in *Buddenbrooks* leaves her marriage to the Münchener Permaneder, it isn't primarily because he has drunkenly tried to assault the maid. As Thomas charges, and as she acknowledges, it's not the man but the place, of which her husband is only a symptom, that disgusts her and to which she has been unable to adjust. "I can't live down south, by God and all His heavenly hosts, I can't," she angrily insists. "We northerners should never leave here. . . . Adjust to that? No, not to people who have no dignity, morals, ambition, elegance, or discipline, not to impolite, unkempt, slovenly people, people who are lazy and frivolous, sluggish and superficial all at the same time."[99] Toned down to discount the naïveté of Tony's emotional expressiveness, and understood more deeply than the superficiality of her familial snobbery allowed, these comments could have spoken for Mann himself.

By the alchemy of Mann's redescription of Munich, however, the artist was no longer the lonely sick individual isolated from the culture but the organic expression of the culture. From here it was but a quantitative shift to identify the unit of cultural community with the nation rather than the city, though more than quantitative expansion was involved in the way in which he reified and mystified it. "The human being is not only a social but also a metaphysical being," Mann began—a proposition that might have been the motto of *Buddenbrooks* were it not for what followed. "The nation, too, is not only a social but a metaphysical being. . . . [T]he nation, not 'the human race' as the sum of the individuals, is the bearer of the general, of the human quality; and . . . of the intellectual-artistic-religious product that one calls national culture, that cannot be grasped by scientific methods. . . . The metaphysical nation is the bearer of the general element."[100] That these were the commonplaces of late nineteenth-century German "mandarin" ideology,[101] aimed against "Western" individualism and sharpened by the polemics of wartime does not explain how Thomas Mann could come to mouth them when they ran against everything he believed about the relation between the artist and the collectivity. Even in his prewar polemics against his brother's Enlightenment humanism he had never vested the "metaphysical" quest that he felt his brother ignored in anything but the individual.

But his comments about German nationalism also ran counter to what he himself knew, had always known, about contemporary Germany. "No radical literary man is necessary to teach us that the 'man of power,' Bismarck, was a misfortune," he conceded, trying to score a point against his brother at the expense of undercutting his whole argument, "and that the reality of his Reich was not exactly the governmental form to further the national tendency to pure humanity, spiritualization and intellectuality, as did the abstract condition of Germany a hundred years ago [i.e., during Goethe's time]."[102] As for the state of Europe, had Germany won a quick victory in the war, "no doubt it would have offered a more decent sight— serious, respectful of the state, social, official, organizational, masculine-soldierly; but also hard, inhospitable, rather gloomy, rather brutal, 'militaristic' to the point of pitilessness. . . . The idea of humanity in this German Europe would perhaps really have come off badly" (358–59). That being the case, he could justify patriotic nationalism only by depoliticizing it, divorcing his patriotism from the "empirical" Germany whose economic and political ambitions he fully recognized. "I have no life-and-death interest in Germany's trade dominance, and I even entertain oppositional doubts about Germany's calling to grand politics and to an imperial existence," he asserted. "With my heart, I stand with Germany, not as far as she is competing with England in power politics, but as far as she opposes her intellectually" (19). The "real" Germany was not *about* politics or interests in the ordinary sense. It was about an idea, his idea. But if that were all, he would lose the identification that would supply him with the masculinity he so much wanted. That is why he returned, again and again, to a defense of the political Germany, the authoritarian would-be world power whose desire to overcome others was made to mean, by intellectual force majeure, the triumph of Mann's idea of self-overcoming. If the virile *Machtstaat* was the bearer of his idea, then he in turn was a virile man. Mann almost explicitly avowed the need behind the equation. The "patriotic democrat," he announced, is "moved by reason and current events to demand the identity of people and state, the politicization of minds and hearts, so that Germany can live . . . powerfully and masterfully" (205). He was willing to accept a "brutal" Europe, "militaristic to the point of pitilessness," as the price of being one with the victor-nation that had created a Europe that was "masculine-soldierly."

153

Throughout the work, everything good, everything German is identified with traditional masculinity, everything bad, everything Western European is identified with femininity. Weren't the greatest and most German attributes of his philosophical hero Nietzsche "the colossal manliness of his soul, his antifeminism, his opposition to democracy?" (57). Heinrich Mann had attacked his brother's fearful precocity in publishing so young, but was it "necessarily a misfortune, does one pay so dearly for having been spurred on so early by the manliness of work?" (137–38). And in any case, wasn't Heinrich's "ruthless Renaissance aestheticism, that hysterical cult of power, beauty and life . . . no longer quite masculine?" (13). Certainly one could not understand the democracy Heinrich favored "if one does not understand its feminine touch. 'Freedom and a whore are the most cosmopolitan things under the sun'" (223). An Entente victory would have created a Europe of the opposite gender of that of a German victory; "the result," according to Mann, "would have been a Europe that was—well, a somewhat amusing, somewhat insipidly humane, trivially depraved, femininely elegant Europe . . . a Europe of tango and two-step manners, a Europe of business and pleasure à la Edward the Seventh, a Monte-Carlo Europe, literary as a Parisian cocotte" (44–45).

It was precisely Germany's antidemocratic, antipacifistic characteristics that were the manly things about her. "Pride, honor and pleasure in obedience seem today to be peculiarly German," Mann claimed with pride; "here is a psychological fact that proves that 'lack of freedom' is quite compatible with masculine dignity." More than compatible; the essence of masculine dignity.

> Whoever, for example, observes a German cadet standing obediently and rigidly at attention before a comrade of officer rank who is scarcely older than he, will notice that this happens with a certain enthusiasm. . . . [I]n short, there is romantic play in it: the expression of knightly-masculine obedience is obviously bound up with an elevated zest for life, and, particularly as far as the feeling of honor is concerned, it is probably more strongly felt in the one who salutes than in the one who receives the salute. Honor as a life stimulus exists only where there is an aristocratic order, the cult of distance, hierarchy. . . . Whoever is something honors himself by stepping back expressively before someone who is something more. (354)

154

Here was alchemy indeed; the very submissiveness that in *Death in Venice* was for Aschenbach—and Mann—a badge of the femininity of passion is transmuted into the highest form of manliness. The philosopher's stone that accomplished the transformation was the desexualizing of the passional hierarchy in military aggressiveness, or rather its sublimation, for something of "romantic play" still exists in the military. The officer and his subordinate are a couple united in a common purpose that is best served by inequality, which, however, enhances the masculinity of the subordinate because it enables him to honor that which is higher. Homosexual love does not feminize even the dependent member of the couple when its purpose is war.

For war itself has a "terrifying masculinity" (338). It is in fact only in war that men are truly masculine. One can read in this notion the widespread critique of late-nineteenth-century European effeteness; urbanization, the commercial life, and the pursuit of material comfort were making modern man soft, decadent, feminine. But that was a critique from the outside, from those who feared the loss of the aristocratic ideal of the manly warrior in a nonaristocratic age when it was needed more than ever, in the age of rival nation-states whose survival in global capitalist and imperialist competition depended on the size of its populations and the military capacities of its armies. For Mann, the fear was internal, the fear of his own passion, whose all-consuming passivity he knew so well. War channeled the submissiveness of passion into active, masculine aims.

> The human being does not perceive civilization, progress, and security as absolute ideals; beyond doubt there lives immortally in him a primitive-heroic element, a deep desire for the fearful, for which all the desire and sought-

after exertions and adventures of individuals in peacetime: mountain climbing, polar expeditions, wild animal hunts, and daredevil flying stunts, are only
expedients. "Intellect" presses for humanity; but what would humanity be
that had lost its *masculine* component? . . . After all, there is no antithesis between civilization and masculinity. . . . In any case, whoever honors, loves
and affirms human nature must above all wish for it to remain *complete*. He
will not want, in its variety of forms, to miss that of the warrior, he will not
want human beings to divide up into merchants and literati—which admittedly would be democracy. (341)

Merchants and literati are feminine, or at best eunuchs—like Tonio Kröger's
genuine artist. The way for the artist not to be either one is to be a warrior,
not a symbolic but a real one. This is the deepest reason for the conservative
stance Mann adopted during the war. Writing had proved to be fragile ar-
mor for the would-be masculine warrior; it either documented feminine
passion or substituted for it at the cost of a loss of living experience. The
only way to masculinity was to don the real thing.

155
•

It did not take very many years for Mann to become aware of the moral ugliness and political dangers of what he had committed himself to in the real
political world by his wartime ideological transformation. The reality of
postwar German domestic politics made it impossible to project the dualistic mythology of "good" spiritual conservatism and "bad" materialist
democracy onto the warring factions as he had done on the international
scene from within wartime fortress Germany. The increasingly violent anti-
Semitism of the militant right—which included attacks on Albert Einstein
by students invading his classroom and culminated for Mann in the assassi-
nation of Walter Rathenau—made it perfectly plain that real-life conservatives were not the cultural philosophers of the *Reflections* but the enemies
of freedom and the mind. It was not a simple thing, however, for Mann to
abjure his conservatism, not because he had believed in its politics—he had
never really known or cared much about actual conservative politics—nor
because he was worried about consistency, but because of what his conservatism had meant to him in personal terms. If it was a serious wrenching of
his own understanding of spirituality to politicize it in the first place, his
having done so had given him the foundation for his problematic masculinity that he had not found in writing. Furthermore, there was no possibility
of a simple retreat from politics with the acknowledgment that he had made
an error in identifying his brand of psychological "pessimism" with existing
right-wing ideology. Having lent aid and comfort to what he was increasingly recognizing as the enemies of both culture and civilization by identi-

fying their stance with his own, he had to find a way to defend those values upon which he now understood his own work to be founded. Given his quest for masculinity, however, the problem he faced was breaking the identification he had made between manliness and authoritarian militarism, and finding a way to identify it instead with equality, democracy, and pacifism.

It is this need that accounts for the peculiarities of the speech in which he announced his conversion from conservatism to support of the Weimar Republic. "On the German Republic" is, from the viewpoint of political theory, as odd an argument for democracy as his essay on Frederick the Great was a defense of German militarism. Its heroes are not the canonical political thinkers of liberalism and democracy but the German Romantic poet and mystic Novalis and the American poet, singer of democracy, and homosexual, Walt Whitman. It was above all Whitman, whom Mann had recently read in translation, who offered him a way of thinking about the manliness of both democracy and homosexuality by linking them together in the vision of a polity of free men bound as courageous and creative equals by the ties of Eros.

We know we are on the same terrain as *Reflections of a Nonpolitical Man* by the speech's initial preoccupation with the manliness of war. Four years later, however, the values are reversed. Mann now criticized the revanchism of those who claimed that Germany had not really been defeated in the Great War and were calling for a renewed effort at national military self-assertion. "The world, its peoples, are old and wise today, the epic-heroic stage of life lies far in the past for every one of them," he declaimed in a period whose length is a relentless hammer blow against his former position; "the attempt to go back signifies a desperate resistance against the law of the present, a spiritual untruth, war is a lie, even its results are lies, it is bereft of all honor, however much individuals want to invest it with honor, and therefore it presents itself almost wholly to the eye that does not deceive itself as the triumph of all the brutal and common populist elements that are by disposition the archenemies of culture and thought, as a blood orgy of egotism, destruction and evil."[103] Lest his own manly credentials for making this negative judgment about war might be considered insufficient, or suspect, he pointed out that "even the manliest among contemporary spirits, whose poetry is an austere cult of manliness . . . has also seen in the reality of war today 'only destruction without value'" (123). But refuting the manliness of war was not in itself sufficient to establish the virility of democracy, associated as it was with the pacifism that before the war had been so widely condemned in Germany, and by Mann, as lax, weak, voluptuous, and feminine. "Freedom is not a game, not a recreation," Mann insisted. "Its other name is responsibility—and so it becomes clearer that it is a heavy burden:

and particularly for the spiritually talented. There is reason to doubt that everyone who calls for it . . . is up to the task" (128–29). The maintenance of freedom is an arduous exercise in masculine self-mastery.

The democratic republic, however, is even more than virile ethical discipline. It represents the unity of state and culture. This was Mann's most dramatic reversal; culture was the supreme virtue he had previously claimed for the aristocratic monarchy. But in reassigning "culture" to the republic, he also identified it with another value, humanity, thus expanding its previous definition. By humanity Mann meant the unity of the worldly and the supernatural, a "third way" between what had earlier seemed unbridgeable opposites that reconciled the social and the individual-spiritual (*innerlich*), the universally human and the aristocratic. What made that dialectical third way possible was the understanding of Novalis and Whitman that the binding cement of a truly egalitarian polity was love, "not in some pale, anemic, ascetically sympathetic sense of the word, but in the sense of the obscenely symbolic root that Whitman used for the title of his wildly pious sequence of poems" (150)—in other words, sexual love, however spiritually sublimated.

But Mann did not stop with the notion that Eros was the binding force of society. When he spoke of the politicized erotic, he boldly went on to claim, he was in the "zone of Eros in which the generally accepted law of sexual polarity proves to be invalid, and in which we see like with like, whether mature masculinity and adoring youth, joined in a dream of themselves as gods, or young manliness drawn its own mirror image, bound together in a passionate community." Despite common opinion, this homosexual community is not contrary to nature; it has appeared in all times and peoples and is explained aesthetically by the fact that "objectively, the masculine is the purest and most beautiful expression of the idea of humanity." And not only aesthetically; politically too, the masculine community is the highest form of humanity. Hadn't the war, for example, with its experiences of the comradeship of blood and death, of the hard and exclusive masculinity of its lifeform and atmosphere, greatly strengthened the empire of Eros? That didn't mean, however, that the ideal masculine brotherhood had to be nationalistic and militaristic. Its former devotees (Mann did not need to mention that he himself had been foremost amongst them) used to claim that such relationships were the binding force of monarchical unity. But Whitman is the modern counterexample who shows that a manly vision of continental unity and power is possible through the egalitarian love of comrades in a democracy (154–55). Nor is there anything "unhealthy" about such a homosexual vision. On the contrary, Whitman's celebration of the love of young men, just one province of his "all-embracing empire of holy and exuberant phallic fervor," is much healthier than the sickly heterosexual

157
∎

Romantic pining of a Novalis for his dead Sophie; the difference between Whitman's "Calamus" poems and Novalis's *Hymns to the Night* was the difference between life and death (155–56).

This was another of the astonishing reversals of Mann's address—not of course his equation of Romanticism with sickness and death, but his siding with Goethe's condemnation of its morbidity. It was not a position Mann could sustain without overturning his entire life understanding and life work, and he immediately equivocated within the speech itself. Whitman too, he claimed, knew that the love of beauty and wholeness is nothing other than the love of death, a truth shared by aestheticism since Platen, Mann's favorite German poet. The difference between healthy and unhealthy sympathy with death was that in the first, death is not opposed to life as an independent spiritual power but taken up within life as a challenge that leads to a deeper understanding of what it means to be human.

Even this formulation, however, superficially plausible as an account of Mann's long struggle with the relationship between "masculine" individuation and the de-individualizing, "feminine" quest for transcendence, was too optimistic a concession to the easy humanism he had always reviled. Necessary as it was for his support of democracy, it flew in the face of both his experiential understanding and his philosophical definition of passion as feminine worship and surrender. He could never abandon it. Homosexual lovers might join in a dream of mutual divinity, but this was a form of narcissistic self-idolatry that Mann had early repudiated as inconsistent with the true meaning of transcendence, which entailed worshiping something greater than the self. On the other hand, he now clearly recognized the dangers of translating the religious quest for transcendence into politics. It could only lead to the deification of and submission to a person, political entity, or movement who like Hitler and Nazism licensed the destruction of culture itself.

From this point on there were in effect two Thomas Manns, the political polemicist for democracy against fascism and the creative writer exploring the awful depths of desire, though the two would meet and cross constantly within his fictional work. As a political thinker, Mann made no concessions to the romanticizing of death. In this persona, his watchword was the sentiment, so often erroneously quoted as his final word on the subject, that he assigned to Hans Castorp in the chapter "Snow" in *The Magic Mountain.* Caught between the liberal humanism of Settembrini and the pessimistic conservatism of Naphta, Hans resolves, after a hallucinatory vision of cannibalism and death not unlike Aschenbach's orgy dream in *Death in Venice,* "for the sake of goodness and love, man shall let death have no sovereignty over his thoughts." It is the failure to adhere to that conclusion in both artistic creativity and politics that is the awful message of *Doctor Faustus*. But in the sphere of the erotic, Mann's equally uncompromising position is summed up in the words of Diane Philibert, the middle-aged French novelist, when she has sex with the young servant Felix Krull in Mann's last novel, and who is clearly Mann's alter ego. "Be familiar with me, degrade me!" she screams as she approaches her climax. "I adore being humiliated! I adore you! Oh, I adore you, my stupid little slave who dishonors me." In postcoital afterglow she only confirms what she called out in her mounting erotic fever. She is an author who has written many novels full of psychological insight, an author of extreme intelligence, she adds ironically. "And yet the intellect—oh! . . . how could you understand that? The intellect longs for the delights of the non-intellect, that which is alive and beautiful in its stupidity, in love with it, oh, in love with it to the point of idiocy, to the ultimate self-betrayal and self-denial, in love with the beautiful and the divinely stupid, it kneels before it, it prays to it in an ecstasy of self-abnegation, self-degradation, and finds it intoxicating to be degraded by it. . . . Love is perversion through and through, it can't be anything else. . . . I live in my so-called perversion," she says to Felix, representing at last Mann's lifelong passion in so many words, "in the love of my life that lies at the bottom of everything I am. . . . I live in my love for all of you, you, you image of desire, whose beauty I kiss in complete abnegation of spirit." And suiting actions to words, she requests that he whip her till she bleeds; when he refuses in horror, she settles for the humiliation of allowing him to rob her of all her jewelry.[104]

Nothing could rescue the hope for traditional masculinity from such an expression of masochistic desire. Certainly not writing, which not only did nothing to assuage the compulsion but promoted its repetition. Nor did Mann *wish* to rescue it at the price of surrendering desire. But such a compulsion could not be allowed to invade the sphere of politics, where abnegation to a divinity could easily become worship of the devil. In the last thirty years of his life, Mann *was* truly a warrior who faced the danger of death and suffered lifelong exile battling on behalf of an Enlightenment humanism that understood the temptations of escape from freedom as perhaps none before it. More even than his writing—indeed now as part of his writing—and without the sacrifice of his homosexual desire, it was his war against political sadomasochism that offered him the countervailing traditional masculine self-image he also so deeply desired.

CHAPTER THREE

Wassily Kandinsky and the Origins of Abstraction

Not one of the great masters had attained the exhaustive beauty and ingenuity of natural modeling: nature herself remained untouched. Sometimes, she seemed to me to be laughing at these efforts. But more often she appeared to me, in an abstract sense, "divine": she created as she saw fit; she followed her path toward her goals, which are lost in the mists; she lived in her domain, which existed in a curious way outside myself.

161
■

I was conscious of the weakness of art in general, and of my own abilities in particular, in the face of nature. Years had to elapse before I arrived, by intuition and reflection, at the simple solution that the aims (and hence the resources too) of nature and of art were fundamentally, organically, and by the very nature of the world different—and equally great, which also means equally powerful.

I learned to struggle with the canvas, to recognize it as an entity opposed to my wishes (= dreams), and to force it to submit to these wishes. At first, it stands there like a pure, chaste maiden, with clear gaze and heavenly joy—this pure canvas that is itself as beautiful as a picture. And then comes the imperious brush, conquering it gradually, first here, then there, employing all its native energy, like a European colonist who with axe, spade, hammer, saw penetrates the virgin jungle where no human foot has trod, bending it to conform to his will.

—Wassily Kandinsky, "Reminiscences"

It was only after others had begun to paint in an abstract style that Wassily Kandinsky claimed priority. In his "Self-Characterization" (1919), he referred to himself as "the first painter to base painting upon purely pictorial means of expression and abandon objects in his pictures," and dated his first abstract painting 1911.[1] Years later, when abstraction had become an even more respected current within Modernism, he was even more emphatic. His *Picture with a Circle* (1911), he wrote his New York dealer in 1935, was "actually the first abstract picture in the world, because no other painter was painting in the abstract at that time. So it is a 'historic picture.'"[2] Whether or not Kandinsky was literally right—claims have been made for works of other painters, though for none before him was abstraction the explicit aesthetic-philosophic concern it was for him—the implications of his claim for personal recognition go well beyond vanity. Because European painting had been moving away from "naturalistic" representation since Impressionism, because abstract painting has sometimes seemed the very definition of "modern art" in the twentieth century, there has been a strong tendency to think of abstraction as a cultural inevitability. One account, for example, argues that Kandinsky's discovery was the ineluctable working out of the logic of nineteenth-century literary Symbolism. The nucleus of abstraction in this view can be found as far back as Baudelaire's theory of "Correspondences," which held that material existence is a translucent veil that both conceals and hints at the existence of abstract, spiritual truths. This notion animated the Symbolist painters' belief that color, line, and pictorial organization communicated meaning directly, independently of subject matter; and while Symbolist painting still retained strong naturalistic ties, it was inevitable that art influenced by Symbolist theory would eventually reject Symbolist practice.[3] The purely formalist interpretation of Modernism epitomized by Clement Greenberg saw in abstraction a Whiglike natural progress in the evolution of painting from "accidental" concern with the world to essential preoccupation with its own proper elements: color, line, and space. And though such pure formalism has long since fallen into disfavor, the sociohistorical approaches that challenged it, even those sensitive to psychological implications, similarly emphasize the inescapable impact of large-scale forces—in this case economic, social, and cultural—on the artistic sensibility. Donald Kuspit, for example, argues that the first abstract painters wanted to create an enigmatic aesthetic language as a narcissistic defense of their belief in the timelessness, uniqueness, and omnipotence of art against the threat posed to it by the modern industrial world.[4]

But Kandinsky himself said more than once that for him the move to abstraction was anything but obvious or easy. Even after he concluded that objects "harmed" his pictures—on that perhaps symbolic occasion when he was stunned by the mysterious beauty of one of his own paintings lying on its side, its subject unrecognizable—he remained terrified by the "abyss" that his conclusion opened up. He didn't know what could "replace the object" in painting, so entrenched was the representational metaphysic. "I sometimes look back at the past and despair," he wrote after painting his first completely abstract work, "at how long this solution took me."[5]

Before he arrived at it, however, he had already insisted that the zeitgeist alone could not produce genuine artistic innovation. "Inner necessity," the only source of true art, originated from three elements, he claimed. First, every artist, as a creator, had something in him that demanded expression—the element of personality. Secondly, every artist, as a child of his time, was impelled to express the spirit of his age, its style. Finally, every artist must pursue the pure and eternal in art. This third, "objective," element was the true essence of all great art, but it could only work through the individual and historical. "The effect of internal necessity, and thus the development of art," he concluded, "is the advancing expression of the eternal-objective in terms of the temporal-subjective."[6]

There was, furthermore, a close connection between the historical and the subjective. By "spirit of the age" Kandinsky meant more than style. He certainly aligned his argument against naturalism and for abstraction with the widespread contemporary critique of a soulless modernity that had replaced the eternal with the mere timeliness of material progress. Modern society had turned life into an "evil, purposeless game" of selfish egos; even artists were caught up in the wild competitive chase for external success. There was nothing to be gained for the "eternal-objective" from representing the chaos of contemporary social life. At the same time, all the other supports of absolute truth had cracked as well. Nietzsche had undermined morality and religion; the very substantiality of matter had been dissolved by the discoveries of modern physics. But the ultimate evidence of contemporary loss and fragmentation was subjective and emotional. As Kandinsky maintained:

163

> Not only actions that can be observed, thoughts and feelings that can find external expression, but also perfectly secret actions that "no-one knows about," unuttered thoughts, and unexpressed feelings (i.e. the actions that take place within people) are the elements that constitute the spiritual atmosphere. Suicide, murder, violence, unworthy and base thoughts, hatred, enmity, egotism, envy, "patriotism," prejudice are all spiritual forms . . . that go to create the atmosphere. And on the contrary, self-sacrifice, help, pure, high-minded thoughts, love, altruism, delight in the happiness of others, humanity and justice are also such entities, which can kill the others as the sun kills microbes, and can reconstitute the pure atmosphere.[7]

Painting could hope to achieve such a reconstitution primarily through the agency of color because color expressed all of these psychological, and psychosocial, states, from yellow's manic frenzy and violence to the complacent cowlike "bourgeois" restfulness of green.[8] Colors, in a word, represented the psyche in strife; the task of painting was to harmonize them—and it. "Clashing discords, loss of equilibrium, 'principles overthrown,' unexpected drumbeats, great questionings, apparently purposeless strivings, stress and longing . . . chains and fetters . . . broken (which had united many), opposites and contradictions—this is our *harmony*," Kandinsky claimed. "*The composition arising from this harmony is a mingling of color and drawing, each with its separate existence, but each blended into a common life, which is called a picture by the force of internal necessity.*"[9]

But how to achieve this harmony? In fact, Kandinsky had an ideal model in mind when he talked about the aesthetic harmonizing of psychological opposites. That very model, however, made the problem of realizing his painterly goal seem insuperable. It introduced a cultural and personal issue that both illuminates the state of inner conflict he described and goes far to explain why the problem of representation weighed so heavily on his art for so many years.

In all of his paintings, Kandinsky wrote in his "Reminiscences," he had been trying to catch the essence of one particular scene:

> I was actually hunting for a particular hour, which always was and remains the most beautiful hour of the Moscow day. The sun is already getting low, and has attained its full intensity which it has been seeking all day. . . . The sunlight grows red with effort. . . . [It] dissolves the whole of Moscow into a single red spot, which, like a wild tuba, sets all one's soul vibrating. No, this red fusion is not the most beautiful hour! It is only the final chord of the symphony, which brings every color vividly to life, which allows and forces the whole of Moscow to resound like the *fff* of a giant orchestra. Pink, lilac, yellow, white, blue, pistachio green, flame red houses, churches, each an independent song—the garish green of the grass, the deeper tremolo of the trees, the singing snow with its thousand voices, or the allegretto of the bare branches, the red, stiff, silent ring of the Kremlin walls, and above, towering over everything, like a shout of triumph, like a self-oblivious hallelujah, the long, white, graceful, serious line of the Bell Tower of Ivan the Great. And upon its tall, tense neck, stretched up toward the heaven in eternal yearning, the golden head of the cupola, which among the golden and colored stars of the other cupolas, is Moscow's sun.

"To paint this hour," he concluded, "must be for the artist the most impossible, the greatest joy."[10]

The greatest joy because in that scene all opposites, all spheres of being, all the seasons of the year were united in a timeless synaesthesia of sounding color. The most impossible, however, because what nature did, the painter could not do. Even simply reproducing nature was out of the question. "In my student days," Kandinsky wrote, "I sought—impossible though it might seem—to capture on canvas the 'chorus of colors'. . . that nature, with staggering force, impressed upon my entire soul. I made desperate attempts to express the whole power of its resonance, but in vain."[11] This was not just an after-the-fact reconstruction of his state of mind prior to abstraction. Years before, he had given even more poignant private expression to his frustration. Visiting Venice in 1903, he was overwhelmed by the city's visual beauties, which thrust in his face the inability of painting to reproduce them. "Color! Color! Noble, dark shining, explosively loud and deeply harmonious color! You show so clearly how impoverished, weak and dirty our palette is," he wrote in ecstatic anguish.[12] But even if he were able to duplicate natural color, he would still not be a genuine creator. True creation to Kandinsky meant creation ex nihilo, like nature's own. It was for that reason he felt that his two most basic impulses, his "love of nature" and his "indefinite stirrings of the urge to create" were "fundamentally different" from one another.[13] To copy nature, even faithfully, even brilliantly, was not truly to create.

165

But the obstacle that nature's inimitable power represented to Kandinsky's creative ambition was even greater than these remarks alone indicated. Nature's creativity was inextricably intertwined for him with his figuration of nature as feminine divinity; her accomplishments were by their very origin apparently unattainable by the (male) artist. Of his reaction to the great paintings he had seen in Munich's Alte Pinakothek, he wrote despairingly, "I . . . noticed that not one of the great masters had attained the exhaustive beauty and ingenuity of natural modeling; nature herself remained untouched. Sometimes, she appeared to me, in an abstract sense, 'divine': she created as she saw fit; she followed her path toward her goals, which are lost in the mists; she lived in her domain, which existed in a curious way outside myself. . . . What relation had she to art?"[14] And nature's divinely feminine unattainability was implicitly sealed for Kandinsky by his explicit identification of the idealized Moscow of his painterly inspiration with his mother's personal qualities:

> My mother is a Muscovite by birth, and combines qualities that for me are the embodiment of Moscow: external, striking, serious, and severe beauty through and through, well-bred simplicity, inexhaustible energy, and a unique accord between a sense of tradition and genuine freedom of thought, in which pronounced nervousness, impressive, majestic tranquility, and heroic self-control are interwoven. In short: "white-stone," "gold-crowned," "Mother Moscow" in human guise. Moscow: the duality, the complexity, the extreme agitation, the conflict, and the confusion that mark its external ap-

pearance and in the end constitute a unified, individual countenance; the same qualities in its inner life . . . and yet, just as unique and, in the end, wholly unified—I regard this entire city of Moscow, both its internal and external aspect, as the origin of my artistic ambition. . . . I have simply painted, and am still painting, this same "model" with ever greater expressiveness, in more perfect form, more in its essentials.[15]

There is a significant equivocation in Kandinsky's metaphor here. Though his mother is ostensibly its tenor or subject and Moscow its vehicle, the descriptions of city and person are at the least mutually informing; in the second half of the passage their roles in the metaphor actually appear to be reversed. If the city has formal rhetorical priority, the maternal persona had temporal priority, and the personified characterization of Moscow in the second half seems directly derived from it. "Mother Moscow" was a perfectly conventional usage,[16] but there was nothing conventional either in Kandinsky's image of his mother or in that of his Mother Moscow.

His description of his mother is strikingly androgynous. The sense of tradition typically associated with women in the nineteenth century is balanced in her by stereotypically masculine freedom of thought; she masters her "feminine" nervousness and agitation by quintessentially masculine qualities of "majestic tranquility" and "heroic self-control." This is a very different picture of femininity from the concept of unindividuated maternal plenitude that Rita Felski argues was the nostalgic recourse of some Modernist artists protesting against the anxious individuation of modernity. Kandinsky's construction of nature, whether as an abstract creative force or in its manifest urban incarnation, meant an enormous challenge to male creativity because it ascribed the highest form of being—integrated individuality and totality, absolute creative agency—expressly, and exclusively, to the feminine.[17]

As he described her "masculine" qualities, Kandinsky's mother appeared to be a more positive version of the New Woman so much agonized over at the end of the nineteenth century.[18] In fact, though she remained a housewife all her life, Lidia Kandinsky was not a traditional "Victorian." Shortly after the family's move from Moscow to Odessa in 1871, she divorced her husband and married another man, with whom she would have four more children. Four-year-old Wassily was left with his father, who never remarried. Divorce in that time and place was uncommon enough, divorce at the woman's instigation even less so. Relations between the former spouses remained amicable; Wassily was raised by his mother's sister, who had lived with the family previously, and mother and son exchanged frequent visits in one another's homes. But his mother certainly lived in a domain outside

Kandinsky's own, following what must have seemed to the young child "mysterious paths" toward her own goals. Though he was very close to his mother all his life, and later tried to give the impression that the divorce did not disturb the harmony of his childhood, the sense of an arbitrary and unreachable *dea abscondita* haunted his early adult relationships with nature and with women. "When I was very young," he acknowledged to his lover Gabriele Münter in one of his early letters, "I was often sad. I sought something. I was missing something, I wanted to have something unconditional. And it seemed to me impossible ever to find what was missing. At that time I called the state of mind 'the feeling of paradise lost [*das Gefühl des verlorenen Paradies*]'" (October 11, 1903). Kandinsky's early experience of femininity was of autonomy, initiative, and strength of will, but those qualities were also associated with an unappeasable longing for the security of unconditional being. In his "Reminiscences," Kandinsky connected black, which in his color theory represented utter annihilation, with vivid memories of two episodes from a trip to Italy when he was three, both of which threatened him with separation from his mother.[19] In the context of the letter to Münter, they look very much like screen memories for the impact of his mother's leaving home for good a year later. The great yearning that he described in the letter to his young lover reveals by implication the magnitude of the hopes he invested in love. But its explicitly religious language, the language of lost paradise and unconditional being, also shows that his hopes for love had more than psychological resonance. Kandinsky's idea of love, as of femininity, was refracted through distinctively Russian philosophical and Symbolist notions that had influenced many members of the late-nineteenth-century Russian intelligentsia. It entailed not only personal emotional fulfillment but a philosophical, and political, worldview.

Femininity and Creativity: The Symbolist Background

> *The transformation of an individual feminine being into a ray of the divine eternal feminine, inseparable from its radiant source, will be the real, both the subjective and the objective, reunion of the individual human being with the Deity.*
>
> —Vladimir Solovyov, *The Meaning of Love*

Kandinsky was hardly alone among European artists in worrying the problem of the gender of creativity. Despite almost universal lip service to the conventional nineteenth-century axiom that masculinity represented the active creative principle and femininity the passive, created one, there was a widespread feeling of anxiety among artists, writers, and critics toward the end of the century about its tenability. Its most fanatic exponent testified to the extent of his doubts in the very extremism of his position, as well as in its incoherence. Otto Weininger insisted that only men are creative because they alone have a relationship to the spiritual, the "Absolute," while women, totally consumed by the sexual drive to reproduce, "have no existence and no essence; they are not, they are nothing."[20] But this rigid polarity of the sexes contradicted his central hypothesis, on which he staked his claim to originality, that "living beings cannot be described bluntly as of one sex or the other" because all were by nature bisexual.[21] The insistence on absolute difference was an obviously defensive reaction against his own assertion that each sex possessed anatomical vestiges and psychological characteristics of the other, which denied the creative potential of men who had a "disproportionately" large feminine component in their personality, such as homosexuals and Jews. The ostensibly opposing view held by Weininger's fellow Viennese Karl Kraus represented to an extent a more positive evaluation of the role of femininity in creativity and thus a greater threat to the traditional view. He associated creativity not with male reason but with feminine fantasy and imagination. Reason was simply the source of energy; in itself it lacked direction and could be turned indifferently to good or evil.[22] But Kraus's equation of femininity with sexuality and masculinity with reason preserved the old paradigm of masculinity as the active creative force. It was specifically intended as an argument against the "masculinizing" of the modern woman by the contemporary women's movement, which was destroying the true femininity necessary for artistic inspiration, represented for example by Wedekind's Lulu.[23] Kraus's position thus politically rejoined that of Weininger, who openly acknowledged that he wrote his book to combat the movement for woman's emancipation.[24] A third view of the issue of creativity and femininity, whose implications haunted the work of writers like August Strindberg, not only granted the reality of female creativity inherent in childbearing and nurturing, but seemed awed by and envious of its effortless naturalness. Men had to struggle to create and always faced the possibility of failure. Those who took this position, however, allayed its anxieties by demeaning the very naturalness they envied; mere "organic" creativity that was not achieved by the effort of reason, imagination, and will did not earn moral credit.

Kandinsky's initial sense of the weakness of art in the face of nature was thus one version of a European-wide concern about the power of feminine creativity. If anything his dilemma was greater, for more than even the most "feminist" of these writers, he believed in the superior creative agency of the feminine principle. On this point he represented a peculiarly Russian sensibility. That the Russian cultural elite shared many of the gender constructions and anxieties of their Western counterparts is evident from the enormous interest roused by Weininger's book when it appeared in Russia shortly after it was published in 1903.[25] But there its themes converged with indigenous concerns about sexuality to intensify a culturally specific version of masculine nervousness. Perhaps nowhere else in Europe was the relationship of femininity to the needs and prospects of spiritual transformation examined as thoroughly as in late-nineteenth-century Russian religious and philosophical thought, which in turn influenced both Symbolist aesthetic theories and the cultural-political aspirations of the progressive intelligentsia.

Russian Symbolism, like its French and Belgian models, aspired to penetrate the husk of material reality to the spiritual core within and transform the world by representing higher spiritual truth in art. In the West, however, Symbolist antimaterialism, linked to a wholesale critique of bourgeois civilization that included its interest politics, largely repudiated political and social engagement in favor of aestheticism, the modern substitute for a dying religiosity. Russians, inhabiting the most politically backward regime in Europe, could not afford such a luxury. Russian Modernism of the "Silver Age," the period from about 1892 to 1917, blended its aestheticist critique of materialism with a utopian social criticism based on a peculiar, apparently contradictory mix of Nietzscheanism and religion.[26] The ambitions of Russian artistic Modernism to produce a "new man," a divinely creative individual freed from enslavement to material nature, converged with the liberal intelligentsia's desire to throw off the dead weight of Russia's Old Regime. Enemies of the traditional paternalist order and partisans of European enlightened ideals, the liberal intelligentsia called for education and social reform to combat the tyranny of authoritarian custom in Russian life.[27] However, though they generally adopted the liberal ideal of the autonomous subject, they sharply differentiated it from what they saw as Western bourgeois ideas of self-interest and concern for purely individual gratification. Their Western values were tempered by a commitment, however ambivalent, to Russian folk culture, with its strong communal traditions, and to an Orthodox religious strain of deep suspicion of the material world.[28]

The key to both personal and social transformation for the religious philosophers Nicholas Fyodorov, Vladimir Solovyov, and Nicholas Berdyaev lay in the creative potential of human beings in the spheres of art and love.[29] In both of these spheres—by contrast with the economic, for example—the spiritual and the material could be united to produce a new kind of human being, who in turn could create a new kind of world. Through art the human imagination was potentially able rise above blind natural necessity to imitate God in the creative act; the true artist was the Nietzschean overman, limited by the body but spiritually unbounded.[30] The actualization of this potential for transcendence, however, was possible only through love. Love fused the feminine and the masculine, spirit and flesh, into a truly androgynous being that was neither one nor the other, but a new, higher creation, what Solovyov called a "spiritual corporeality." Solovyov in particular grounded his notion of androgyny in the deification of the feminine principle—Sophia, the Eternal Feminine—as spiritual knowledge or wisdom that alone could elevate the earthly masculine to divinity.[31]

The emphasis on the need to spiritualize the material could lead this highly charged erotic vision of human rebirth through the merger of male and female to quite paradoxical reactions. For Nicholas Berdyaev and those Symbolists influenced by him, for example, it involved the repudiation of physical sexuality in favor of purely Platonic love; the instinctual drive to reproduction was the very essence of blind nature. This meant the rejection of the sexual woman and above all the mother, the very epitome of the principle of flesh. In this context the enthusiastic Russian reception of Weininger, who also preached the end of sex and the sexual woman, is fully intelligible. If anything, the Russian response outdid him in disgust at female sexuality. Where sexuality and maternity were equated, all sexual desire was suffused with the shame and horror of incest.[32]

Berdyaev's conclusion, however, was not the only possible one to be drawn from the vision of corporeal spirituality; in any case his influential work only appeared after Kandinsky left Russia to begin his artistic career. For the older Solovyov, the vision of human spiritual elevation through male-female union was distinctly sexual. In fact, he argued that sexual love is "the finest flowering of the individual life"[33] because it alone allows individuality to reach its highest spiritual potentiality, the awareness of universal unity, through the overcoming of egoism. The flaw of egoism is not in the recognition of the subject's own absolute significance and value, which are wholly legitimate, but in the fact that he unjustly denies it to others. Through love one comes to know the truth of another person not as an abstraction but in reality. But if the other is truly to liberate one's individuality from the fetters of egoism, it must differ from oneself in every way, so as to be wholly other; hence the priority of sexual (meaning of course heterosexual) love.

Despite the apparent symmetry of role for the lovers in this description, Solovyov ascribed a different meaning and function to male and female in sexual love. Though he offhandedly reaffirmed the "elementary truth" that man stands for the active and woman the passive principle, which entails that the man have a formative influence on the mind and character of the woman, he was not interested in this "superficial relation." He was concerned rather with the "great mystery" of the two "differently acting" potencies of husband and wife in the attainment of perfection, a relationship analogous to that between the human and the divine.[34] Though the opacity of his prose retains much of the mystery, it is clear enough that woman is not simply equated with the human and man with the divine. God *is* explicitly the masculine principle that infuses the empty potentiality of otherness, feminine passivity, with fullness of being. But in the human love relationship, the idealized woman is the incarnation of the absolute perfection and fullness that God has created; thus "the transformation of an individual feminine being into a ray of the divine eternal feminine, inseparable from its radiant source, will be the real, both the subjective and the objective, reunion of the individual human being with the Deity."[35] As the idealized object of sexual love, woman is the visible incarnation of divinity, and union with her unites man with God. In the analogy with God's relation to His creation, it is the male who is in the passive "feminine" role, and woman is *in loco dei*.

Fulfillment in love was the precondition of the creative individuality that could produce true art, the material, tangible realization of the lover's experience of wholeness. But subjective expression was not an end in itself. The purpose of true art for the Symbolist artist was in turn the transformation of the world. Just as the individual, in order to fulfill his individuality, had to transcend egoism in a love relationship to reach the experience of wholeness, he also had to actualize the idea of wholeness beyond himself by linking it to the world and to the rest of humanity. All art aimed at such a transforming connection with the world, the Symbolists believed, whether self-consciously or not. In an essay attempting to define the essence of his movement, the poet Bely argued that all past movements in the history of art represented stages on the way to Symbolism's explicit awareness of this goal. Classicism had "discovered" the ideal forms of visible nature. The Romantic poet recognized that the external world was created in the image and likeness of the inner world of the imagination. Symbolism was a sublimation of the two: the image of harmony and totality, the creation of the artist's transformed inner consciousness, was embodied in the artistic artifact, and thereby became part of the real world.[36] The world was thus materially changed through and in accordance with the artist's vision of harmony, as the artist himself had been. By the same token, the artist's life was not separable from the art that was both to reflect and further transform it. It was the raw, chaotic material on which art worked. As one historian of the movement has put it, "The events of the life were never experienced [by the Symbolists] as merely and solely life's events. The events of life immediately became a part of the internal world, a piece of creation."[37]

171

Kandinsky's aesthetic theory reflected these Symbolist norms. The work of art, concerned with the creation of aesthetic harmony out of psychic discord, functions on two levels, in relationship to the artist himself and in relationship to the viewer. In relationship to the artist, a painting expresses his current spiritual state in the struggle for harmony and at the same time represents one step in his further spiritual transformation: "A certain complex of vibrations [in the soul]—the goal of a work of art. The progressive refinement of the soul by means of the accumulation of different complexes [in the work]—the aim of art."[38] The formal aspect of painting served the spiritual and was essentially instrumental. Kandinsky's position on this matter explains why he could praise the "naïve" paintings of the composer Arnold Schönberg, whose expressionism was so different from his own increasingly abstract work at the time, in terms that were more than mere politeness to an amateur friend: "In reality, the artist's progress consists not of external development (the search for a form that corresponds to the unchanging condition of the soul), but of internal development (reflection of spiritual desires attained in pictorial form)."[39] As for the work of art's relationship to the viewer, Kandinsky asserted that painting necessarily consists of an inner and an outer element: "The inner element, taken in isolation, is the emotion in the soul of the artist that causes a corresponding vibration . . . in the soul of another person, the receiver. . . . [But] [t]he vibration in the soul of the artist must . . . find a material form, a means of expression, which is capable of being picked up by the receiver"[40]—in order, that is, to effect the corresponding spiritual refinement in him. Art is not an exercise in solipsism; it must be able to communicate its vision of harmony to the viewer and transform him as it did the artist.

By contrast with these remarks on aesthetic purpose, Kandinsky had nothing to say theoretically about the erotic preconditions of inner harmony that had been laid out by the religious philosophers and Symbolist writers. Those preconditions were, however, not only implicit in the Symbolist origins of his aesthetic; they were even more directly entailed by his conceptualization of the aesthetic problem of creativity. Since he had identified absolute creativity with the feminine principal, he also believed, at least initially, that it was only by joining in love with the idealized feminine that the absolute harmony he aspired to could be achieved. Though he did not, like the Symbolists influenced by Berdyaev, repudiate sexuality, the fact that his idealized femininity was also identified with a maternal image faced him with deep ambivalence about his sexuality, inevitably tinged with incestuous overtones. Even more problematic was the danger of the loss of autonomy, the dissolution of self, in the merger with a maternal woman. Kandinsky did not write about these issues in his theoretical work, but he did live them out in his life, which in good Symbolist fashion was not only a source for but a vehicle of his art. And he did actually express them in another kind of writing, his intimate correspondence with his lover.

Politics and Feminism

> *Up to my thirtieth year I longed to be a painter, since I loved painting above all else. . . . [But] it appeared to me at that time that art was an unallowable extravagance for a Russian.*
>
> —Wassily Kandinsky, "Autobiographical Note"
>
> *Ladies and gentlemen of all ages accepted.*
>
> —prospectus of the *Phalanx*

Kandinsky's critique of materialism in *On the Spiritual in Art* includes a list of targets that go beyond the generalities of aesthetic criticism and would appear to stamp him as a conservative or even reactionary political and cultural anti-Modernist. They include republicanism and democracy in politics, socialism in economics, positivism in science, realism in art, and atheism in religion. In fact the animus of this list points to a very different ideological origin.

173

Kandinsky was a trained economist and legal scholar, and something more than an amateur ethnographer, before he became a painter. However much contemporary aesthetic theory ultimately aimed at social transformation, art was not the most direct path to it; and in any case the first emphasis of contemporary aesthetics was on self-fashioning. Persuaded like so many of his generation that the hopelessly backward Russian polity required urgent reform, Kandinsky had put aside an artistic passion dating from his earliest years to train in the social sciences, which he believed would be most useful in the modernization of his country. His brand of liberalism, however, was also distinctively Russian. Putting its emphasis on personal moral as well as social/political regeneration, it was close in spirit to contemporary Russian philosophical and aesthetic theories and significantly influenced by them. In turn the sociology of his liberalism casts light on the concern of those theories with the problems of egoism, ethical individuality, and community.

Kandinsky's father, the well-to-do director of a tea shipping company, was part of the progressive commercial middle class pressing for Russia's adoption of Western European freedoms and institutions. His son's inherited liberalism was shaped by his choice of career as a member of the professional and academic intelligentsia. Virtually excluded from political power,

Russian professionals were both resentful of the state and dependent on it, drawn into alliance with disgruntled groups socially below them yet culturally related to those socially above them.[41] Ideologically, their ambivalence produced not only a conflicted attitude toward the masses but disdain for the self-interested, self-indulgent individualism of the modern West,[42] and a commitment to a distinctively populist liberalism that combined modern constitutionalism with traditional Russian communalism. These values were especially marked in the legal profession, where a strong strain of opposition to "rational" legal systems in favor of customary law was reinforced by the long-standing Slavophile reaction against Westernization.[43] Kandinsky's legal thinking, which rejected the abstractions of Roman law in favor of Russian peasant law, typified this attitude perfectly.[44] Especially when his patriotism was provoked, Kandinsky could be quite sharp, even nasty, in his contempt for utilitarian individualism. Writing to Gabriele Münter in the bitter aftermath of Russia's unexpected defeat by a modern Japanese navy in 1905, he expressed open schadenfreude at reports of Japanese domestic repression: "The Japanese government (constitutional) betrays its own people, suppresses newspapers and uses violence if the people express their will. I am genuinely happy. And not only as a Russian but also as a human being to whom purely practical and superficial progress is disgusting and hateful. To the devil with the practical sense, which leads only to the temporary success of one's own egotistical purposes. . . . A people gifted chiefly in this respect I find alien and repulsive. As I find the Messrs. Englishmen and their dearest friends, the Japanese" (September 9, 1905). His contempt for modern material progress, however, was completely consistent with his almost millennial sense of joy at the news of the promulgation of a liberal constitution for Russia just over a month later: "Ella, Ella, congratulate me! It has happened, finally, finally. We have a real constitution and are no longer subjects, but citizens, real citizens with all the important rights. After twenty-five years of anticipation I now experience this day. There are tears in my eye. . . . Congratulations, joy. At last, at last, freedom. There are parties that immediately want much more. For what purpose, now that legislative right belongs to the people? Happiness, Ella, happiness! Beloved, dear one, you will rejoice with me . . ." (October 30, 1905).

Whether or not they were directly engaged in politics, liberal professionals were actively concerned with propagating the liberal values of independence and self-control, the latter based on scientific rationality and professional expertise, in the norms and daily exercise of their professions.[45] The two values were equally emphasized because Russian liberals—in this respect no different from their European predecessors—feared the consequences for morality and social order of the very liberation they sought. In

174

no sphere of life was this fear greater, professionally and personally, than in sexuality. The liberal ideal of autonomy entailed relaxation of the traditional rigid restraints on sexual expression, but unbridled desire and limitless gratification threatened rationality and communal order. No longer able to count on the old natural order of traditional society to restrain the impulses, the Russian educated elite could achieve virtue only by submitting desire to intellectual control, a precarious bulwark that demanded constant vigilance and effort. Partly as a result of their ambivalence, they also had conflicted attitudes toward women and the cause of female emancipation. Enemies of patriarchy, they necessarily stood for a greater degree of social freedom for women, but their habitual paternalism constrained their permissiveness. "Like liberals everywhere," Laura Engelstein concludes, "Russians persisted in their custodial attitude toward women while persisting on expanded autonomy for men."[46] To the extent that women were still identified with the flesh, sexual temptation could also be dealt with by excluding women from the public sphere. As one critic has observed, "Progressives who seemed to be expanding their worlds to encompass the flesh also believed they were expanding the circle of socially significant beings to include women. Inclusion and exclusion often went hand in hand."[47] Liberal and even radical male attitudes to the New Woman of the late nineteenth and early twentieth century showed a corresponding ambivalence: even men who desired the end or at least the mitigation of traditional male power over women feared that it would mean the rule of women over men.[48]

From the little evidence we have, it seems that Kandinsky himself was at the more radical end of the spectrum of liberal attitudes toward contemporary women's issues during his university years. In some of his ethnographic publications, written during the period he was caught up in student politics for a variety of radical causes, he engaged in feminist polemic not the less sharp for being masked as scientific debate. One of his book reviews attacked anthropological theories that posited the primacy of patriarchy, and defended the theories of Bachofen and Kovaleskii, who had argued that matriarchy was the first form of human community.[49] Years later, when Kandinsky had the opportunity to do something concrete about women's exclusion, his actions matched his ideological predilections. The official art academies at the end of the nineteenth century did not admit female students, and even in the private art schools that did, there reigned what Kandinsky castigated as a strong "misogynistic element."[50] It was in militant defiance of established norms that the prospectus of the *Phalanx* art school that Kandinsky began in late 1901, proclaimed, "Ladies and gentlemen of all ages accepted";[51] the majority of its students were in fact women. As Gabriele Münter would testify years later, his professional egalitarianism

175

was not a pure formality. "He loved, understood, protected and furthered my talent," she wrote in her diary in 1911.[52] And even toward the end of her life, despite her undying sense of betrayal by him, she never recanted her appreciation of Kandinsky as a teacher who from the beginning had treated her like a fully rational adult. "[That] was a new artistic experience, how K., quite unlike the other teachers—painstakingly, comprehensively explained things and regarded me as a consciously striving person, capable of setting herself tasks and goals. This was something new for me, it impressed me."[53] Even her more ironic recording of his exasperation at her stubborn independence acknowledged his admiration for it and his concern to foster it: "K. the great art teacher despaired of his mission in the case of G. M.—he said, 'You are hopeless as a pupil. All I can do for you is guard your talent and nurture it like a good gardener, to let nothing false creep in—you can only do what has grown within you (yourself).'"[54] Kandinsky's attraction to Münter was perhaps the most obvious sign of his advanced attitudes toward women.

176

Art and Love

> This woman was the internally necessary correlate of his human and artistic existence.
>
> —H. K. Roethel, *Gabriele Münter*

Kandinsky's abrupt decision to give up his academic career on the eve of taking a university appointment, leave Russia, and start a career as a painter at the age of thirty without previous formal training was even more radical than it appears. It has been suggested that art was simply the medium Kandinsky ultimately chose to realize the project of cultural and spiritual reform that had animated his professional ambitions. The break between the careers was actually much greater. Choosing art meant the choice of what he had previously thought of as an unallowable personal extravagance. However, after six years of academic preparation, he would write later, "I began to notice that my earlier belief in the beneficial value of the social sciences . . . had seriously diminished. . . . [T]he thought came to me: now or never. . . . [I]nwardly I was sufficiently mature to realize . . . that I had every right to be a painter."[55] However much his painting would be marked by the spirit of social-cultural crusade, the leap into this new career meant addressing what felt like a long-deferred personal and aesthetic need—and problem.

Kandinsky made great strides in his craft in his first years in Munich—by

1901, five years after he arrived, he felt confident enough to stop apprenticing himself to others and start his own art association and school—but his output before 1902 was relatively small. It consisted of land- and townscapes, including numerous scenes of Schwabing and Munich, beautifully colored in rich, deep hues and thickly painted, often with a palette knife, representing by far the bulk of his work; a very few "anecdotal" paintings of Symbolist fairy-tale and German medieval themes, and a small number of Jugendstil graphic works like the poster for his newly founded *Phalanx,* with its classical allusion.[56] In March 1901 he was complaining that for all his desire to paint, he felt inhibited by a need to work provisionally and was producing only "scraps."[57] Within a short time, however, he dramatically increased his productivity and introduced new ranges of subject matter and styles. The changes coincided closely with his meeting and falling in love with Gabriele Münter in the summer of 1902.

Kandinsky was married when he moved to Munich, to a cousin, Ania (Anna) Chimiakina, in whose home he had stayed while attending the University of Moscow. Little is known about her or their relationship, other than that she was a traditional nineteenth-century wife in her willingness to subordinate herself to him, and that however much real affection he had for her, theirs was not a passionate love match.[58] Gabriele Münter was, in sharp contrast to Anna, one of the "New Women" of the time.[59] She was the daughter of a politically radical German father, who had been shipped to America by *his* father to avoid trouble with the authorities, and an American-born woman of German descent used to the relatively freer ways of the New World.[60] Though her parents became more conservative after they returned to Germany, they retained a somewhat relaxed attitude toward Gabriele, born when her father was fifty-one. She showed artistic talent early on, and while she and her family expected that she would marry in due course, she was in no hurry to do so; encouraged after her father's death by her mother and brother to develop her talent, she left home to study. Like other independent young women of her generation, she took up cycling, which gave women unprecedented freedom of movement, with a passion. After her mother died, she made an extensive tour of the United States, with no chaperone other than her sister, to visit her American relatives. Upon her return she moved to Munich to study at the academy of the Women Artists Association, living in Schwabing, Munich's bohemia, where she came into contact with lively discussion and debate on women in the arts, feminism, and women's suffrage. Nonetheless, when the opportunity came to study in a coeducational school run by a forward-looking male artist, she was among the first to enter. It was on a *Phalanx* painting excursion in the country south of Munich during its first summer that teacher and student, twelve years apart in age, fell in love. An otherwise ordinary class photo taken at the time unintentionally displays one reason for their affinity, and the means that enabled them to go off together alone: standing side by side, they are the only two with bicycles.[61]

Kandinsky's passion for Münter developed with a rapidity that frightened her despite her own attraction to him. It was in fact a passion in waiting, a long-unfulfilled need whose personal and ideological roots were, in appropriate Symbolist fashion, closely intertwined. He openly acknowledged his yearning for the lost paradise of childhood,[62] but he also believed that it was only through union with an ideal woman that he could achieve his artistic goal of creating objective harmony out of subjective chaos. In 1902 Münter became that woman. She was in some ways at least well suited for the role, admirably independent, an artist, whose identity mirrored his own, yet enough younger that she could look up to his greater achievement. These traits reflect what would almost immediately become the conflicting poles of Kandinsky's feelings for Münter: an idealizing dependency so complete that any threat of distance completely unnerved him and a need for independence so desperate that he was constantly contriving to avoid too much closeness, physical and psychological. He was aware of the conflict, though its deeper source remained a troubling mystery to him. "You don't understand me—you always say," he wrote her early on. "Yes, sometimes I don't understand myself. What is unclear to you, however, is, I believe, mostly the various contradictory elements that constitute my so-called 'soul'. . . . I don't want to remain lonely, apart from the world, and yet I really shouldn't get close to anyone, because I can *only* bring that person unhappiness" (March 13, 1903; italics in original). The "contradiction" in his relationship to Münter paralleled exactly the conflicting attitudes to nature—the desire to assimilate, the need to stand apart—that both drove and stymied his artistic ambition. It was to prove an unbearable burden for the loving though baffled young woman, and ultimately for the relationship. But out of its failure came an aesthetic reaction that produced an artistic revolution.

The letters that Kandinsky wrote Münter over the years—necessitated first by the clandestine nature of the affair and later, after Kandinsky left his wife, by their frequent separations for visits to their families—are intimate, vulnerable, and revealing, but their significance is not only psychobiographical. They display as nothing else could the inner experience of a crisis of masculinity in which personal and aesthetic issues cannot be separated out from one another. For Kandinsky, the personal *was* the aesthetic.

The tone of desperate intensity was established early on, following a tryst on their return to Munich in which the lovers shared their first kiss. His love for her had made him lose his "peace of mind and inner balance," he wrote Münter. He pressed her with urgent declarations and demands for reciprocation while she was still fighting a confused inner battle between her attraction to him and her desire for a more conventional, respectable friendship with this older married mentor.[63] Her hesitations heightened both his desire and his anxiety about her love and brought out the insecurity and the recriminations that would mark his side of the relationship to the end. "It seems to me that you love me far, far too little and perhaps not at all," he wrote. "When you are not here, I talk to you in my thoughts. . . . And then I'm silent when we're together. It always seems to me that you don't understand me and that you think me worse than I really am. I can't help it. I would only like to hear from you that you really love me and that you will be patient with me. I am so sad now. I can't do anything and I can't think logically" (October 31, 1902). Not only her absence but her difference frightened him. Inviting him to join her at the opening ball of the Fasching season, Münter innocently related how much she had enjoyed the events of the previous holiday season with friends. The information upset him. Carnival and dancing, he wrote, were enjoyments that left him "completely cold," but his dislike of them made him feel "powerless and weak" because he could not join with her in such pleasures. "What do you get from me?" he asked bitterly. "I am seldom able to be fun." The self-recrimination masked an anger that he expressed through barely suppressed contempt for the crudeness of her amusements. "It hurt me," he wrote, "because I knew that something like that could give you so much joy," and went on to protest his own—superior—capacity for happiness. "I have much joy in life and nature, and sometimes thank the unknown power that has endowed me with joy with all my heart. This joy one can read in my paintings" (November 5, 1902).

The impact of the relationship colored his sense of the world at large. The remarks on carnival are preceded by a sweeping, but puzzled, observation: "Lately I see in people only a lust for murder. And that changes the whole picture of nature for me, the old picture that I loved so much. Here my thoughts get even more confused. What does all this mean? I have terrible dreams and scream every night like a crazy man. And I feel alone in life. It seems to me that I have to get away, away from people. Stupid! Isn't it? After all I can't bring happiness to anyone on earth. I only bring suffering to those I love." The sequence suggests that Kandinsky's new "perception" of the world was excited by new feelings within himself, not necessarily as a crude projection of his own rage but as an attunement to the murderous rage in the world that he had previously ignored. What apparently made him so angry was the evidence Münter's invitation unwittingly offered that he was not the sole object of her interest or the sole source of her happiness. But his anger went beyond the personal to disrupt the harmonious image of nature that he wanted his painting to capture, potentially posing aesthetic as well as personal problems.

Murderous rage was not the only troubling impulse he had to accommodate in his newly shaken world picture. In her initial efforts to ward off an erotic attachment, Münter had accused Kandinsky of hypocrisy for kissing her while saying that he wanted to be friends. Kandinsky's wounded reaction betrayed guilt not at the correctness of her frightened reductionism— he knew how much more than just sex he wanted—but at the idea of desiring her sexually at all. "It's not just kissing that I need," he protested. "'It's not appropriate to it,' you say, that is, to friendship. That's true too: I don't kiss my other friends. But it isn't my fault that my feeling is bigger than friendship. It will always remain so internally. Externally I can certainly control myself, if that's what you really want. I am not as bad as you think. I'm also capable of higher feelings. Maybe too idealistic, which doesn't suit our times well—in this respect I'm quite old-fashioned. And to the devil with modern filth" (November 7, 1902). Kandinsky's disgust at "modern filth" was as genuine as his desire for Münter. He seemed caught between Solovyov's valorization of sexual love and Berdyaev's fear that physical love would obliterate the spiritual. Throughout their relationship Kandinsky never forgot Münter's early reproach, which she renewed at times of strife. In one of his last letters to her, he defended himself against it yet again: "You have often thought it was your body, but no, no! It was for all that a spiritual liaison" (May 27, 1916). Physical desire versus spirituality was yet another conflict he, and his work, had to accommodate. If "materialism" was the enemy, the enemy was also him.

The intensity and volatility of Kandinsky's feelings are the measure of how much was at stake for him in the relationship with Münter. "I know well enough . . . that I give you no peace," he acknowledged. "But what am I supposed to do with myself? . . . Everything in me has changed. I've lost my peace of mind, my desire for perpetual work, my free thoughts, dreams and ideas. . . . Oh! What's the use of complaints? After all . . . it's not your fault that I'm so completely attached to you . . ." (December 1, 1902). Every precious encounter with her was potentially either paradisiacal fulfillment or apocalyptic disaster. "Oh, my dear good friend, my good golden little heart, if you only knew how happy you can make me," he wrote after one early meeting. "My heart is still celebrating, you were so good, so dear, so kind. . . . I still hear, as if you had just said it, the 'I love you'. . . . Dear, dear, dear Ella. Do you know that Ella in Italian means 'She'? And you are indeed my 'She' who holds my heart in her slim, delicate hand" (December 9,

Plate 1

Riding Couple (1907). Copyright © 2000 Artists Rights Society (ARS), New York /
ADAGP, Paris. Courtesy of the Städtische Galerie im Lenbachhaus, Munich.

Plate 2

Mountain (1909). Copyright © 2000 Artists Rights Society (ARS), New York /
ADAGP, Paris. Courtesy of the Städtische Galerie im Lenbachhaus, Munich.

Plate 3

Picture with a Circle (1911). Copyright © 2000 Artists Rights Society (ARS), New York / ADAGP, Paris.

Plate 4

Improvisation 27 (The Garden of Love) (1912). Copyright © 2000 Artists Rights Society (ARS), New York / ADAGP, Paris. Courtesy of The Metropolitan Museum of Art, The Alfred Stieglitz Collection, 1949. (49.70.1). Photograph copyright © 1987 by The Metropolitan Museum of Art.

Plate 5

Composition IV (1911). Copyright © 2000 Artists Rights Society (ARS), New York / ADAGP, Paris. Photograph courtesy of Art Resource.

Plate 6

Composition VI (Deluge) (1913). Copyright © 2000 Artists Rights Society (ARS), New York / ADAGP, Paris.

Plate 7

Composition VII (1913). Copyright © 2000 Artists Rights Society (ARS), New York / ADAGP, Paris.

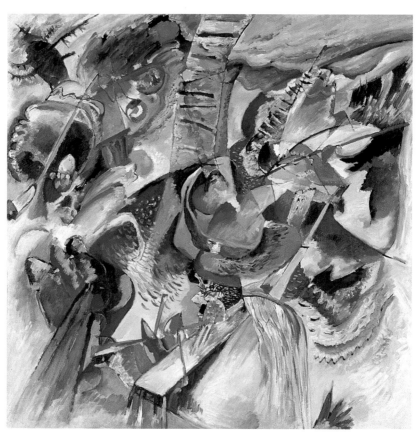

Plate 8

Improvisation (Gorge) (1914). Copyright © 2000 Artists Rights Society (ARS), New York/ ADAGP, Paris. Courtesy of the Städtische Galerie im Lenbachhaus, Munich.

1902). His reaction six months later to the collapse of a rare opportunity to spend three days together, which went awry through a series of miscommunications, was equally extreme in the opposite direction. "You must know after all what it means to wait so endlessly long," he wrote frantically when the first arrangement fell through. "I had crazy thoughts: that you were sick, that you didn't want me anymore, that you had an accident, etc., etc., that you got engaged. O God, it's not a laughing matter. . . . I won't die? Yes! But it hurts, it hurts very much . . ." (May 31, 1903). A few days later he broke down crying as he wrote, "I am ashamed. This is just childish. In addition, the old ghosts pop up. . . . Stupid, stupid, childish, senseless. And when on top of that I reflect that you love me so little . . . I am alone and must remain alone. That is my role in life" (early June 1903; exact date uncertain). Though he meant the term judgmentally, of course, Kandinsky's reaction was also "childish" in the literal descriptive sense of the word. That Münter could awaken the "old ghosts" of his childhood, the devastation of early loss, is sure evidence on the other side of the promise that her love held for him.[64] It is not surprising that he wanted to reorganize his life around her. In the summer of 1903, during another painting expedition outside Munich, on the anniversary of their falling in love, they became lovers for the first time and entered into a "marriage of conscience," complete with an exchange of rings that was the pledge of a future formal union.

Despite its internal and external storminess, perhaps indeed because of it, Kandinsky's relationship with Münter had an immediately galvanizing effect on his art. The number of his woodcuts and watercolors increased substantially; most of the former, and many of the latter, as well as some of the oil paintings, were devoted to scenes of medieval "Old Russia." At most only the two earliest of this genre, *Russian Knight* and *Russian City,* may predate the relationship with Münter, though this seems unlikely; they are ambiguously dated 1901–2, but they were first exhibited in November 1902, months after Kandinsky and Münter began their affair.[65] In any case the number and variety of the Old Russia works increased substantially from 1903, and especially after Kandinsky's return that year from his first trip to Moscow since he had left in 1896.

The trip marked the revival of powerful childhood feelings for the city. "I have a quite remarkable feeling here in Moscow," he wrote Münter shortly after his arrival. "Hundreds of memories, partly forgotten images, the whole character of the authentic Russian city, which I can still feel to this day, these churches, carriages, dwellings, people, which are so near to me and so far. I have been gone from here seven years and only this time and for the first time I unexpectedly get these feelings" (October 9, 1903). "Only this time and for the first time" because Kandinsky's return to Moscow took place in the aura of his recent "engagement" to Münter, which had revived the hopes of recovering the lost paradise of his life there, before its disruption by transplantation and divorce. The connection between Münter and Moscow is made clear in a letter written two days later, after an angry exchange in which he had expressed his customary reproaches at her deficient love and she had responded in her usual defensive way by raising doubts about their future together. His half-apology hardly concealed his anger, but his attempt to explain his anxiety offered a look into the deepest meaning of her love for him and its connection with his origins.

> I am sometimes childish and naive. When I have a strong feeling, I think about absolutely nothing. I feel. I suffer. But I cannot think even when I make a great effort. My feelings were at a high pitch, so high that I found no more energy in me for thought. "Does she love me"—that was the only thing that I could think about. . . . And you only thought. You wanted to know what would become of it. . . . I wanted only to feel . . . where one should think. Frivolity? Egoism? . . . Ah! Love, you hurt me. Sometimes it seems to me that you do not know what joy, JOY is, the most beautiful, purest joy, that does not come from human beings, which human beings cannot cause. But the divine feeling, which suddenly makes the eternally unclear almost completely clear. . . . When I was very young, I was often sad. I sought something, I was missing something, I wanted to have something unconditional. And it seemed to me impossible ever to find what was missing. At that time I called the state of mind "the feeling of paradise lost." Only much later did I acquire eyes, which could sometimes look in through the keyhole of the gate of paradise. I am too bad and weak and am not always able to keep these eyes open. I seek too much on earth. And whoever looks for something down here seeks indeed absolutely nothing up above. (October 11, 1903)

If it was contradictory to criticize Münter for not recognizing that the highest happiness comes from above while simultaneously telling her that all he could think about was whether she loved him, he unwittingly accused himself of the same error. He too was seeking too much on earth through her love. But this was to acknowledge that he was seeking more than the earthly in her. With its reference to both early childhood sadness and the lost paradise, his letter in fact offered an oblique explanation for the confusion of earthly and heavenly. The eternal, the maternal, and the erotic had been inextricably interwoven for him from his earliest life, and Münter was their present embodiment. Her power irradiated the city of Moscow as it had been illuminated for him in childhood, not simply now as a memory of the past but "this time and for the first time," as a recoverable possibility.

Night (Promenading Lady) (ca. 1903). Copyright © 2000 Artists Rights Society (ARS), New York / ADAGP, Paris. Courtesy of the Städtische Galerie im Lenbachhaus, Munich.

Moscow and Münter make frequent appearances in Kandinsky's painting and graphic work in the next few years, usually in medieval and romantic guise, with Münter as often Western European as Russian. Kandinsky made the meaning of these images explicit when in 1904 he gave her as a first gift the painting *Night (Promenading Lady)*. It depicts an elegant young woman in festive medieval costume standing in the foreground before a tiny walled castle toward which a column of knights on horseback rides, blowing fanfares. The painting, he wrote her, represented his love for her.[66] Kandinsky later explained his attraction to the themes of these paintings in purely technical and ideological terms. Painting images of the past gave him the freedom to use colors as he felt them within himself rather than realistically, while, by representing the past, he could turn away from the soulless content of modern life to a time that nurtured the nonmaterialist strivings of the thirsty soul. The second reason, however, hinted at another, more personal aspect of his attraction to the past. His idealized images of noble ladies and knightly riders, the many paintings and woodcuts of hidden trysting places, brides and marriage scenes, sad farewells and happy reunions, triumphant processions and dramatic duels, figured the inner story of his love affair with Gabriele Münter.[67] One of the most striking and suggestive of these is a gouache called *The Bride* or *Russian Beauty in a Landscape,* painted in 1903, which shows a young woman in medieval Russian dress seated in a flowery meadow below a church on a hill; beside her are birch trees, an old Russian symbol of love and marriage. The canvases of larger scope—*The Arrival of the Merchants, Song of the Volga,* several versions of the theme *Sunday (Old Russia)*—depict the harmonious premodern society that was for Kandinsky the necessary social matrix for the spiritual love, the communion of souls, that he longed for. In a society governed by the religious spirit of *Sunday (Old Russia),* with its grave and stately figures solemnly passing on foot and horse before the walls of Moscow, the busy activities of the merchants and crowds represented in the other paintings were an enrichment of life, the occasion of cheerful sociable hubbub, not its spiritual impoverishment in the greedy competition of atomized individuals. Though there is careful formal and color composition in the Old Russia paintings, the work of harmony is carried as much by the subject matter, the evocation of an idyllic past, as by painterly means. Along with scenes of Old Russia and medieval Europe, Kandinsky also painted more contemporary scenes of courtly life and high society, equally idealized, equally romantic. The chivalric and populist sentimentalizing of these works elevated love above the "modern filth" he hated, and that he seemed to have feared had tainted him as well.

184
■

Kandinsky's need for concealment also played a part in the medievalized representation of his love. The need was characterological as well as practical; perhaps he had learned that there was no return but disappointment and hurt for revealing desires that could not be met and emotions that would not be welcomed. "Even aside from my wife," he had written Münter just after their aborted tryst in 1903, "I would really prefer that people not know about us, talk about our love, dissect it and dirty it. Stick their fingers into our souls and grope around in our feelings. I hate that, I hate it with all the force of my soul. And I have always hated it, as long as I can remember. The soul must be guarded, no outsider should be able to see inside. Mourning, enjoying, loving, hating, shivering inside from happiness—and not letting it be noticed" (June 5, 1903). This attitude was so fundamental to Kandinsky that it had become an aesthetic. He wrote Münter a few months later:

> It's funny that people only see decorativeness in my drawings and notice nothing of the content. But I don't want to emphasize it more strongly. One should only sense the content, the internal. For me, obvious content is ugly, unhealthy, unrefined. . . . Much should be unintelligible at first. . . . The thing must "sound" and through this sound one gradually approaches

the content. But the content must never be too clear and one-dimensional: the more possibilities for fantasy and interpretation the better. It is best to mix various oppositions of form-feelings if one wants to express deep and serious content. And the deaf and blind must walk on by peacefully without noticing anything. If such a person notices something, it's bad: then the thing is certainly ignoble and cheap. There you have my philosophy of art, about which I don't usually like to speak. But I want you to know it, my little one, my love. (January 31, 1904)

He wanted to share everything, even the secret of concealment, with Münter because he wanted complete transparency between them. He fantasized an immediate oneness so complete that it would inaugurate the new era anticipated by the Symbolists. "In my feelings you are already my wife," he wrote her before he had even broached the subject of separation to Anna. "I feel you so near to me and want to have you here bodily as well. . . . I think the transition to our life together will come easily and naturally, because it cannot be otherwise" (November 15, 1903). During the long, anguished discussions with his wife when he did finally tell her—he could not leave without trying to make sure that his decision would not shatter her— he sounded even more hopeful. "The two of us will have a fine, harmonious life," he wrote Münter; "we live together as one being. We understand one another, have the same feelings, enjoy life, nature, God. I would like to transfer my belief to you. . . . We belong together. A great power has united us. . . . The golden age is coming when we go through life hand in hand. It is coming, Ella, it is coming" (March 1904; exact date uncertain). "You, my love, my happiness, my joy, I thank you also for the future," he wrote again a few weeks later. "We climb together hand in hand up the high mountain of the world and look around and see the beauty of the world, the great world. From above too one no longer sees the ugliness" (April 12, 1904). If the tone of certainty was partly an effort to reassure an anxious Münter, who frequently despaired at the length of time it was taking for Kandinsky to leave his wife, partly an attempt to make up for the harshness he sometimes showed at her impatience, the vision he offered her was genuinely his own. It describes a fusion of two selves in a symbiotic union with just one set of feelings between them, a fantasy of seamless unity whose wishful intensity is evident in the abrupt shift from future to present tense. It was a promise with millenarian overtones, its realization ordained by divine destiny.

Separation from his wife made Kandinsky's dependency on Münter even more explicit. He now avowed openly what had always been implicit for him: Münter's love was the very condition of his creativity. "The more I think about it," he told her some months after he left Anna, "the more strongly I feel that I can't make it without you. . . . I only hope that until our wedding I somehow find the right way. But I wish you were already my wife" (April 20, 1905). Whether lonely and self-doubting or confident and optimistic, he sounded the same note. On his trip to Russia the next year, he begged her in a moment of despair, "Be with me and be good to me. I need your support so much. . . . I implore you, my Ella, help me, help me for God's sake to find myself again. You can do a lot, you can do everything, beloved. . . . [H]elp me with your love . . . to regain my old powers. Do you want to? You must want it, or otherwise I will be ruined" (September 21, 1905). Reporting more cheerfully the next month that he had won a prize for best painting in an Odessa exhibition, he again invoked her indispensability. "If we only have more peace, I will paint something great qualitatively and quantitatively. A few more years and I will win. But you, my Ella, my shining star, you must believe in me. Then I will accomplish something. I repeat what I once said: a lot depends on you. You alone can't do everything, but only through you can I achieve true greatness" (October 30, 1905). There is no reason except discomfort with his pleading vulnerability or inhuman idealization of genius to doubt that Kandinsky meant exactly what he said; the "truth" of his dependency on Münter cannot be separated from his belief in it.

The Crisis

I would like to be able to feel again, to be able to cry again before nature as I once did, to kneel and give thanks. I let it go, however, and torture myself as little as possible about it. But it must, it absolutely must return, or take on new forms.

—Wassily Kandinsky, letter to Gabriele Münter

Kandinsky was never to have the peace with Münter that he said he needed for greatness. From the beginning he questioned the completeness and even the reality of her love, and the events that followed the separation from his wife only confirmed his doubts. Unquestionably Münter's behavior in the early phase of the relationship, as well as certain aspects of her character, played into Kandinsky's fears. Her pangs over the illicit liaison, the warnings of her family, her self-doubts coupled with her awe at being loved by someone she thought a "wonder,"[68] finally and not least her uncertainty about Kandinsky's ultimate intentions, combined to make her frequently tense and edgy. She was easily angered when she felt taken for granted or ill-used and would regularly threaten to end the relationship even after he left his wife. Despite her admiration, she could be more open about her ambivalence than he was. "Doubt over and over again," she acknowledged months after their relationship had been consummated. "You are after all so different from me. I understand you intellectually, but lack the love for understanding and tolerance. You know well how I am—never satisfied with you. Or is it perhaps that you could try rather more to listen to me? To understand me and to please me?"[69] But these words were written during the difficult period of "conversations" between Kandinsky and his wife—when all his concern seemed to be for her feelings rather than Münter's situation—and, as the plaintive last sentences show, were meant not to cast doubt on her commitment but to plead for his attention. Months earlier, after their engagement, she had expressed her sense of being committed to a relationship in which she was destined to give more than she got, and in which her only recourse was passive aggression. "If you want me, you must win me wholly," she wrote, "but I will never be able to get away from you."[70]

Measured against the unconditional, uncritical devotion he wanted from her, however, there was psychological truth in Kandinsky's fears. His fantasy was of total and totally voluntary union. Early on he warned her that he would not be quick to marry her even apart from the legal difficulties he faced in securing a divorce.[71] "You do everything I want, you always say. Yes, my Ella, it is so," he acknowledged. "But I don't want to bind you fast to me until I see that you do it because you also want it. And not just I alone. I have made a firm decision about this, even if it hurts. You are my fiancée. I will not set you free. But I will make you my wife only when I am convinced that you are unhappy otherwise" (December 24, 1903). His hesitation, however, also served his ambivalence; because his all-consuming desire threatened his own autonomy, he needed to keep her at arm's length. He warned her consistently that he was an "egotist" who really ought to live alone because he brought nothing but pain to those he loved. While these warnings were especially frequent when he was angrily attacking her shows of coldness or her "flirtations" with other men—more fantasized than real—they were sounded too often to be merely retaliatory. A minor contretemps provoked a supposedly joking admission that revealed the deepest source of his fear. Begging forgiveness for sending her something later than promised, he wrote, "You make me so anxious [*So eine Angst habe ich vor dir*]. . . . And really it should be (if I were a good Russian) the other way around: 'and the woman must be-e-e a-a-afraid of the man!!' I fear that my wife is right and that you would rather be approached in your men's clothes" (February 14, 1904).[72] There could be no clearer expression of the threat he felt to his masculinity than this reaffirmation of the traditional relationship between men and women, and the slam at the masculinity of the New Woman occasioned by his fear of her displeasure.

The relationship became much more strained during the seven months Kandinsky took to leave his wife. While he was concerned with lessening the blow to Anna as well as vindicating himself, Münter was upset at his delays, taking his failure to inform his mother of the divorce, among other things, as a sign of his lack of seriousness. Kandinsky responded to her threats with outbursts of rage. "You are really strange. . . . [W]hat do you mean when you say I am renouncing you? . . . Do I have to explain in detail that I am overturning *everything* for you (to put it better, in order to get you), destroying everything, taking absolutely nothing else into consideration? Everything! Should I on top of that now harry my wife out in disgust in order to make a quick end of things? . . . Put yourself in my situation. I feel terrible, terrible. I did not expect this blow from you precisely *at this time*. It was very, very malicious of you" (July 28, 1904).[73] Two months later he was writing in the same vein:

> How can you do such a thing to me, Ella? Just think, both of us have no one else in the world who is as close to us as we are to one another. And you can hurt this person, who loves you so, who is giving up his life and everything he has for you, over such a paltry thing. . . . I have to muster all my strength not to show my wife how unbearable I sometimes find it, how I sometimes wait for the end of this life so as not to *humiliate* her anymore. Do you think that I should spit on everything? . . . Don't you understand that the injury I have inflicted on my wife is deep and serious, and that I *may* not simply run away? . . . Just imagine yourself in her place, but not as you are now—fresh and full of strength—but beaten down, without strength, half sick in body and completely sick in spirit, not knowing what to do, how you can go on living. And I should say to her: beat it! (September 6, 1904)

His rage at Münter was a measure of his guilt. What he was doing to his wife was nothing less than a crime.[74] In his mind there could be nothing worse than abandonment, as he knew at firsthand, and now he was the abandoner. It was almost intolerable.

Over the next while, his unrelenting guilt drove him into an increasing depression that only his ability to work and to vent his feelings to Münter could lighten. Not surprisingly, she found it difficult to listen constantly to the self-accusations and suicidal feelings for which she was, after all, the occasion. His feelings of closeness to her oscillated wildly with his moods and her responses. Writing from Russia shortly after leaving his wife, he bitterly castigated himself for the badness in him that had made him a sexual adventurer and was now making him an enthusiastic supporter of Russia's war against Japan:

Sometimes I would prefer to be all alone in the world. . . . And have no one who is well inclined toward me. . . . A thousand torturous thoughts, a thousand ugly pictures before my eyes. Filth and tears. And my own guilt before many people. My own evil. And my own pain. Am I after all not alone? No one understands me. . . . I feel, think, dream, and desire differently from others. I want to speak the same language and I can't. But I do understand myself, it's just that I can't explain what I am. "You don't have to hurry, death will come all by itself." And I want death, and I don't. . . . [I,] who *want* to be alone and *am* Don Juan. Who persists in believing in God and finds war useful. Who believes in beauty and finds the ugly. Ugliness [?] and beauty. The music of the spheres, and diarrhea. (November 12, 1904)[75]

Being together with Münter did not lessen his depression, or his ambivalence. After his return from Russia, they began a peripatetic existence because Kandinsky would not further humiliate his wife by living with his lover in Munich. Two letters written during one of their separations in this period reflect ambivalence at an almost comical peak. "I think: I will marry you, so that we belong to one another, but we will not live together," he wrote. "I find that that would be the best. But to have you far from me is so difficult and painful that I can't find the courage to act as I think right" (April 18, 1905). And two days later, "I feel that I will not survive without you. I would like at least to be in the same city. I find my life in this suffering, and sometimes my very self, unbearable. . . . My Ella, my friend, advise me what to do" (April 20, 1905). Just a few days after that, he wrote Münter from Munich that he had arranged to meet his wife later that summer: "Again . . . you can see how unashamedly egotistical I am: not Anna but I need our meeting, and I want her to come to me though she says explicitly that it is difficult for her" (April 22, 1905). To assuage his guilt, Kandinsky contrived a triangular situation (which continued into the years he and Münter lived in Munich, where the two women met and occasionally dined together) that effectively kept both women bound to him while he committed fully to neither.[76]

The reestablishment of relations with Anna did not solve the problem of his guilt. "This year, which I wanted to spend far from you, will hardly help me," he acknowledged to Münter, "since the longing for you will constantly rob me of my peace of mind. What can one do, beloved? Promise me, if you can, that you will come immediately if I ask you to. The certainty of being able to have you with me will indeed somewhat ease my situation. Am thankful for the inhuman patience you have with me" (April 27, 1905). That it was he who kept her at a distance did not protect him from continuing jealousy at fantasized flirtations with other men, even innocent intimacy with relatives. Under the pressure his masculine vulnerability broke through with a force whose primitiveness, which he ambivalently expressed in conventional nineteenth-century racist terms, embarrassed him. "I can't stand that anyone touches you!" he said in apology for his overreaction to one such event. "That is perhaps a stupid Asiatic jealousy, but after all I am somewhat Asiatic. Would you be so *completely* indifferent about something like that? You European woman, you!" (August 28, 1905).

It was on a trip to Russia later that same year to tell his family about his divorce and to start the legal proceedings for it that he made the confession to Münter of his total dependency on her quoted earlier, the most abject he was ever to utter. His behavior when he did not get a letter from her was, as he described it himself, almost crazed.[77] Nor could his peace of mind have increased when his father responded to his news of the divorce with the words, "You are now experiencing everything that I once experienced" (October 5, 1905)—a perhaps unintended sting since Kandinsky was doing what his mother did to his father, not reliving his father's fate. In any case, after an unhappy reunion with Münter, Kandinsky, in an almost Freudian caricature of unconscious conflict, lost the ring he had worn since their spiritual "wedding." He himself called it a "bad omen," but immediately thought of some rings they had seen together the day before. "It was coincidental, but I see something deeper," he wrote trying to put the best face on it. "Doesn't this mean that our earlier life together until these last few days is gone, that a new, beautiful, happy period of our life is beginning?" He would purchase the rings, then go to the cathedral "to find peace and to pray to the unknown God for both of us" (November 17, 1905). He did not find it, and the hoped-for new life did not begin. The crisis reached its peak during their stay in and near Paris in 1906–7.

To be in Paris with Münter was a dream whose realization he had looked forward to from the time he decided to leave his wife. Since he would not live with her in Munich, where he was an active and important force in the city's artistic avant-garde, it would be no small consolation to be at the heart of modern developments in painting while testing what life with her would be like. "Paris tempts me," he had written her at the end of 1903, "because I will be there with you, and will live there peacefully and undisturbed, and much joy waits for us there. . . . This year and the next in Paris will be the best [last] test. I believe, however, that your love for me will gain all the elements that are now lacking in it. I *believe* it . . ." (December 24, 1903). As it turned out, they went to Paris later than originally planned, in 1906. By then Kandinsky had already exhibited there; the tempera "anecdotal" works such as *Sunday (Old Russia),* whose stylistic device of bright spots or dabs of paint showed the influence of Signac's Neo-Impressionism, had been favorably noticed by French critics, and he had made a connection with the Symbolists and Neo-Impressionists associated with the review *Les Tendances Nouvelles*.[78] From an artistic point of view, the trip seemed to promise even more than previously; its emotional circumstances, however, made it less likely than before that it would be a successful test of Münter's love.

After a brief stay together in the city, Kandinsky and Münter took up residence in Sèvres, on the outskirts. Four months later, however, she left him at his request and took an apartment in Paris, visiting Kandinsky on weekends. The only direct explanation of the separation came in an angry letter of Kandinsky's written in 1910. If its tone was clearly colored by contemporary events, the continuity of the issues over time suggests that it is a trustworthy version of what had happened four years earlier:

> Don't forget the years when the whole world, life, nature, the cosmos were like bottomless blackness for me, seemed to me like black walls that had buried me alive, when I had no fear of death, only of the possibility of life. At that time I had in you no support. I told you often how difficult my burden was, the burden of my bad life of many years, my faults, my sins. When I think of these burdensome times (it is not <u>fully</u> overcome even now) I am amazed how <u>I</u> could stand it, I who was not used to pain. I had no one but you with whom to talk about it. Do you know what you once said about it? It was in Sèvres, and I asked you to go to Paris so that I would not have to continually control myself. That evening, when I brought you to the train station and came home, I lost control over myself, fell on the floor, tore at my hair and cried so wildly. . . . Don't forget what I was, a person who since childhood was spoiled and idolized (I may use that word here) by everyone. . . . (December 8, 1910)

191

Allusive as these remarks are, their import is clear enough. Wracked with obsessive self-reproaches for leaving Anna, he felt compelled to ruminate and confess his sins over and over again. Münter seems to have indicated at one point that she would no longer indulge him, and Kandinsky decided that he would be free to indulge himself only if he were alone. Nonetheless, though it was he who sent her away, he felt abandoned. Even years later his furious disappointment at her failure to patiently listen to and contain his feelings of pain and guilt during that time was virtually undiminished. He had always wanted from Münter the loving, selfless imperturbability of a mother; in his depressed state he desperately needed it. Only occasionally was he able to see beyond his need to its impact on her. One weekend when she failed to show up, he came back from the train station and broke down, crying uncontrollably. "My whole life passed before my eyes," he wrote describing his reaction. "The unhappy faces that I have created stood before me. And I saw your dear face, your dear eyes full of tears, as clearly as if you were really there. Everything I hurt you with, all the unkind things I did to you awoke in my memory. I say without exaggerating that what I wanted most at that moment was to die." At that point he recalled a night during the last months with Anna in which she had cried bitterly, able to empathize with his mistress most readily when he could assimilate her suffering to his wife's. "To what end should I cause pain to the best, the very best people whom after all I love so much?" he lamented. "Am I a sinner who deserves no forgiveness? What is all this? And why do these best, purest people love me? The best thing is—not to come into the world. Or is that too much to ask?" (February 20 or 21, 1907). When, however, Münter reacted to his re-morseless self-punishment not with suffering but with criticism, his guilt turned into anger and hopelessness at her inability to understand the full depths of his despair: "You are not right when you accuse me of making no efforts to control myself. Can't I will to free myself from this pressure? . . . But I can't, Ellchen. I tell you, earlier on I could. . . . Now, however, I don't lead my own life any more. A power outside myself has torn the reins out of my hand and I have to . . . go along. Don't scold me over it and forgive me as much as you can that I don't control myself sufficiently, which is my duty, for whose fulfillment I am too weak" (March 7, 1907). This was an almost clinical description of severe depression, and in a classical response it had frightened his companion into anxious insistence that he pull himself together. By the time the Paris sojourn ended in June 1907, Kandinsky was in such a bad way that he found it necessary to go to the health spa at Bad Reichenhall for a rest cure. For a while, he was completely unable to work.

Up to that point, however, not only had he been able to work; he had painted his two masterpieces in the vein of Old Russia. The first, *Riding Couple* (plate 1), is a gorgeous paradigm of fairy-tale romance. In the lower foreground, a knight in a bright red cap holds his lady gently on his lap atop a large prancing charger across a river from a walled town of colorful buildings topped by gold cupolas. Above them in the upper half of the painting is a canopy of birch limbs. The magical feel of the painting is created by the soft yet luminous pastels of the sky seen through the branches in the upper half hovering over the darker lower half, and especially by the jewel-like dots of color, including many of gold and silver, which render the foliage of the birch trees and ground cover, the reflections in the water, and the decorated coverings of lovers and horse. The style blends Symbolist and pointillist influences in a wholly original way. But for Kandinsky the magic was also in the meaning of the images. "I am working on the sketch for the tranquil couple on the steed [*Ross*]," he wrote Münter from Sèvres, "and I am enjoying it. I have embodied much of my dreams in it: it really resembles an organ, there's music in it. This awakens in me once again the courage to try other things, and twice already I have experienced that peculiar throbbing of the heart which I had so often before, when I was much more the painter-poet" (December 4, 1906). What Kandinsky meant by his cryptic reference to his "dreams" may be inferred from the painting itself. It brings together as no work of his had previously done an ideal representation of Moscow with an ideal representation of love. The bell tower of Ivan the Great, rising above the other buildings, subtly identifies the city.[79] The romantic image is of courtly love, intimate yet chaste, but the lovers are strikingly positioned. The young woman, though pliant and affectionate, boldly faces the viewer with composed features, while her knightly protector, face averted, pays her homage with a kiss to the temple. It is a deeply nostalgic representation; the warrior-knight is the very embodiment of traditional aristocratic mas-culinity. But it is the unquestionable virility signaled by his role and his cos-tume that permits him the tenderness and submissive devotion his attitude displays. The identification of artist and knight leaps back over the materi-alistic present, which equated masculinity with mastery and productivity and had no place for masculine softness, aesthetic appreciation, and the urge to worship. The image of the knight harmonizes masculine and feminine, submission and dominance through possession of the ideal, independent woman. And the harmony of love is paralleled in the harmony of nature, both rendered through the harmony of color.

193

The second painting, *Motley Life,* a much larger canvas that brought to a climax the theme of harmonious social life in Old Russia, was expressly painted, according to a letter Kandinsky wrote years later, "to ventilate my nostalgia for Russia."[80] A very busy canvas, much different from the tran-quillity of *Riding Couple,* it nonetheless represents the kind of society that makes the love depicted there possible. The lower half presents a bright throng of people converging on a town bordering a river; above them in the background of the upper half there is a dark hill topped by a walled town. The crowd is densely populated with figures from every social station and every walk of life, working, playing, fighting, loving, and praying. The sup-posedly structured hierarchy of medieval society, the picture suggests, does not preclude variety, individuality, and energy. But the apparent chaos of in-dividuality is organized both thematically and aesthetically. The painting, as one critic has noted, is built upon a series of contrapuntal contrasts: life and death, old and young, love and hate, peace and war[81]—the reconciliation of opposites that Kandinsky would soon make the explicit theoretical goal of painting. Stylistically, the painting is unified by the dark background against which the colorful costumes and flowers are painted. The pointillist tech-

Motley Life (1907). Copyright © 2000 Artists Rights Society (ARS), New York/
ADAGP, Paris. Courtesy of the Städtische Galerie im Lenbachhaus, Munich.

nique is similar to that of the *Riding Couple*, but the effect of bright bustle in
the lower half is very different; only the brooding darker hill of the upper
half projects a parallel if different kind of spiritual mystery.

These two paintings, representing the culmination of Kandinsky's work
under the aegis of his hopes, personal and aesthetic, for the relationship with
Münter, were done during the time when those hopes were being fatally
undermined. It is difficult to disagree with Gisela Kleine's judgment of *Riding Couple*, and indeed not to extend it to *Motley Life*: "It was a working
through of suffering. It was wish fulfillment. It was a preservation in art of
what had failed in life."[82] But it was also more than that. It was the end of an
aesthetic program. Kandinsky would never paint in the theme or style of
Old Russia again. The hope of reproducing divine nature's effects through
possession of the eternal feminine in the guise of the ideal lover was
doomed by the revelation of her stubborn otherness, her unattainability, in
Paris. However one judges the success of these paintings in purely aesthetic
terms, for Kandinsky they were thematically a dead end.

A number of minor works done around the same time are more direct
expressions of the darker feelings of despair that overcame him. *Panic* and

Alarm Bell show people fleeing from some unnamed danger. *Snake,* an unusually pessimistic representation of Kandinsky's favored theme of Saint George, depicts a very small rider attacking a huge and terrifying serpent. Whatever it was that he was fighting threatened to overwhelm him completely. At Bad Reichenhall, Kandinsky's depression reached a point where he found himself completely unable to work, cut off from nature herself by a spiritual wall. "I have become dull [*stumpfsinnig*]," he wrote from the spa.

> And only music can wake me. I don't want this death, since aside from everything, through this death comes the one after life too. I would like to be able to feel again, to be able to cry again before nature as I once did, to kneel and give thanks. I let it go, however, and torture myself as little as possible about it. But it must, it absolutely must return, or take on new forms. I can never live blind and deaf after I have had eyes and ears. And I feel so far from everything. . . . I hang in the air. That is indeed good but for that I need wings. I peer from above into everything and see misery, ugliness, filth. But also tranquility, purity. You belong to the latter. And an infinity ago so did I, to some extent. . . . (July 10, 1907)

In the midst of this bleakness, his reference to the possibility that his old feelings might take on new forms gleams like a surprise. The "death" Kandinsky was experiencing was the death of his old hopes and expectations; yet even at that moment, he hoped that it might be the prelude to a rebirth psychologically and artistically.

Toward Autonomous Painting

> *Art which conceals no future potentialities, and which is therefore only a child of its time and can never become mother of the future, is a castrated art.*
> —Wassily Kandinsky, *On the Spiritual in Art*

It was a rebirth. While in Paris, Kandinsky discovered that the French avant-garde had gone beyond Neo-Impressionism in the even more radical color experiments of Matisse and the other Fauves. The discovery coincided with the crisis in his relationship with Münter that showed him it could never create the paradise he had dreamed of and that made him keenly aware of the emotional dangers of depending on it as completely as he had up to then. Deprived of the possibility of possessing absolute femininity as the way to reproduce nature's wholeness, he was free to explore a way of creating ex nihilo on his own. It was only after the emotional-spiritual trauma of Paris that he could begin to work through the artistic acquisition of Paris.

195
∎

There would be no overt break with Münter for years, and they would soon even begin living together in Munich as he would not let them do earlier, but the tenor of their relationship had changed forever. He acknowledged the change even as he tried to reassure Münter that it still survived. "If our life doesn't turn out as one might wish, nevertheless you are not alone. And in me you have someone who is immensely close to you, and who can sympathize with you . . . and who is always prepared to do everything for you that is in his power. . . . If we can't create a *proper* family, are proper ones so easily come by?" (June 20, 1907).

It was during the stay in Paris that Kandinsky first showed interest in what he called the "spiritualist movement," the European theosophical movement that some critics have claimed provided the spiritual subject matter he used to replace the object world in his painting.[83] Though its influence on his evolution toward abstraction has been exaggerated, and the emotional context of his attention to it ignored altogether, this was a significant turn. Without giving up wholly on the idea of a future with Münter, he was beginning to look to versions of spiritual wholeness and unity that did not depend on the grace of another person. Kandinsky had yet to take the giant psychological and ontological step that would make abstraction possible: the liberation from dependency on *any* external version of cosmic unity into the idea of a unity created by the painter alone in pure painting. But from this point on, the struggle for that liberation would be carried out much more self-consciously than before on the plane of metaphysics and aesthetic theory. In the years after Paris, Kandinsky pushed against the limits of representation, which were still for him the limits of art, by extending his artistic experimentation into drama and music, where as an amateur he was less bound by convention, and by conceptualizing its results in scripts, reviews, manifestos, and theoretical treatises as he had never really done before.

Kandinsky painted nothing between his departure from Paris in June 1907 and his arrival with Münter in Berlin in September, where they stayed until the spring of 1908. Of the few paintings he did there, one in particular, *With Yellow Cloud,* seems to mark the closure of a phase. Though its whereabouts are unknown, and the mood can only be guessed from a black-and-white reproduction, the "yellow" of the title perhaps points to the significance he would soon attribute to the color in *On the Spiritual in Art.* The painting shows clouds billowing up ominously above a dark landscape with four figures, two tall thin women standing on the left in long robes and dark hats with cowls obscuring their faces, their arms outstretched in an undecipherable gesture, and two smaller figures, completely apart and farther back on the right, at least one of whom is a male; it is an image of separation and distance. In the summer and fall of 1908, however, which Kandinsky and Münter spent in the town of Murnau an hour south of Munich on the Staffelsee, Kandinsky had a sudden outburst of creativity. He produced a large number of works, almost exclusively land- or townscapes without human figures, in a style utterly unlike anything he had done before. They were bold, bright, brilliantly colored, filled with an electricity that tended to blur the shapes of objects in the landscape, though the scenes remained clearly recognizable. Kandinsky's stay in Murnau was so productive that they repeated it in the spring of the following year, and later that summer Münter bought a house there that both had admired the year before, a retreat from the city.

So abrupt was the transition of Kandinsky's work in 1908 that art historians have felt hard-pressed to explain it. It has been variously attributed to the Fauve influences of Paris, perhaps further mediated through Alex Jawlensky and Marianne von Werefkin, Kandinsky's friends from the early years in Munich, with whom he and Münter spent a good part of the summer in 1908; to Werefkin's more spiritual, abstract interests; to Kandinsky's own growing interest in theosophy and spiritualism; and to the intense experience of nature that their sojourn in the countryside afforded them.[84] All may have played their role; none alone nor even all together are sufficient to explain what happened in 1908–9, which is unintelligible outside the context of the psychological crisis that by his own avowal made a new turn in Kandinsky's work necessary. Deciding to settle in Munich (at first in separate residences) and then to have a place of their own after the years of traveling undoubtedly ushered in a happier phase in Kandinsky's and Münter's life together, and contributed to the color mood of the new paintings. Looking at the repeated images of kremlins atop steep hills in many of these works, one can hear echoes of Kandinsky's words to Münter from an earlier letter, "Why can one not build a tower where one hears nothing of the world, of life?" (February 17, 1904). The brilliantly prismatic *Mountain* (1909) (plate 2) also evokes an earlier wishful anticipation: "We will climb hand in hand together the highest mountain of the world, the great world. From above one no longer sees the ugly" (April 12, 1904). *Mountain,* however, is as troubled as it is wishful. At its foot there is indeed a couple, a motif that appears in so many works of the next five years, but the two figures face one another in an attitude of strife; in particular the black figure, apparently the male, seems to thrust aggressively, even menacingly, toward the other. And to the left, separated from the couple by a little hill, is a rider, Kandinsky's most common self-representation. The painting is a graphic representation of the growing split between two different possible destinies, the lover as an inextricable member of a pair and the lone knight-rider on a

197

spiritual mission to the world. "Murnau," what it came to stand for in the history of Modernism, was more result than it was cause.

In fact the "Fauvist" works were only a relatively brief stopping place. By 1909 the paintings began to change again, becoming less and less obvious as landscapes, more and more difficult to read, filled with "objects" that even when recognizable were mysteriously allusive, with no obvious pictorial or narrative context. That same summer also saw the beginnings of a new and sweeping theoretical undertaking. *On the Spiritual in Art* would not be published for over two years, but the original draft, not to be changed materially, was completed in the fall of 1909. It was Kandinsky's first substantial writing on art since his letters from Munich to the Saint Petersburg periodical *Mir Iskusstva* (World of Art) in 1902, apart from scattered comments in the letters to Münter and some rough notes that are no longer available. As striking as the new turn in his painting was the emergence of an almost full-blown aesthetic theory with very little in his previous work to herald it. Kandinsky now knew both what art had to achieve and how it had to achieve it. A major reason for the delay in publication was that publishers found Kandinsky's arguments too abstract and unclear. But its thesis that the task of art was the reconciliation of inner strife through the creation of a harmony of opposites on the canvas retroactively takes on much more specific meaning in the light of Kandinsky's enactment of Symbolist issues in his own life. It was of their intimate essence that Kandinsky would not further specify those "secret happenings of which no one knows; unspoken thoughts, hidden feelings" that required sublimation into a spiritual synthesis, but he had spoken too often to Münter of the "low and unworthy thoughts" and the "egotism" that bedeviled him to mistake either the psychological/moral meaning or the autobiographical roots of his aesthetic concerns.

The vehicle for accomplishing the task of art was primarily pure color, though he did not ignore the expressive possibilities of form. Kandinsky's shift in the direction of abstraction was possible because color was at this point in his thinking both subjective and objective. Color expressed the painter's subjectivity, but it did so "objectively" since colors had objective emotional correlates, as much rooted in the nature of things as the object world. For the moment, this objective signification of color could take the place of objects, provisionally supplying Kandinsky with the foundation he feared to lose if he did away with representation, at least in principle. At the same time this belief marked the limits of the artist's liberation into pure "inner necessity." For if colors had predetermined meanings, their dissonance and consonance were still dictated by nature. Though *On the Spiritual in Art* was a defense of abstraction, it could not yet be fully realized either in theory or in practice; Kandinsky had not given up at this point on the idea of an external support for internal necessity, or internal harmony. "[The] emancipation [of painting] from direct dependence on 'nature' is in its very earliest stages,"[85] he acknowledged. But that needed external support was detaching itself from concrete objects, and particular persons, in the world to the more universal and timeless entity of color.

The tone of *On the Spiritual in Art* was visionary and militant. At stake for Kandinsky in his polemic on behalf of an art produced out of "inner necessity" rather than out of considerations of prevailing style, pure technique, competitive ambition, or the market was nothing less than the future of art, on which he believed depended the future of the human spirit. But what saving the future required of the artist, Kandinsky expressed in an extraordinary metaphor that exposed the concerns about gender implicit in his enterprise from the very beginning. "It has been said earlier," he wrote, "that art is the child of its time. But the kind of art just described can only repeat in artistic form that which already quite clearly constitutes the content of the contemporary ethos. *This art, which conceals no future potentialities, and which is therefore only a child of its time and can never become mother of the future, is a castrated art.*"[86] The mixed and apparently thoroughly confused metaphors fit too well with Kandinsky's onto-aesthetic and psychological conflict to be dismissed as mere clumsy style; they evoke the figure of the male artist as phallic mother.[87] Only an originary, nonimitative, art, he was saying, could be truly fecund, maternally generative, but only a noncastrated art could be truly creative. The crisis of sterile dependent imitativeness in which contemporary art found itself could only be solved if the artist united within himself virile male and maternal female in a hermaphroditic, self-contained whole that did not depend, childlike, on anything outside itself. The artist must be his own origin, and he could be this only if he, as male, internalized the feminine. This was, in Kandinsky's own words, the thrust of abstraction. Abstraction was the only nonimitative art, and hence the only art that could produce an independent masculinity powerful and creative enough to spiritually transform the world.

But as Kandinsky acknowledged, he was not yet ready for a fully abstract art. "Today," he conceded, "the artist cannot manage exclusively with purely abstract forms. These forms are too imprecise for him. To limit oneself exclusively to the imprecise is to deprive oneself of possibilities, to exclude the purely human and thus impoverish one's means of expression."[88] At the time he first drafted *On the Spiritual in Art,* he had not yet painted a truly abstract work (oddly he did not change this sentence when the work was published, though by then he had). Even the "natural" signification of color was not a secure enough foundation to enable him to paint without continuing reliance on the external world, however much it continued to be volatilized in many of his works of 1909–10. That reliance paralleled his continuing, if ever more tenuous reliance on, his relationship with Münter.

Nevertheless, Kandinsky's militancy, artistic as well as theoretical, upset the art world of Munich. The mutual stimulation of working with Jawlensky and Werefkin led Kandinsky and Münter to join them in forming the New Artists' Association of Munich, dedicated to bringing the avant-garde of European art to the attention of the artistically conservative city. The Association mounted two exhibits in 1909 and 1910 that were met with venomous ad hominem attacks and literally spitting fury by Munich critics. More disturbingly, Kandinsky's work soon became too extreme even for some of the Association members, who voted against including his *Composition II* in the second exhibition of the Association. His painting was evolving more and more rapidly away from accepted canons of intelligibility and "beauty," and the evolution was accompanied by increasingly radical public statements. Reviewing a Fauve exhibit in the same gallery that had hosted the Association, he criticized the Fauves' failure to extend their color radicalism to line and form. "Why is it only color that undergoes these modifications, violations, substitutions?" he asked. "What prevents the artist from likewise submitting the linear and planar aspects of nature to the same artistically necessary transformations? . . . Why is it necessary to 'paint' nature in different colors? If it is to derive pictorial composition, the inner sound of the picture, then why does this 'composition,' this 'sound,' extend only so far as the transformation of color? And why is drawing, that is to say, the nonpainterly, incidental aspect of art, so carefully avoided, thus, as it were, clipping the wings of the artist's creative imagination?"[89] But Kandinsky's criticism of the Fauves was friendly fire from within the avant-garde, aimed only at their residual conservatism in painting recognizable objects. Their achievements had to be measured against what he regarded as the dead end of German art represented by Secessionist artists like Slevogt and Corinth, whose recent Munich exhibit was everything that disgusted him about modernity. "Here," he wrote, "one's imagination leads nowhere, or rather, if it leads anywhere, then it is not into artistic realms, but rather . . . anatomical or even gynecological . . . for example, Corinth's much vaunted 'Bathsheba.' A large, soft, female is lying on her back. Naturally, with her legs apart. Naturally, naked. For some reason, around her waist a scrap of what appears to be black fur hangs down, disappearing between her large, soft thighs. In her right hand she holds a flower. A noble picture!"[90] While Kandinsky was perceptive about the prurience so frequently hidden in "respectable" biblical and mythical themes, his disgust was also determined by his own long-standing conflict over sexuality and by his recent recoil from his own erotic dependency, both of which lay behind the push to spirituality and abstraction. It is perhaps telling that his somewhat ambivalent collaborator of the following year, August Macke, thought he detected repressed phallic fantasies in Kandinsky's paintings. "When I see your towers in your picture," he wrote Kandinsky, "I sometimes think of Beardsley. Towers, flowers, or . . . ?"[91]

Still, even as late as 1910, Kandinsky was not prepared to go all the way to the total concealment of abstraction, as his exemption of Matisse from his criticism of the other Fauves shows. Matisse, he claimed, had gone "'beyond the accidental forms of nature,' or better expressed, only he has succeeded in entirely discarding the inessential . . . aspect of these forms, replacing it with his own forms. . . ."[92] For all his deformations of reality, of course, Matisse was recognizably representative; and while "replacing it with his own forms" is more aptly applied to Kandinsky's own work of 1910, the notion of "inessential" aspects of natural forms implies a distinction with "essential" ones still to be preserved in the painting. One clue to his continuing hesitation lies in the phrase with which he chastised the hesitation of the Fauves. If failing to extend abstraction beyond color to form meant "clipping the wings of the artist's creative imagination and power," doing so would mean soaring with the artist's own wings, and this Kandinsky did not yet feel able to do. What after all could possibly hold the artist aloft? For what was at stake in the total liberation of the artist from nature was a godlike autonomy and isolation that seemed too much for him to claim. In the essay "Content and Form"—which was probably written before his first abstract painting, though published after—Kandinsky unabashedly asserted the solipsistic consequences of adopting the criterion of inner necessity for judging a work of art. "Only that form is correct," he wrote, "which expresses, materializes its corresponding content. . . . Thus, only its author can fully assess the caliber of a work of art; only he is capable of seeing whether and to what extent the form he has devised corresponds to that content which imperiously demands embodiment. The greater or lesser degree of this correspondence is the criterion by which the 'beauty' of the work of art may be judged."[93] To claim the creator's sole authority over aesthetic judgment demanded absolute self-certainty, but this was not simply a psychological state. Achieving that kind of self-sufficiency required the apparently impossible, the internal unification of male and female, of the finite/active and the infinite/generative—or in Kandinsky's own words, referring to the way Persian miniatures miraculously combined simplicity and complexity, refinement and sensuousness, "the unification of the irreconcilable."[94]

201

On some level Kandinsky had long been aware of the implications of such an ambition. Years before he had made them clear to Münter, and in doing so also the necessity of her role for him. Münter had criticized his work in woodcuts, one of his favored genres before 1907, as not artistically serious, as mere "fooling around." Kandinsky's response shone a brief but brilliant flash of light on how he understood the artist's creativity:

> You say "fooling around [*Spielerei*]." Indeed! Everything the artist does is also only fooling around. He torments himself, tries to find an expression for his feelings and thoughts, he speaks with colors, form, drawing, sound, word etc. To what end? A big question! . . . Externally, only playing around. For him, for the artist, the question "to what end?" has little meaning. He only knows a "why?" In this way there arise works of art, in this way also things that are not yet works of art, but only way-stations, paths to works of art, but which already have a small light, a sound within them. The first and just as much the second (the first are after all so rare) *must* be made, because otherwise one has no peace. You saw in Kallmünz how I paint. That is how I do everything that I must do: it is ready within me and it must find expression. When I play that way, every nerve in me trembles, throughout my entire body music sounds, and God is in my heart. I don't give a damn whether it is hard or easy, whether it takes a long or a short time, whether it has any use or not. . . .

At that point in the letter Kandinsky asked Münter to come to him, "And we shall be like gods" (August 10, 1904). Here in a phrase was the meaning for Kandinsky of his painting, his relationship with Münter, and the connection between the two. The description of the artist as merely playing, which sounds so contemporary, actually highlights the difference between Modernist and Postmodern conceptions of art. For Kandinsky, it was only to the external, superficial eye that the artist played. The true artist is called by divinely inspired necessity, and when he answers the call, he is like God Himself. Except that, since nature alone was the source of color vibrations and color harmony, the task was too large for Kandinsky (or any artist) to accomplish alone. The appeal to Münter to come to him so that they could together be like gods was an appeal to the fantasized all-powerful alter ego, the idealized mother/lover/painter who represented totality in her own being and whose love could confer on him the painterly power to reproduce it. To create alone, in view of such fantasies, would be a declaration of independence from and equality with this other; it would also be a reduction of her superiority, a form of conquest. In 1904 Kandinsky still believed in his utopia of love and felt no need of, indeed felt utterly incapable of, such a declaration; by 1911 he was ready to take the momentous step.

The Breakthrough

> *I felt, with an exactitude I had never yet experienced, that . . . the innate inner character of color can be redefined ad infinitum by its different uses. . . . This revelation turned the whole of painting upside-down and . . . tore open for me the gates of the realm of absolute art.*

—Wassily Kandinsky, "Cologne Lecture"

The inner separation from Münter that had begun during the Paris crisis was completed in the years 1910–11. The next turning point was ironically Kandinsky's trip to Russia in late 1910, during which he saw Moscow for the first time since the crucial visit of 1903 that had cemented the link between the city and his lover. Even en route he seemed to have anticipated some kind of major change in himself. Visiting Goethe's house in Weimar, he was most moved by the bedroom in which the great German genius spoke his last words that "were not 'more light'," he wrote Münter, "but . . . 'now begins the transformation to the other transformations'" (October 10, 1910). His reaction to Moscow was even more powerful than seven years earlier, in part because of his disaffection with Munich, where his work had so recently been savaged. "So many things almost make me cry and cause my heart to beat more strongly," he wrote. "Why is life here . . . more intense and gripping. . . . I breathe Moscow in really deeply. . . . Every city has a face. Moscow—10. And the same goes for everything in it. And something like that has an impact. How will the old church art affect me? Will I find the essence, which I want to seek, to touch? Moscow is—whiplash. Moscow is—balsam" (October 14, 1910). In Moscow Kandinsky was finding kindred spirits and the acclaim he was refused in Munich.

But Moscow also worked its exciting and consoling effects in the context of the tension between the lovers, further exacerbated by separation. Münter did not receive any letters from Kandinsky for some time after he left Germany—he had mailed them to Munich and the concierge of their apartment had failed to forward them to Murnau—but her violent reaction, as she later acknowledged, came from a deeper sense that something had changed between them in the last year. "You know," she wrote him, "if you hadn't been so cold & often not nice to me more or less the whole of this year it would undoubtedly not have affected me so deeply—but in the end it looked as if you had changed toward me, as you no longer seemed to want to write to you as you used to, at length. . . ."[95] Kandinsky was highly irritated by her distrust. "You ought not to be so sensitive," he admonished her. "After all you know how I depend on you, how sincerely and well and despite everything how properly I love you ('despite everything,' which means

203
■

despite my bad character). And you ought to trust me more and think: something must have happened, that's why there aren't any letters. You must also know that I was totally swallowed up by Moscow and my impressions and still am" (November 3, 1910).[96] But he had also acknowledged that his behavior toward her had been unsatisfactory and hinted that there were more than superficial reasons for it: "You are right, my Ella, I am irresponsible and so often mean, sharp, hard and absent. I long myself for equilibrium, for a life with you that breathes peace, with a constant accord of our souls and our bodies. But then there always comes 'something' or 'somebody' and gently lays its fingertips on the scale, and the sound of equilibrium is gone" (October 28, 1910). The lability he confessed was dramatized a few days later in a letter full of jubilation at the actual launching of divorce proceedings: "What really makes me happy are your relations with Ania. If I am so cheerful here, so young (as everyone claims), so much a 'fiancé' . . . if I'm such an 'all-around good guy'. . . one of the main reasons, the main causes is this feeling of happiness. And that had to be so, had to come with the divorce—I *know* that now especially clearly (before I *felt* it only dully). You too trust the 'powers' and you too let everything 'ripen.' Then the right results come 'by themselves'" (November 22, 1910). Compared with the tone of letters from earlier years, however, even Kandinsky's reassurances did not sound convincing, and it could not have helped that he stressed the importance of Münter's relationship with Anna even as he celebrated his impending divorce from her. Appropriately, his remarks on painting paralleled the volatility of his feelings. Commenting on some work that Münter sent him, he wrote, "The sketches please me. Now, as you know, I am altogether against hard, too precise form, which 'today' cannot be and really results in a dead end. . . . What form is I have defined precisely and will in my brochure [*On the Spiritual in Art,* not yet published]. Outwardly—delimitation; inwardly—external expression of the internal. When you really feel what I mean by that (not philosophize, but simply understand, feel!) then you also find form. One must allow form to affect one and forget all the Picassos and his imitators [*alle Picasso und Picassore*]" (November 8, 1910).[97]

Clearing up the misunderstanding over the belated mail only postponed an explosion. An apparently trivial provocation ignited Kandinsky's anger and brought the underlying issue of the relationship to the surface. Münter had been studying Russian in preparation for meeting Kandinsky's family—there had been a notion of her accompanying him on the trip. Kandinsky wrote that he would prefer to teach her himself, and she chose in one of her letters to criticize his pronunciation of the letter "l" in German as too Russian, creating difficulties for her in learning the language. The more serious cause of her resentment was Kandinsky's decision to postpone

204
•

his departure from Odessa by three weeks, missing Christmas with her; in that case, she threatened that he would find an empty apartment when he returned.[98] Kandinsky poured all of his pent-up anger at her criticisms and repeated threats to leave him into a seven-page letter in which he brought his childhood and the history of his relationship with Münter together; it amounted to an explanation of why he could no longer depend on her for the fructifying love he had hoped for. "I am often surprised," he raged, "at the things I put up with from you. All those who are really fond of me show me so much love, consideration, and tenderness all the time and spoil me endlessly (and have spoiled me all my life) that the way you act was very hard to take especially at the outset and had the effect on me of slaps and punches. I have a generally bad character. You should understand how such feelings could and can affect me. . . ." At this point he reminded Münter, in the passage quoted earlier, about the bad time in Paris, which was as fresh as if it had just happened, but which he only now, in Moscow and further down the road to independence, was more fully able to understand.

205

> Don't forget what I was, a person who since childhood was spoiled and idolized (I think that word is justified here) by everyone. This time in Moscow has brought me back again into that old atmosphere. Now, however, I have reached the point that I feel ashamed when I see this undeserved love . . . which is unjust, which pains me. That's how far I have come. Perhaps, and I hope so, I will go even further. And that is perhaps your mission. You know that in Munich I am not spoiled, not treasured . . . and that for that reason it is difficult for me there (since I am just not that far advanced yet). Why do you want to make my home a bitter place too? Well, perhaps that's necessary. I mean, to begin with, it would be enough if I swallowed my pride and accepted the fact that you love me much less than I love you. Or should I just bear these "little" blows? I feel very depressed now and the night makes me shudder. It frightens me like those earlier nights when you slept and I tossed and turned in bed for hours and was pushed away by you when I came to you in despair. . . . I would like to live in solitude and push away life's adversities. Fine! I know it's mean-spirited. I know it very well. But I'm tired of being "generous." I am just tired of many things. I wish I could live only for art. Oh! To beard the "lion." I'm ready to beard the lion. I just don't want to have to beard the mouse. (December 8, 1910)

"I wish I could live only for art." Kandinsky was confronting the implications of accepting his ultimate disappointment with Münter. She would never love him enough to justify him wholly and unreservedly, to accept him despite his "evil" character. Indeed, her mission seemed to be quite the opposite, to force him to develop further, which meant in his own terms to become less narcissistic, by punishing him with criticisms and unavailability for his sense of entitlement. The sincerity of Kandinsky's guilt at the "undeserved" idolatry he got was not any the less for all his obvious rage at Münter's failure to spoil him like everyone else; the letter virtually proclaims his ambivalence about the hard necessity of leaving emotional childhood. Kandinsky seems to have been protesting rather too much the unconditional love he got as a child. At any rate, a curious coda to the letter, in which Kandinsky mentioned the immediate occasion of the bad mood in which he wrote it, offers some insight into the childhood origin of his expectations. "My bad mood came," he explained, "when I saw how much my mother is suffering (her wound opens so suddenly: we were talking at afternoon tea about Alex's childhood and she undoubtedly thought about other children), so that she retired after dinner. If I think about her burden, my heart bleeds. And she was certainly much more spoiled than I. That has to be paid for. With interest, without pity. Excuse me. I am hurting you. My heart hurts too. And properly so." [99] Identifying with his mother's suffering over her lost child, he expressed his own sense of being lost as well as the desire for his mother to grieve for him too—that at least is what seems to be hinted at in the enigmatic reference to her "undoubtedly" thinking about her "other children." She was paying the price for having had everything her way—a bit of wishful punishment—as he was paying the price in Münter's deficient love for his wanting everything his way. The alternative to this state of eternally frustrated desire was to live only for art—that is, to become totally self-sufficient in his art. He was ready to tackle that, he said, if he were up to it, but what if he were merely a mouse rather than the king of beasts? For the task of becoming an artist required not just self-sufficiency but greatness; it meant displacing nature from her primacy and forcing her to share the throne. And that represented not only self-conquest but conquest of the other, the feminine.

It was in this frame of mind that Kandinsky, not long after his return from Russia, met the two men whose support and example would help him to take the final step beyond dependence on nature, coincidentally but auspiciously on the occasion of the New Year of 1911. The young painter Franz Marc was the one artist who had come publicly to the defense of the New Artists' Association exhibit in the fall of 1910; Kandinsky met him for the first time on New Year's Eve and began the personal collaboration that would shortly produce the *Blue Rider Almanac* and the associated exhibitions. Marc was not only in crucial respects a kindred spirit but a practical facilitator; he persuaded his own publisher to publish Kandinsky's manuscript *On the Spiritual in Art,* which had lain in a drawer for two years after its initial rejection.

The second encounter was even more fateful from a theoretical point of view. On New Year's Day 1911, the members of the Association, joined by Marc, went to hear a concert of new music by Arnold Schönberg. Kandinsky, for whom painting had always "sounded" in musical resonance, conveyed the enormous impact of Schönberg's atonal music on him in a letter to the composer two weeks later: "In your works you have realized what I, albeit in uncertain form, have so greatly longed for in music. The independent progress through their own destinies, the independent life of the individual voices in your compositions, is exactly what I am trying to find in my paintings." What made for that "independent life," in Kandinsky's view, was Schönberg's break with traditional harmony.

> At the moment there is a great tendency in painting to discover the "new" harmony by constructive means, whereby the rhythmic is built on an almost geometric form. My own instinct and striving can support these tendencies only halfway. *Construction* is what has been so woefully lacking in the painting of recent times, and it is good that it is now being sought. But I think differently about the *type* of construction.
>
> I am certain that our own modern harmony is not to be found in the "geometric" way, but rather in the anti-geometric, anti-logical way. And this way is that of "dissonances in *art*,['] in painting, therefore just as much as in music. And "today's" dissonance in painting and music is merely the "consonance" of "tomorrow."[100]

Kandinsky's rejection of geometry in painting—so striking in the light of the severe geometry of the Bauhaus period a decade later—was meant as an embrace of radical disharmony and contradiction; the harmony he sought had to answer the problem of creating order out of disorder. Thus he did not fully accept Schönberg's equation of the anti-geometric and anti-logical with the unconscious; the painter had to employ them consciously and purposefully. "Up to now," he replied to the composer, "the painter has thought too little in general."[101] Kandinsky was concerned with more than pure self-expression uncensored by the conscious, rational mind. His was the metaphysical-psychological task of producing unity out of opposites, not only on the canvas, but as the condition of the aesthetic achievement, within himself. Unity required an intellectual solution, but it demanded something else first: a break with the "external feminine," and an internalization of its infinite power. He had not yet fully realized that, and so from his own point of view rightly felt that he had not yet achieved in painting what Schönberg had in music. "How immensely fortunate . . . musicians are," he wrote Schönberg a few months later, "in their highly advanced art, truly an art which has already the good fortune to forgo completely all

207
∎

purely practical aims. How long will painting have to wait for this? And painting also has the right (= duty) to it: color and line for their own sake—what infinite beauty and power these artistic means possess!"[102]

As it turned out, painting did not have to wait as long as Kandinsky's lament suggested. Just a few months after writing this letter, Kandinsky made the breakthrough in color theory that enabled him at long last to achieve the parity with nature and thus the independence he had been striving for. It happened, significantly, while he was alone; Münter had gone off to visit the various members of her family for a few months. It was as if he needed physical distance from her both to assuage the guilt of his emotional distance and to remove the temptation to dependence that her presence always created. The letter he wrote the very day of her departure was both an apology for the pain he caused her by his ambivalence and a projection of his relief at the liberation his solitude brought with it.

> You are sitting in the train now, my poor dear Ellchen. I think of you often and hope you get pleasure and enjoyment from the journey. I, of course, have nothing to report. I just want you to have a greeting from me soon after your arrival. With all my heart (words are always so stupid and feeble) I hope that you feel well in every sense, that you are recovering from me, and are in good, cheerful spirits. It grieves my heart (even though I am sometimes able to suppress it) that I make life so unpleasant for you. What's the use of telling you and myself that I cannot help it? Years ago I seriously thought of going to Siberia and freeing the people I love from me. It would be better if those people were to abandon me and I were alone and could do no damage. Why should I be the sacrificial knife? It is difficult to be defined that way. . . . (June 26, 1911)

A letter a few days later hints even more directly at his ambivalence over the opportunity that aloneness brought. "Your postcard is not yet here. Your room is empty—how strangely empty rooms sound—frozen, questioning, secretive. They act as if nothing had happened, but one can tell about them that they know. Often they look like a dog, which lies on its back with its legs in the air, tail tucked in and indicating: do what you want with me!" (June 30, 1911). Even his encouraging remarks to her projected his own inner workings. As she was on her way to Bonn, he wrote, "I should like you to achieve much good in general on your trip, that is, internally too. Such a trip (especially made alone) enriches the inner view and induces reflection. One collects much unconsciously, and only later does one know it . . ." (August 1, 1911).

He did not, however, expand on these gnomic remarks. When he did have something to report, it was the details of house-husbandry, the minutiae of gardening and housework that he genuinely enjoyed and shared with his companion. What he did not relay to her was the great discovery of that summer. That he described only a few years later, in a lecture that was scheduled for Cologne in 1914 but because of the outbreak of war was never given.

> The summer of 1911, which was unusually hot for Germany, lasted desperately long. . . . Suddenly, all nature seemed to me white; white (great silence—full of possibilities) displayed itself everywhere and expanded visibly. . . . Since that time, I know what undreamed-of possibilities this primordial color conceals within itself. . . . This discovery was of enormous importance for me. *I felt, with an exactitude I had never yet experienced, that the principal tone, the innate, inner character of a color, can be redefined ad infinitum by its different uses. . . . This revelation turned the whole of painting upside-down and opened up before it a realm in which one had previously been unable to believe. I.e., the inner, thousandfold, unlimited values of one and the same quality, the possibility of obtaining and applying infinite series simply in combination with one single quality, tore open for me the gates of the realm of absolute art.*[103]

It was sometime around this epiphany that Kandinsky painted *Picture with a Circle* (plate 3), his first abstract painting.

It is of telling significance that Kandinsky made his discovery through the color that represented to him the silence of aloneness, but it was not simply about one color. It was a discovery about the lack of objective foundation for the meaning of color altogether. That meaning, which for so long he had felt was given in nature, was, he now realized, defined only by the uses that the painter made of it. From a Postmodernist point of view, Kandinsky's revelation ought to have shattered his belief in the ontological soundness of "inner necessity" as an objective criterion for art. This is not at all how he interpreted it. On the contrary, it opened for him the "gates of the realm of absolute art." Its meaning for him was conditioned by the historical and conceptual context of his original dilemma—the problem posed by the artist's crisis of masculinity. His insight freed the painter to become a true creator who, godlike, self-sufficient, defined the meaning of color through his own usage without external constraint. Kandinsky's breakthrough almost reads like the origin of Clement Greenberg's famous comment on the metaphysical significance of Modernism: "The avant-garde poet or artist tried in effect to imitate God by creating something valid solely on its own terms, in the way nature itself is valid, in the way a landscape—not its picture—is aesthetically valid; something *given*, increate, independent of meanings, similars or originals"[104]—except that claiming ultimate creative power for Kandinsky was a struggle not with God but with the feminine, as well as with his own belief in her supremacy and his own readiness to worship her in return for her blessing. Now he was her equal, no longer needing to possess her in order to match her achievement. For a long time, he said in the autobiography he could now write from the vantage point of journey's end, he had been "conscious of the weakness of art, and of my own abilities in particular, in the face of nature. Years had to elapse before I arrived, by intuition and reflection, at the simple solution that the aims (and hence the resources too) of nature and of art were fundamentally, organically, and by the very nature of the world different—and equally great, which also means equally powerful."[105]

Intuition and reflection, however, had not been the whole story. The reason it had taken Kandinsky so long to arrive at abstraction was precisely that the issue for him *was* one of power, absolute power, not simply of knowledge. Painting was for him from the very beginning an expression of the will to power, in both the masculine and the Nietzschean metaphysical sense. The power originally vested in the feminine was the source of his aesthetic and personal difficulties. It was when she "refused" to grant it through unconditional love that the struggle shifted from obtaining it from her to freeing himself from the necessity of doing so. It was not a mere stylistic flourish that Kandinsky figured his artistic triumph over the canvas, pristine as nature herself, as a double conquest, of woman and of colonial empire.

210

> I learned to struggle with the canvas, to recognize it as an entity opposed to my wishes (= dreams), and to force it to submit to these wishes. At first, it stands there like a pure, chaste maiden, with clear gaze and heavenly joy— this pure canvas that is itself as beautiful as a picture. And then comes the imperious brush, conquering it gradually, first here, then there, employing all its native energy, like a European colonist who with axe, spade, hammer, saw penetrates the virgin jungle where no human foot has trod, bending it to conform to his will.[106]

The notion of conquest did not really contradict Kandinsky's assertion of equality with nature; before he could become her equal, he had to reduce her in his own mind. Nor did it contradict his liberalism, which in the years before World War I was far from precluding imperialist sentiments. Kandinsky is not on record directly on the subject of empire, but here he uttered one of the commonplaces of European imperialist rhetoric. Its masculinist orientation, the subject of a good deal of interpretation in recent postcolonial studies, is here almost openly avowed, if not in full self-awareness: the European colonist is exposed as a sexual violator. Though Kandinsky would have been horrified that such an inference could be read from his words, it is not inappropriate to their context. It took an act of emotional violence against Münter to free himself from his self-imposed tutelage to the feminine. It is not an accident that Kandinsky analogized the painter in terms of two contemporary icons of true masculinity, the virile "seducer" who takes women against their will and the heroic colonizer whose conquest of "virgin" nature is a sexual conquest.

Gabriele Münter was the midwife for Kandinsky's birth into aesthetic independence because she had been emotionally disqualified from becoming his wife. When his divorce became final in 1911, he did not marry her; and though they continued to live together until Kandinsky was forced to leave Germany as an enemy alien at the outbreak of the war, their relationship was effectively over as a love affair. The letters reveal the same recriminations as before on Münter's side and the same unconvincing efforts to reassure her on Kandinsky's. Münter remained invaluable to him as a friend, artistic companion, and ally in the Blue Rider years, and habit was difficult to break. It was finally the enforced separation of war that sealed what had been true for some time emotionally: he no longer needed her in the erotic-spiritual and aesthetic ways he once had.

211

The Garden of Love

> *My ideal of love is greater than my ability to embody it. Perhaps I once loved truly and never met "her" again. Perhaps I am searching for her.*
> —Wassily Kandinsky, letter to Gabriele Münter

But if the breakthrough to abstraction was the end of one story, it was only the beginning of another. Finding an autonomous creative language did not mean that Kandinsky had solved the problem of harmony he had set himself; he had only found the aesthetic means with which he might at last address it on his own terms. The enormous output of the years from 1911 to 1914 documents the struggle for aesthetic harmony along two axes. One of these might be labeled dualistic, the attempt to reconcile opposites; the other, harder to characterize in a word, was the effort to create order out of a disorder that was no longer simply seen as the conflict of opposites but as infinite multiplicity, or increasing chaos and fragmentation.

Since the work of Rose-Carol Washton Long, it has been generally recognized that Kandinsky's work was far from completely abstract before World War I. He not only gave thematic titles to many of his abstract paintings; many paintings with nonthematic titles, particularly the numbered series named *Improvisations* and *Compositions*—musical terms Kandinsky deliberately chose to emphasize their nonrepresentational intent—abound with discernible objects, though often stripped to bare suggestive lines: human figures, horses, lances, cannons, boats, angels, trumpets, mountains, kremlins. Long noted two main sets of themes in the titles and images. One includes representations of conflict, battle, and destruction, above all images of deluge and storm, with frequent overt biblical references to Noah's flood and the Apocalypse of Saint John. The second includes various representations of paradise. Two of the paintings in this group are titled *The Garden of Love*; they employ images of loving couples to represent the vision of harmony, rather than, she points out, the more traditional angels, and she remarks on their filiation with contemporary Symbolist ideas about sexuality.[107] The larger and better known of the two, the brightly colored *Improvisation 27 (The Garden of Love)* (plate 4), shows three couples spaced widely apart, anchoring the canvas at strategic places, two lying down and one seated and embracing. Kandinsky had not given up on the idea of love as the vehicle and embodiment of cosmic unity, however problematic it was personally. In fact the painting, darkened with patches of black, one representing a snake and another a member of one of the couples, introduces its own aesthetic disharmony into paradise. Oblique references to the situation with Münter are present even in very different representations of paradise. One of his glass paintings of the period called *Hellhound and Bird of Paradise* neatly compresses the opposing themes of evil and salvation into a pair of mythic creatures, a gorgeously plumed bird hovering with an open, perhaps angry beak over a magnificently menacing black panther. According to Münter herself, Kandinsky painted it in response to her wish that he should create something especially beautiful for her.[108] Whatever the exact provenance of the hidden and not-so-hidden images in the works of these years, whether Symbolist, theosophical, Christian, shamanistic,[109] or a syncretism of all four, they are concerned with the healing of strife, violence, and egotism through love. The testimony of *On the Spiritual in Art* argues explicitly that the dissonance that required healing was not only a matter of the external political and social world, but even more so of the inner and psychological world. The motif of the couple in the Murnau period points to the continuing importance of the idea of love as the path to cosmic harmony, even as the increasing vagueness and dematerialization of the representation of love indicate its emotional and aesthetic abstraction from its former concrete embodiment.

On a grander scale, dualism also structures the earliest surviving of Kandinsky's *Compositions,* the larger, carefully planned works in which he tried to work out his most difficult puzzles and that he regarded as his most important works.[110] *Composition IV* (plate 5), painted in 1911, is divided into two distinct sections by two vertical black lines, representing Cossack lances, which bisect the painting from top to bottom. Even Kandinsky's notes to *Composition IV,* which interpret the painting almost exclusively in formal terms, point out that the painting has two centers, one represented by "entangled lines" on the left and the other by the "acute form modeled in blue" on the right. He further emphasizes the work's formal dualism when listing the contrasts among its central formal features and points out that "the juxtaposition of [the] bright-sweet-cold tone [of the colors] with angular movement (battle) is the principal contrast in the picture."[111] The dualism, however, is even more strikingly apparent in thematic and iconographic terms, terms that Kandinsky expressly licensed not only with the references to "lance" and "battle" in his exposition, but in subtitling the composition *Battle.* The left side of the painting contains many images of conflict: the entangled lines Kandinsky mentioned, but also two horses leaping at one another in the upper left, lances, guns, and armed boats. The right side of the work represents the "Garden of Love," with its two couples, one reclining on the lower right, the other climbing a hill. The distinction between the two halves isn't absolute; a brilliant rainbow, more reminiscent of paradise, bridges the distance between two mountains on the left or battle side. But the overall effect, almost a diptych, is unmistakable. There is a unity of color tones across the whole painting, and portions of the hill and castle bisected by the lances appear in both parts, unifying them in that way; but neither the painting itself nor Kandinsky's comments suggest a successful harmonizing, if such was even the intention. The difficulty of unification is inherent in the dualistic project itself. The meaning of the "Garden of Love" symbolism is the sublimation of individuality, with its conflicting, embattled egotisms, into a higher unity, canceling out strife. Juxtaposing the two images, however, affirms the reality of strife and the utopian nature of love as a wishful response.

213

But Kandinsky was simultaneously wrestling with an even more encompassing problem that included but went beyond reconciling the forces of strife and love to harmonizing the infinite multiplicity and whirl of the universe. The succeeding prewar *Compositions, V* (1911) through *VII* (1913), show a progressive development toward a much looser, more chaotic structure and a corresponding effort to unify radical fragmentation. The tension is particularly striking in *Composition V* because the central unifying device, a thick black line that appears to whip out from the center of the painting toward the left, then loop around all the way to the right as if to contain the chaos, seems imposed upon the painting rather than emerging organically from it. Kandinsky explicitly said that the subject of *Composition V* was the Resurrection, and a close examination of the painting can reveal a detailed structure of iconographic allusions. These are so well concealed, however, that their interpretation is a matter of some controversy; more to the point, they are so thoroughly dissolved into the formal organization of the picture that the overall effect is of an abstract image.[112] The animating spirit of the painting is best caught in a remark about totality that Kandinsky himself made in a letter to Münter written between the painting of *Composition V* and *Composition VI*. "Yes, I also believe that at bottom or in the final analysis everything is one," he wrote her in late 1912. "It is simultaneously a double movement: 1) from the complex to the simple 2) the reverse. That is why I always sought unconsciously*—[note at the bottom of the letter: '*I understand it just now, in this instant']—to unite these two currents in my painting. I always wanted to combine these two incompatible principles. All revelations are like rays that in the end make up just one 'sun' = truth." To preserve particulars while unifying them in the one—little wonder that Kandinsky went on to remark in Platonic spirit that "numbers are just a bridge to number," but also that elementary forms like the triangle are too simple for the complexity of the cosmos that needs to be unified. Because of that, he concluded with an epigrammatic paradox, "today the inexact is more exact."[113] The paradox reflected both the formal problem and the personal situation out of which it emerged. The further Kandinsky got away from the concrete possibility of love while still retaining its afterimage, the more abstract its representation had to become, and the more difficult it became to represent unity out of the whirl of chaotic multiplicity.

The difficulty is apparent in Kandinsky's exposition of *Composition VI* (plate 6), subtitled *Deluge*. More dramatic, more active than *Composition V,* the painting, especially under the suggestion of the title, easily conveys the sense of storm and flood with roiling clouds and billowing waves. Kandinsky, however, insisted that it was not meant as a representation of the event that the word referred to, but rather as the evocation of the inner sense associated with the sound of the word, so that its interpretation had to be purely formal. Yet formalist interpretation yields thematic meaning, intrinsically and in the metaphors used to clarify it. This turbulent picture has two centers, Kandinsky pointed out, one on the left, delicate, rosy, somewhat blurred with weak, indefinite lines in the middle, the other on the right, a crude blue, discordant area with sharp, "rather evil, strong, very precise lines." There seems to be a natural association with the dualistic elements of *Composition IV* in this analysis, but here Kandinsky was explicit that there is a third center. Nearer to the left of the painting, vague and indistinct, is a center that one "only recognizes subsequently as being a center, but is, in the end, the principal center"—that is, the unification of the opposites, which enables the picture to "inwardly attain total equilibrium." In describing the nature and location of this center, Kandinsky volatilized it even further. The pink and white of this third center "seethe in such a way that they seem to lie neither upon the surface of the canvas nor upon any ideal surface." The center is somewhat like a man standing in the steam of a Russian steam bath, who is "neither close to nor far away; he is just *somewhere*. This feeling of 'somewhere' about the principal center determines the inner sound of the whole picture."[114]

What was this mysterious center, which was rendered here not so much by a some*thing* as by an indefinite some*where*? Pictorially it appears as the major element in two of Kandinsky's most important paintings in his last years before leaving Germany, *Composition VII,* from 1913, the climax of the *Composition* series in that period, and *Improvisation (Gorge),* from 1914. Conceptually its meaning emerges directly in the amazing letter that Kandinsky wrote Münter from Russia in 1915 that effectively announced the end of their relationship, though they would be together one last time for a period of some months at the end of that year.

Composition VII (plate 7), the most complex of them all, appears to be spatially organized around a vortex in the form of two rounded ovals at the center of the picture, but because of the extraordinary busyness of the painting, many other centers of action attract the viewer's attention. A more subtle point of organization is the lower right-hand corner of the painting, set off by a broad, sweeping light yellow band. Both it and the brown ground of the corner itself are relatively less busy than the other parts. Between them, two purple ovals represent, in their most abstract version yet, the couple of *The Garden of Love.* Throughout the rest of the painting can be discerned the shapes that suggest the other major themes of the paintings of these years, the Apocalypse, the Last Judgment, and the Resurrection. If the corner of *The Garden of Love* is the spiritual terminus of the painting, the point on which the chaos converges, or stops, it is nonetheless not the spatial point of gravitation; the vortex in the middle still carries the eye, visually undermining any notion of a final harmony. It is as if the image of the couple does not carry the conviction of the chaotic mass of the painting.

This last impression is borne out by *Improvisation (Gorge)* (plate 8), which Kandinsky painted in the summer of 1914, after a trip with Münter to Hell's Valley Gorge [*Höllentalklamm*] in the Bavarian Alps, a wildly spectacular ravine with a roaring waterfall created by glacial runoff crashing down the precipitous rocky face. The picture presents the chaotic spirit of the scene rather than a realistic representation, though concrete images from the actual location are easily discernible. In the words of one of Kandinsky's most knowledgeable commentators, "A whirlwind of the most heterogeneous patterns, with no relationship to each other, seems to have been let loose upon the canvas." Eventually the viewer discerns a very small image of a couple in Bavarian dress standing by a small boat dock in the lower center of the painting, overwhelmed and all but obscured by the chaos around and above them. A figure on horseback holding aloft a scale suggests its meaning: the Apocalypse.[115] But, as another commentator perceptively notes, the title and the entire ambience of the painting, bathed in yellows and reds, suggest that what he had in mind was the late afternoon Moscow of his artistic inspiration,[116] and Kandinsky did refer to the painting as "his Moscow."[117] In *Improvisation (Gorge)* the couple is clearly identifiable both iconographically and biographically, a rarity in the Murnau period; Kandinsky's identification of the painting with Moscow suggests that he had here explicitly linked Münter with his idealized inspiration. Even more obviously than in *Composition VII,* however, the couple does not represent a point of rest, a response to the chaos; rather it is threatened with annihilation. Taken together with *Composition VII, Improvisation (Gorge)* suggests that where the "center" is concrete and identifiable, it is powerless to organize chaos and fragmentation; where it is vague, it is as unlocatable as a shadowy figure in steam.

216

The key to this dilemma is to be found in the letter that Kandinsky wrote to Münter from Russia in 1915 explaining the collapse of their relationship even as she waited for him to rejoin her in Stockholm, where they were both to have exhibits of their work.

> I am not at all good at being clear about my personal life. Here I am too impulsive, too flighty, and too moody. Only in art do I know truly, definitively and infallibly what I want. That's why I also accomplish something. In my personal life, I don't know what I owe to whom, or to whom I would like to give. Only one thing is clear, that I don't want anyone to suffer because of me. And this desire to do right by everyone leads to the exact opposite result; I do everyone wrong. In art I am infallible, like the Pope, and despotic, like a king. In life I am like a feeble stream, that doesn't flow strongly anywhere because it wants to flow in all directions at once. Such a person should be alone. In one point only do my art and my life agree, in that I want to have complete freedom. Every limitation is real suffering for me. I sometimes envy terribly people who go out together, come home together, spend the night together and wake up with the feeling, the knowledge, "he is here," "she is here." I know that this envy is unfruitful, because that kind of life can only satisfy me for a short time—I immediately long for freedom and aloneness. Aloneness above all. That is perhaps because my ideal of love is greater than my ability to embody it. *Perhaps I once loved truly and never met "her" again. Perhaps I am searching for her.* If these words hurt you, don't forget that they pain me no less. I would like to surrender my heart and I can't. Perhaps it is not my line. Love, according to my ideal, must be boundless and in every way fruitful. In that way, I love

only art. Perhaps two such loves in one heart are impossible. Perhaps, however, I am impotent in human love. You also never experienced the love of which I speak and never had it for me. That's why I said to you (perhaps half unconsciously) that you never really loved me. And a life together as man and wife without this love is a compromise with a smaller or greater aftertaste of a lie, or a sin. (March 12, 1915; italics added)

With astounding acuteness, if not full self-knowledge, Kandinsky offered here the vital clue to his quest both in love and in art, and the reason for the failure of the former. He was searching for a lost yet indefinite "someone," who alone could supply him with the wholeness he had lost with her departure. The one he had chosen for that role had disappointed him—even this last confession is an accusation—and he turned more wholly to the sphere in which he could exert complete control once he had stopped depending on her. Abstraction had made him "infallible, like the Pope." Yet, as he also acknowledged, he had not even at that point given up the quest for the lost "her," the vision of love that would harmonize his life and enable him to create the artistic harmony that could inspire the whole world. As much as anything, that continuing quest explains Kandinsky's continuing to resort to objective imagery for some years after the breakthrough to abstraction.

217

Whether it also explains his sudden marriage to a young Russian woman early in 1917, just a few months after his last letter to Münter, is harder to answer. Nina Andreevskaia was about the same age as Münter had been when she and Kandinsky met and according to her fell passionately in love in September 1916. But it does appear to explain an extraordinary mirror image of *Improvisation (Gorge)* that Kandinsky painted that same year. This oil is explicitly titled *Moscow I*—he did a second version a little later that year—and it centers on a small couple very much like the one in the *Improvisation*. The couple is much more immediately visible, however, not overwhelmed by chaos but the focus of a clearly structured though highly detailed cityscape that wheels about them and a burst of yellow light just in front of them. In an astonishing letter to Münter, Kandinsky described the spirit of the painting without any mention of Nina, about whom Münter would only learn years later. "You know that I had this dream of painting a large picture inspired by happiness, joy of life, or of the universe," he wrote. "Quite suddenly I am aware of the harmony of colors and forms, which come from this world of joy" (November 26, 1916). Finally, and with an abruptness that was nothing short of breathtaking, it appeared that Kandinsky had arrived at his long-sought goal.

The apparent climax was in fact an anticlimax. Within a few years Kandinsky's style was to change radically once again. After a brief "regression" in 1917–18 in which he painted a series of Rococo, Biedermeier, and high society genre scenes reminiscent of his work between 1903–7, he began working toward the geometrical style that would characterize his work during the 1920s when he taught at the Bauhaus. Once again the relative rapidity and radical nature of the shift, from chaotic, biomorphic forms to rigid geometry, challenges critical analysis. And yet it would seem in the logic of Kandinsky's original breakthrough to abstraction that the satisfaction of his quest for love on the emotional level could no longer have the impact on his work that he had thought it would. He would have to find the sources of order not in allusions to the "Garden of Love" but in the formal means of line and space itself, in the cool and highly structured forms of geometry. There were signs of this reality even in the continuity of representation in the period between 1911 and 1914. Alongside the image of the couple there was another recurrent image, of the solo rider, the warrior, Saint George, the prophet, the shaman, who would bring the spiritual message of aesthetic order to humankind. Whatever their roots in the different traditions from which Kandinsky worked, they were all representations of a masculinity not empowered by love but by the strength of its own artistic message.

That Kandinsky thought of abstraction as a specifically *masculine* style precisely because it had freed itself from representation, hence dependency on the feminine, he made almost explicit in an introductory essay that he wrote for an exhibition of Münter's work in April 1913. In the very compliments he paid her there lay an implicit judgment of the inferiority of a body of work that remained, despite his example, resolutely representational. When the visitor first walks in, Kandinsky wrote,

> he feels himself surrounded by a feminine soul. It is especially pleasant to note that it is impossible to explain the origin of precisely this feeling. Gabriele Münter does not paint "feminine" motifs; she does not work with feminine material and does not allow herself feminine coquetry. Here one sees neither sentimentality [*Schwärmerei*] nor refined external elegance nor attractive weakness. But on the other hand, no manly allure, that is, no "forceful brushwork," no "brusquely dashed off heaps of color". . . . The robust, inner, let us say directly the genuine German talent of Gabriele Münter should be characterized from the beginning and exclusively as a purely feminine one.[118]

Kandinsky never said exactly what he meant by her femininity, as distinct from the stereotypical femininity that he said she rejected. In the light of the history we have traced here, it seems highly probable that it refers to the continuing dependency on the natural world that he had had to overcome to become, at long last, himself—a truly creative, truly masculine, painter.

CONCLUSION

We poor plebeians and outcasts who honor a feminine cultural and artistic ideal despite the contemptuous laughter of the Renaissance-men . . . can expect from woman as artist the most remarkable and interesting things, that indeed at some point she can even reach a position of artistic leadership amongst us. . . . The eternal feminine draws us onwards.

—Thomas Mann, "The Eternal Feminine"

That Mann may not have really meant what he wrote about women and artistic leadership is less surprising than the fact that he wrote it at all. Whatever tactical role the statement played in his private battle with contemporary literature, and especially with his brother's work, for the acceptance and preeminence of his own, proclaiming the superiority of a feminine cultural ideal was a complete reversal of contemporary gender norms and stereotypes. A similar reversal is at the heart of the work of Wedekind and Kandinsky as well.

It is true that Mann's equation of true passion with the feminine was precisely what made it problematic for him as a man. It is also true that the Modernist image of woman contained many traditional elements. Kandinsky yearned for a lost paradise of unity and harmony that could only be created by the love of a long-lost but always unconsciously known maternal figure. Even Wedekind's idealized circus riders and tightrope walkers could be argued to reduce to the tired cliché of female sensuality. But these are at best superficial readings. Wedekind's tightrope walker was hardly the simple embodiment of traditional feminine grace. She was the Nietzschean *Übermensch,* a psychological and ethical model of individualistic self-sufficiency, flexibility, and courage as she crossed the abyss of life unsupported by any-thing except her own exquisite sense of balance. Kandinsky's "Mother Moscow" and nature were also not conventional nineteenth-century femi-nine images; they were the absolute creative force that both produced the chaotic, conflicting multiplicity of the cosmos and integrated it into a harmonious aesthetic whole, the "All" that the arch-misogynist Otto Weininger explicitly attributed to masculinity. And even Mann's yearning femininity was not traditionally passive but ragingly Dionysian, a demand-ing, voracious, sexual, destructive striving for unity with the ground of be-ing, while his ideal of the writer entailed the incorporation of the Dionysian as an indispensable element. All three of the figures, two of them explicitly, identified with the Nietzschean standpoint and the Nietzschean ideal of human creative mastery and self-overcoming. This was not uncom-mon for artists and intellectuals of the period; what is wholly unexpected is the extent to which they identified the Nietzschean ideal with the femi-nine.

220

From another point of view, however, such a conception of the feminine in the high literary and artistic tradition of Europe shouldn't surprise as much as it does. The image of the feminine in European Romanticism was quite different from that represented in the domesticity of Victorianism or in the premodern stereotype that Simmel invoked as the obverse of moder-nity. Whether nature, nation, or erotic beloved, the Romantic feminine was not a figure of unindividuated unity but the, admittedly contradictory, im-age of the omnipotent creative maternal force whose sheltering but em-powering embrace made infinite individuality both possible and safe for the Romantic artist. The continuity of such an image of the feminine into Modernism further justifies the occasional characterization of early Mod-ernism as a late Romanticism.

Of course even on this point, Romanticism and Modernism were not the same. The Romantic artist projected the ideal of totality onto the femi-nine with relatively little anxiety and allowed himself to be enfolded by it without a real sense of threat to his individuality or his masculinity. The Romantics were able to contain a deep contradiction in their sense of masculine-feminine relationships, epitomized in the mother-infant babe analogy on which Wordsworth drew to define the poet's relationship with nature, or the sun-moon metaphor that Friedrich Schlegel elaborated in *Lucinde.* Though the male in Schlegel's construction needs to see himself re-flected in the admiring gaze of the female moon-mirror to sustain his sense of infinite individuality, he is at the same time the sun, the very source of the light that the mirror reflects back to him. The male is the active, creative principle, the female the passive, created principle. Nevertheless it was also the case that for Schlegel only a woman who was herself a creative artist, daring and independent enough to flout society's rules and leave husband and children to live on her own, was able to function for the man as an enabling mirror. It was the Romantic artist's ability to compartmentalize these contradictory elements that made it possible for him to find support for his masculinity in the idea of a powerful femininity.

The Modernist was no longer able to do so as easily. The difference lay in the passing of a century, in the evolution of bourgeois society and the changes in both the role of the artist and the situation of women over that time. Though some of the Romantics, such as Schlegel, were proto-feminists who wanted greater equality and more legal rights for women, they did not have to face the specter of truly independent women entering the public sphere. The power of women for the Romantics was largely notional, emotional, and imaginative. At the same time, Romantics did not feel themselves to be weaker than other men; they were not alienated from the polity or even from political power. A surprising number of Romantics—Wordsworth, Schlegel, Chateaubriand, Constant—held political office, some at fairly high levels; one Romantic poet, Lamartine, even provisionally headed a government. Whether conservatives or liberals politically—depending on how they tilted the Romantic synthesis of infinite individuality and fusion with the infinite whole—they all believed in the continuity of art and politics and in their own ability to use the first to influence the second. The alienation of the artist from economic individualism and bourgeois utilitarianism started with the Romantics themselves, many of whom came to see industrial modernity as incompatible with the development of true individuality, but that tended only to drive them to conservative politics, not away from politics altogether. In Germany a characteristic form of political Romanticism was strengthened by the displacement of the ideal of individuality from the individual on to the collectivity. The retreat of the disappointed French Romantics of 1830 into aestheticism was a harbinger of things to come, but even for French Romanticism there would be a renewal of political hope in the 1840s. Nor did the vicissitudes of politics and society dampen the Romantic's confidence that the artist was the anointed spokesman of true freedom and transcendence and could therefore act as the unacknowledged legislator of mankind, if not the acknowledged one.

By the end of the century, however, the power of capitalist industrialism and the materialist ethos seemed to have swept all before them. Like the Romantics who had turned against the commercial-industrial revolution, the Modernists wanted to be prophets of true individuality against self-interested egoism, of ethical and transcendent spirituality against all-encompassing bourgeois materialism. But precisely because of its triumphant spread, they felt their own position to be more difficult and precarious. Masculinity itself had become identified with material productive power, with sensual repression coupled with hypocritical sexual self-indulgence and exploitation, with competitive egoism. Only women, until then largely excluded from the public sphere, seemed to have escaped the spiritual deformation of modern society without having succumbed to inert passivity. Only the feminine seemed to many artists capable of functioning as a counterimage of sensual spontaneity, self-sufficiency, and transcendental spirituality. Strikingly, of the figures discussed in this study, Wedekind and Mann explicitly saw the defects of masculine modernity embodied in their own bourgeois fathers, and all three saw the saving powers and virtues of femininity embodied in their mothers. Wedekind linked femininity with the recognized countercultural trope of the circus, part of the world of popular entertainment his mother had come from. Kandinsky's "Mother Moscow" was the synthesis of medieval harmonious community and modern individuation, as his mother combined domesticity with a powerful, independent will. Mann's identification with his mother's musical bent, as well as his homosexual passion, sensitized him to the awareness that in a world where masculinity had become synonymous with rational mastery and competitive domination, the urge to worship, the quest for transcendence, was itself "feminine."

At the end of the nineteenth century, however, the idealization of the feminine was far more problematic for male artists than it had been at the beginning. As artists, their own masculinity was more in question, not only for others but even for themselves, in a world where concrete material productivity had joined with military prowess and political power to define the masculine. Wedekind's *Samson* was perhaps the most poignant statement of the "femininity" of art, derived from weakness and yearning, and Mann's *Death in Venice* the most philosophically profound. Furthermore, the very women that Modernists idealized were also part of the problem. Themselves personally drawn to "New Women" artists, writers, actresses because of their energy, creativity, initiative, and passion, the Modernists were also afraid of the New Woman as a social-political phenomenon. Not content to embody the Modernist ideal, she seemed all too bent on joining the enemy, the bourgeois world of work and material success. And even the women they were drawn to were not content to be the personification of idealized abstractions, but in all their humanity made demands, or simply represented demands, that put further strain on their already threatened sense of masculine power. Finally, not the least source of threat to Modernist masculinity derived from the fact that Modernists had not by any means fully relin-

222
■

quished the nineteenth-century stereotypes of feminine passivity and weakness. This pervasive contradiction in their image of women made the desire to identify with a feminine ideal doubly threatening: men were faced with the paradoxical difficulty of appropriating the feminine as men and with the danger of being feminized if they succeeded.

The result of such difficulties was that Modernists often found themselves as much in an adversarial relationship with the feminine as in one of advocacy. The heightened awareness of the power of femininity did not result in a breakdown of gender identity polarization in Modernism, but rather in an urge to appropriate the feminine for masculinity itself, in the hopes of restoring or reformulating masculine creative identity. It was a complex maneuver, bound by its essential contradictions to fail in personal and logical terms, but artistically, where contradiction could be part of the aesthetic effect, enormously fruitful. Wedekind's most successful and influential work—especially *Spring's Awakening,* the Lulu plays, and even *The Marquis of Keith*—was built stylistically and in content on the tension between appropriating and combating the feminine. Mann's very conception of writing was driven by the goal of both incorporating and linguistically mastering "feminine" experience. And Kandinsky's abstraction was perhaps the most dramatic example of the effort to assimilate the maternal ground of being and feminine creativity in the service of the creative, masterful autonomous masculine self. But while all these Modernists held to the desire to reestablish a traditional male potency, their identification of the universal ideals of liberation of the body, unity of body and spirit, psychological self-sufficiency, and yearning for totality with the feminine, not simply as the figuration of abstractions like nature but in the visible figures of real women—artists, performers, mothers, lovers, wives—logically at least prepared the ground for the undermining of gender polarities, and hence of the traditional masculinity they wanted to rescue.

223

NOTES

Introduction

1. A. Strindberg, *The Father: A Tragedy in Three Acts; and, A Dream Play,* trans. V. Anderson (Arlington Heights, Ill., 1964), 40, 56.

2. P. Gay, *The Cultivation of Hatred,* vol. 3, *The Bourgeois Experience: Victoria to Freud* (New York, 1993), 299–300.

3. F. Kafka, *Letter to His Father,* trans. E. Kaiser and E. Wilkins (New York, 1953), 99.

4. W. Rubin, H. Seckel, and J. Cousins, *Les Demoiselles d'Avignon, Studies in Modern Art, No. 3* (New York, 1994), 16.

5. Ibid., 14.

6. S. M. Gilbert and S. Gubar, *The Madwoman in the Attic: The Woman Writer and the Nineteenth-Century Literary Imagination* (New Haven, 1979).

7. Specific mention of individual works in this much contested area risks the charge of omitting all the other important ones. For one recent comprehensive overview of the literature and the issues that also makes its own contribution to the problem of definition, see A. Eysteinsson, *The Concept of Modernism* (Ithaca, 1990). There is a very wide-ranging and useful collection of articles in C. Berg, F. Durieux, and G. Lernout, *The Turn of the Century: Modernism and Modernity in Literature and the Arts* (Berlin and New York, 1995), which, however, does not supplant the older collection edited by M. Bradbury and J. McFarlane, eds., *Modernism: 1890–1930* (London, 1976). Other works on Modernism will be referred to at appropriate places in the discussion.

8. C. Butler, *Early Modernism: Literature, Music and Painting in Europe, 1900–1916* (Oxford, 1994), 3. My preliminary working definition of Modernism is close to Butler's.

9. See for Europe, M. Roper and J. Tosh, eds., *Manful Assertions: Masculinities in Britain Since 1800* (London, 1991); R. S. Nye, *Masculinity and Male Codes of Honor in Modern France* (Oxford, 1993); U. Frevert, *"Mann und Weib, und Weib und Mann": Geschlechter-Differenzen in der Moderne* (Munich, 1995); W. Erhart and B. Herrmann, *Wann ist der Mann ein Mann: Zur Geschichte der Männlichkeit* (Stuttgart and Weimar, 1997); and the pioneering synthesizing work of G. L. Mosse, *The Image of Man: The Creation of Modern Masculinity* (New York and Oxford, 1996). There are also a number of recent studies for the United States by Harry Brod, Kevin White and E. Anthony Rotundo.

At least some anthropological work suggests that there may be limits to the cultural malleability of the idea of masculinity, or, more precisely, that there seem to be some near-universal constraints in the definition of masculinity across cultures. David Gilmore concludes on the basis of both his own fieldwork and his extensive survey of others that "wherever 'real' manhood is emphasized, three moral injunctions seem to come repeatedly into focus. . . . To be a man in most societies . . . one must impregnate women, protect dependents from danger, and provision kith and kin." Furthermore, he argues, most cultures do not regard maturation into manhood as an innate biological development, a fact that crucially differentiates it from maturation into femininity. Virtually all cultures, he notes, have more or less elaborate rites of passage, usually demanding feats of endurance and courage, which boys have to pass through to become men; those same cultures may or may not ceremonially mark the girl's transition to womanhood with the onset of the menses. Gilmore's explanation for this disparity, which in many cultures is seen as the result of an "organic" weakness of masculinity, is biological, cultural, and psychoanalytic. In most societies men have been assigned the tasks of provisioning and protecting that involve physical danger because of their greater bodily strength and the realities of childbearing. These tasks thus often run against the desire for self-preservation, and the natural psychological tendency for men is therefore to wish to regress to the safety of childhood. The purpose of the rite of passage is to counteract this natural tendency through positive and negative social inducements of approval and shame. The virtual omnipresence in cultures of an ideal of omnicompetent masculinity is, Gilmore hypothesizes, counterphobic, a reaction-formation against the ever-present temptation in the male to regression to safety "at mother's side." Gilmore, *Manhood in the Making: Cultural Concepts of Masculinity* (New Haven, 1990), 151–53, 162, 220–28. Even if Gilmore's hypotheses are correct, however, they allow much scope for cultural and historical variety within their parameters. They even offer categories for interpreting the changes historians believe they observe in the ideal of manhood over time in their focus on the needs of procreation, economics, and combat.

10. See for example, P. Gay, *The Education of the Senses,* vol. 1, *The Bourgeois Experience: Victoria to Freud* (New York, 1984); and B. Dykstra, *Idols of Perversity: Fantasies of Feminine Evil in Fin-de-Siècle Culture* (New York and Oxford, 1986).

11. For example, A. Mauge, *L'Identité masculine en crise au tournant du siècle, 1871–1914* (Paris, 1987).

12. See for example, Gay, "The Powerful, Weaker Sex," in *The Cultivation of Hatred,* chap. 4; Mosse, "Masculinity in Crisis: The Decadence," in *The Image of Man,* chap. 5; A. McLaren, "Masculinities," in *The Trials of Masculinity: Policing Sexual Boundaries, 1870–1930* (Chicago, 1997), part 1.

13. McLaren, *Trials of Masculinity,* 2.

14. Mosse, *Image of Man,* 3.

15. Ibid., 17–20.

16. Ibid., 23–39.

17. Gay, *Cultivation of Hatred,* 96. Free trade was defended in the nineteenth century partly as a moral policy that would put an end to war by creating an international network of economic interdependency, but even defenders of capitalism such as Herbert Spencer, who thought the warrior virtues appropriate to an earlier stage of civilization, still saw the economic sphere as a conflict where only the fittest survive.

18. Ibid., 103.

19. See for example, U. Frevert, "Bourgeois Honour: Middle-Class Duelists in Germany from the Late Eighteenth to the Early Twentieth Century," in *The German Bourgeoisie,* ed. D. Blackbourn and R. J. Evans (London, 1993), 224–54; and Frevert, "*Mann und Weib,*" especially the last section.

20. Frevert, "*Mann und Weib,*" 150, which cites explicit letters between the Siemens brothers to this effect.

21. Cited in ibid., 151.

22. On both humanist and Romantic ideals of wholeness, see my *Impossible Individuality: Romanticism, Revolution, and the Origins of Modern Selfhood* (Princeton, 1992). For direct testimony from German bourgeois husbands in the later nineteenth century on this point, see Frevert, "*Mann und Weib,*" 152–54.

23. Mosse, *Image of Man,* 48–52.

24. See for example, M. Horkheimer et al., *Studien über Autorität und Familie* (Paris, 1936). But the same point is also made by E. J. Hobsbawm, *The Age of Empire, 1875–1914* (New York, 1989), 187, citing the 1923 work of the German economic historian A. S. von Waltershausen.

25. Mauge, *L'Identité masculine en crise,* 71–72.

26. J. Le Rider, *Modernity and Crises of Identity: Culture and Society in Fin-de-Siècle Vienna,* trans. R. Morris (New York, 1993); J. E. Toews, "Refashioning the Masculine Subject in Early Modernism: Narratives of Self-Dissolution and Self-Construction in Psychoanalysis and Literature, 1900–1914," *MODERNISM/modernity* 4.1 (1997): 31–67.

27. G. L. Mosse, *Nationalism and Sexuality: Respectability and Normal Sexuality in Modern Europe* (New York, 1985).

28. Hobsbawm, *Age of Empire,* 83.

29. On these issues, see Mosse, "Masculinity in Crisis: The Decadence," in *Image of Man,* 77–106.

30. D. F. Greenberg, *The Construction of Homosexuality* (Chicago, 1988), 408–10.

31. See Frevert, "*Mann und Weib,*" 112.

32. Gay, *Cultivation of Hatred,* 361.

33. O. Weininger, *Sex and Character* (London and New York, 1906).

34. Mauge, *L'Identité masculine en crise,* 74.

35. Hobsbawm, *Age of Empire,* 187–88.

36. See e.g., C. Hilmes, *Die Femme fatale: Ein Weiblichkeitstypus in der nachromantischen Literatur* (Stuttgart, 1990), which focuses on the literary images of Joanna, Judith, Delilah, and Salomé in the works of such writers as Heine, Flaubert, Mallarmé, Wilde, Panizza, Wedekind, and Heinrich Mann. The rubrics and explanations of her background chapter imply a much more general social crisis of masculinity, e.g., "Die Femme fatale als Spiegel einer Krisis des (männlichen) Selbstbewusstseins," vi.

37. Le Rider, *Modernity and Crises of Identity,* 89–90.

38. Ibid., 77–78. Le Rider draws heavily on modern psychoanalytic theory, particularly the "object relations" school of D. W. Winnicott, whom he quotes on the necessity of a sense of being for the sense of self, and the pioneering gender identity work of Robert Stoller, who pointed out the crucial role and problem of male feminine identification for the creation of male gender identity.

39. Ibid., 165.

40. R. Felski, *The Gender of Modernity* (Cambridge, Mass.: 1995), 91.

41. Ibid., 37–38.
42. Ibid., 112.
43. Le Rider, *Modernity and Crises of Identity*, 165.
44. I have done a study of Schiele along these lines that will be published separately.
45. Felski, *Gender of Modernity*, 92.
46. Le Rider, *Modernity and Crises of Identity*, 77.
47. Ibid., 118.
48. On the artists' community in Schwabing, see D. Heisserer, *Wo die Geister Wandern: Eine Topographie der Schwabinger Bohème um 1900* (Munich, 1993); on the network of institutions and ideas that supported Munich's theater, see P. Jelavich, *Munich and Theatrical Modernism: Politics, Playwriting and Performance, 1890–1914* (Cambridge, Mass., 1985).

Chapter One

1. F. Wedekind, *Die junge Welt,* in *Frank Wedekind: Gesammelte Werke,* eds. A. Kutscher and R. Friedenthal, vol. 2 (Munich, 1920), 90. (Cited as *GW.*)
2. F. Wedekind, "Der Witz und seine Sippe," in *Frank Wedekind: Werke in zwei Bänden,* ed. E. Weidl, vol. 1 (Munich, 1990), 342. (Cited as Weidl.)
3. F. Wedekind, "Zirkusgedanken," in Weidl, 362.
4. See for example, S. Gittleman, *Frank Wedekind* (New York, 1969), 35, 52; E. Boa, *The Sexual Circus: Wedekind's Theatre of Subversion* (Oxford, 1987), 82; R. Florack, *Wedekinds "Lulu": Zerrbild der Sinnlichkeit* (Tübingen, 1995), 140.
5. F. Wedekind, *Erdgeist* (1913), in *Werke: Kritische Studienausgabe,* Bd. III, 1, ed. H. Vinçon (Darmstadt, 1996), 405. My translation. I have made no attempt to follow Wedekind's rhyme scheme so as to translate the meaning as closely as possible. For a freer English translation that does try to preserve Wedekind's poetry, see *The Lulu Plays,* trans. C. R. Mueller (New York, 1967), 31.
6. The case for a radical difference between the Lulu of the *Monstertragedy* and the Lulu of *Earth Spirit* and *Pandora's Box* has been made in great detail and quite forcefully by R. Florack in *Wedekinds "Lulu."* I will take up some of the issues at stake in my own discussions of the plays.
7. F. Wedekind, "Zirkusgedanken," in Weidl, 365. The Trakehner was a horse bred in the Trakehnen stud in East Prussia, known for its strength and speed.
8. Ibid., 365, 366.
9. Ibid., 356.
10. Ibid., 365.
11. F. Wedekind, "Im Zirkus: II: Das hängende Drahtseil," in *Werke in zwei Bänden,* ed. Weidl, 375.
12. Ibid., 374–75.
13. F. Wedekind, "Zirkusgedanken," in Weidl, 358.
14. F. Wedekind, "Im Zirkus," in Weidl, 376–77.
15. Ibid., 363.
16. F. Wedekind, *Die junge Welt,* 15–16.
17. F. Wedekind, *Diary of an Erotic Life,* ed. G. Hay and trans. W. E. Yuill (Oxford, 1990), July 20, 1889, 61.
18. R. J. Evans, *The Feminist Movement in Germany, 1894–1933* (London, 1972), 26–28.

19. C. Hilmes, *Die Femme fatale: Ein Weiblichkeitstypus in der nachromantischen Literatur* (Stuttgart, 1990), 53ff.

20. Most of the biographical information about Wedekind's father and mother is taken from Rolf Kieser's indispensable biography of Wedekind's early years: *Benjamin Franklin Wedekind: Biographie einer Jugend* (Zurich, 1990).

21. Kieser, *Wedekind,* 43.

22. Ibid., 51.

23. Ibid., 62.

24. Ibid., 63.

25. F. Wedekind, *Diary,* 1.

26. Ibid., 8. The German version gives the date as February 16, 1888, which the English corrects to 1887, but this cannot be right; the correspondence between Frank and Minna indicates that these entries are even later than the German version suggests, probably the winter of 1888–89.

27. Peter Gay's studies of the nineteenth-century bourgeoisie argues that they were far more sexual than the conventional understanding of Victorianism would have us believe, but it is still necessary to make a distinction between what Victorians did in private and what they said about it publicly.

28. F. Wedekind, letter to Anny Barck, February 1884, *Der Vermummte Herr: Briefe Frank Wedekinds aus den Jahren 1881–1917,* ed. W. Rasch (Munich, 1967), 19. Rasch gives her name as Barte, but Elke Austermühl corrects this in her introduction to the correspondence between Frank and his cousin Minna von Greyerz. See E. Austermühl, "Eine Lenzburger Jugendfreundschaft. Der Briefwechsel zwischen Frank Wedekind und Minna von Greyerz," in *Frank Wedekind: Texte, Interviews, Studien,* eds. E. Austermühl, A. Kessler, and H. Vinçon, *Pharus,* vol. 1 (Darmstadt, 1989), 343.

29. F. Wedekind, letter to Bertha Jahn, April 1885, in *Der Vermummte Herr,* ed. Rasch, 37–38.

30. F. Wedekind, letter to Minna, June 1884, in *Texte, Interviews, Studien,* eds. Austermühl, Kessler, and Vinçon, 380–81.

31. Kieser, *Wedekind,* 220.

32. Ibid., 199.

33. Ibid., 140.

34. Ibid., 261.

35. Ibid., 181.

36. Ibid., 159.

37. F. Wedekind, *Diary,* 5, 8, 11. The dates in both the English and German editions are, as noted, unreliable; the entries seem to be from the winter of 1888–89.

38. Kieser, "The Opening of Pandora's Box: Frank Wedekind, Nietzsche, Freud and Others," in *Frank Wedekind: Yearbook 1991,* eds. R. Kieser and R. Grimm (Bern, 1991), 10.

39. F. Wedekind, *Diary,* July 27, 1889, 67.

40. Liberalism was inconsistent on this issue. The doctrine of free trade promised to end the necessity for war by creating a network of international interdependence upon which the material prosperity of each nation depended.

41. F. Wedekind, *Mine-Haha, oder, Über die körperliche Erziehung des jungen Mädchen,* in *Frank Wedekind: Werke in drei Bänden,* ed. M. Hahn, vol. 3 (Berlin and Weimar, 1969), 113. (Cited as Hahn.)

42. All of these views are canvassed in W. B. Lewis's survey of the critical literature in *The Ironic Dissident: Frank Wedekind in the View of His Critics* (Columbia, 1997), 143–47.

43. F. Wedekind, letter to a critic, December 12, 1891, in *Werke in drei Bänden,* ed. Hahn, vol. 3, 452.

44. F. Wedekind, *Spring's Awakening: Tragedy of Childhood,* trans. E. Bentley (New York, 1960, 1995), 48.

45. Boa, *The Sexual Circus,* 42.

46. It was first published by the German theater magazine *Theater Heute* in 1988, and a scholarly version appeared in Pharus III, edited by H. Vinçon, in 1990.

47. F. Wedekind, *Spring's Awakening,* note 9. In fact, however, the affair began only after Wedekind left Paris, that is, after the composition of the first version of *Earth Spirit.*

48. Florack, *Wedekinds "Lulu,"* 82.

49. Ibid., 163–64.

50. T. Wedekind, *Lulu, Die Rolle meines Lebens* (Munich, 1969), 175.

51. F. Wedekind, *The First Lulu,* trans. E. Bentley (New York, 1994), 88.

52. For an interesting discussion of this and other aspects of the Pierrot figure, see N. Ritter, "The Portrait of Lulu as Pierrot," *Frank Wedekind: Yearbook 1991,* eds. Kieser and Grimm, 127–40.

53. F. Wedekind, *First Lulu,* 35.

54. F. Wedekind, *Earth Spirit,* in *The Lulu Plays,* trans. Mueller, 89.

55. F. Wedekind, *First Lulu,* 45.

56. F. Wedekind, *Earth Spirit,* 77.

57. F. Wedekind, *First Lulu,* 178.

58. F. Wedekind, *Earth Spirit,* 99.

59. F. Wedekind, *Pandora's Box,* in *The Lulu Plays,* trans. Mueller, 123.

60. For the most up-to-date account of facts and theories about Jack the Ripper, see *The Mammoth Book of Jack the Ripper,* edited by M. Jakubowski and N. Braund (New York, 1999).

61. Bentley's stage directions in his English translation locate the first three acts in Munich, but he notes that Wedekind did not do so and that when he wrote the play, Wedekind had not lived for any great length of time in any German city. Bentley's choice is retroactive. Wedekind had, however, spent more time in Munich than in any other city and had written his first plays, including *Spring's Awakening,* there.

62. F. Wedekind, *First Lulu,* 186.

63. See Florack, for whom Jack's act epitomizes the commercial reification of sensuality; she sees this as the central theme of the play. *Wedekinds "Lulu,"* 101. It was the London coroner Wynne Baxter who introduced the story in September 1888 that an American was prepared to pay twenty pounds each for human uteri for inclusion in an unnamed publication. There was no evidence for the story.

64. F. Wedekind, *First Lulu,* 50.

65. But see the last paragraph of this section.

66. F. Wedekind, *Earth Spirit,* 78.

67. F. Wedekind, *Pandora's Box,* 134.

68. F. Wedekind, *Erdgeist; Die Büchse der Pandora: Tragödien* (Munich, 1993), 86.

69. F. Wedekind, *First Lulu,* 207.

70. F. Wedekind, *Pandora's Box,* 161–62.

71. T. Wedekind, *Lulu,* 176.

72. See for example, P. Jelavich, "Art and Mammon in Wilhelmine Germany: The Case of Frank Wedekind," *Central European History* 12 (1979): 203–36; as well chapter 3 of his *Munich and Theatrical Modernism: Politics, Playwriting and Performance, 1890–1914* (Cambridge, Mass., 1985).

73. F. Wedekind, *The Marquis of Keith,* in *Masterpieces of Modern German Theater,* ed. R. W. Corrigan (New York, 1967), 267.

74. F. Wedekind, in *Der Vermummte Herr,* ed. Rasch, 143.

75. Ibid.

76. F. Wedekind, *Der Kammersänger,* in Hahn, vol. 3, 413. Italics in original.

77. F. Wedekind, in *Der Vermummte Herr,* ed. Rasch, 137.

78. F. Wedekind, *König Nicolo, oder, So ist das Leben,* in Hahn, vol. 1, 581.

79. Six years before, Albert Langen, the publisher of the satirical periodical *Simplicissimus,* had allowed a signed manuscript of satirical poems by Wedekind to fall into the hands of the police. Wedekind fled Germany but, unable to support himself, returned and was imprisoned for a few months.

80. F. Wedekind, *Hidalla, oder, Karl Hetmann, der Zwergriese,* in Hahn, vol. 1, 633.

81. A. Kutscher, *Wedekind; Leben und Werk* (Munich, 1964), 215–16.

82. F. Wedekind, *Hidalla,* in Hahn, vol. 1, 638–39.

83. T. Wedekind, *Lulu,* 48.

84. Ibid., 113.

85. Ibid., 156.

86. Ibid., 88.

87. F. Wedekind, *Die Zensur,* in Hahn, vol. 2, 70–71.

88. Editor's notes to *Die Zensur,* in Hahn, vol. 2, 753.

89. F. Wedekind, *Die Zensur,* in "Entstehungszeit meiner Arbeiten," in Hahn, vol. 3, 354.

90. T. Wedekind, *Lulu,* 128–29.

91. F. Wedekind, *Franziska: Ein modernes Mysterium in fünf Akten,* in *Frank Wedekind: Prosa, Dramen, Gedichte,* ed. H. Maier, vol. 2 (Munich, 1964), 446. (Cited as Maier.)

92. F. Wedekind, *Simson, oder, Scham und Eifersucht,* in Maier, vol. 2, 561. I have not attempted to preserve the verse form of the play in my translations.

93. F. Wedekind, "Deutschland bringt die Freiheit," in Hahn, vol. 3, 263.

94. Ibid., 264.

95. A. Martin, "Ein Drahtseilakt: Frank Wedekind und der Erste Weltkrieg," *Text + Kritik,* "Frank Wedekind," vol. 7, no. 131/132 (1996): 147–59.

96. Ibid., 153.

97. F. Wedekind, "Deutschland bringt die Freiheit," in Hahn, vol. 3, 265.

98. Ibid., 263.

99. Martin, "Ein Drahtseilakt," *Text + Kritik,* 153.

100. F. Wedekind, "Deutschland bringt die Freiheit," in Hahn, vol. 3, 264.

101. F. Wedekind, in *Der Vermummte Herr,* 211.

102. Kutscher, *Wedekind,* 321–22.

103. Quoted in Vinçon, *Frank Wedekind* (Stuttgart, 1987), 237.

104. Ibid., 236–37.

105. F. Wedekind, *Bismarck,* in *GW,* vol. 7, 132.

Chapter Two

1. C. Greenberg, *Art and Culture: Critical Essays* (Boston, 1968); A. Eysteinsson, *The Concept of Modernism* (Ithaca, 1990).

2. Russell Berman distinguishes three competing models of Modernist literary aesthetics "all of which are initiated by political motivations"—fascist modernism, epic leftism, and liberal modernism. But aesthetic—that is, formal—innovation remains central to his understanding of Modernism. "The moment of modernism," he asserts, "was marked by the belief in the confluence of aesthetic and political change." R. A. Berman, "Written Right Across Their Faces: Ernst Jünger's Fascist Modernism," in *Modernity and the Text: Revisions of German Modernism,* eds. A. Huyssen and D. Bathrick (New York, 1989), 66–67. Berman classifies Mann as a liberal modernist.

3. T. Mann, *Letters of Thomas Mann, 1889–1955,* trans. R. and C. Winston (Berkeley, 1975), 47. (Cited as *Letters.*)

4. Eysteinsson, *Concept of Modernism,* 3. For a more detailed discussion of the issue, see the section titled "Mann's Relationship to Modernism," in H. Ridley, *The Problematic Bourgeois: Twentieth-Century Criticism on Thomas Mann's* Buddenbrooks *and* The Magic Mountain (Columbia, S.C., 1994), 62–67, as well as 92–100. For a dissenting view arguing that Mann created a Modernist "allegorizing" technique as early as *Buddenbrooks,* see G. Reiss, *'Allegorisierung' und moderne Erzählkunst: Eine Studie zum Werk Thomas Manns* (Munich, 1970).

5. On the issue of the Modernism of *Doctor Faustus,* see H. Lehnert and P. C. Pfeiffer, eds., *Thomas Mann's 'Doctor Faustus': A Novel at the Margins of Modernism* (Columbia, S.C., 1991).

6. Letter of January 5, 1918, in *Letters of Heinrich and Thomas Mann, 1900–1949,* trans. D. Renau (Berkeley, 1998), 128.

7. T. Mann, *Reflections of a Nonpolitical Man,* trans. W. D. Morris (New York, 1983), 9.

8. Berman discerns three characteristics of the literary countermodel against which all the varieties of Modernist innovation were rebelling: a "developmental teleology" as found in the traditional linear *Bildungsroman* and bourgeois drama, a thematics of bourgeois identity-construction for the protagonist undergoing development, and an aesthetics of fictionality separating the work of art from immediate life-practical concerns. Berman, "Written Across Their Faces," in *Modernity and the Text,* 66. The last characteristic is an ideological reading of the *Bildungsroman's* "apoliticism" from a Brechtian point of view; it ignores the explicit cultural purpose of the *Bildungsroman,* let alone the overt, if conflicted, political purpose of much Realist and Naturalist literature.

9. T. Mann, *Reflections,* 225.

10. Ibid., 6.

11. K. W. Böhm, *Zwischen Selbstzucht und Verlangen: Thomas Mann und das Stigma Homosexualität, Untersuchungen zu Frühwerk und Jugend* (Würzburg, 1991), 57. The word *Selbstzucht,* "self-discipline," though more benign than "self-suppression," has the harsh overtones of animal training. A more readable interpretation along these lines that connects the earlier to the later life is A. Heilbut, *Thomas Mann: Eros and Literature* (New York, 1996).

12. Ibid.

13. J. D. Steakley, *The Homosexual Emancipation Movement in Germany* (New York, 1975), 10; D. F. Greenberg, *The Construction of Homosexuality* (Chicago, 1988), 408; Böhm, *Selbstzucht,* 103.

14. R. von Krafft-Ebing, *Psychopathia Sexualis: A Medico-Forensic Study*, trans. H. E. Weddeck (New York, 1965), 309.

15. Ibid., 370.

16. Böhm, *Selbstzucht*, 108.

17. Steakley, *Homosexual Emancipation Movement*, 14–15.

18. Krafft-Ebing, *Psychopathia Sexualis*, 321.

19. E. Hobsbawm, *The Age of Empire, 1875–1914* (New York, 1989), 168ff.

20. On this subject, see Ute Frevert's fascinating discussion "Bourgeois Honour: Middle-Class Duellists in Germany from the Late Eighteenth to the Early Twentieth Century," in *The German Bourgeoisie*, eds. D. Blackbourn and R. J. Evans (London, 1993), 255–92.

21. A. McLaren, *The Trials of Masculinity: Policing Sexual Boundaries, 1870–1930* (Chicago, 1997), 350.

22. Krafft-Ebing, *Psychopathia Sexualis*, 308.

23. T. Mann, "Das Ewig Weiblich," in *Essays, Band I: Frühlingssturm*, eds. H. Kurzke and S. Stachorski (Frankfurt a. M., 1993), 27.

24. Ibid., 28–29.

25. T. Mann, *Notizbücher 1–6*, eds. H. Wysling and Y. Schmidlin (Frankfurt a. M., 1991), 210. The idea is repeated almost verbatim in *Tonio Kröger*.

26. T. Mann, August 28, 1950, *Tagebücher: 1949–50*, ed. I. Jens (Frankfurt a. M., 1991).

27. T. Mann, *Notizbücher 7–14*, eds. H. Wysling and Y. Schmidlin (Frankfurt a. M., 1992), 115.

28. Ibid., 47.

29. T. J. Reed notes the "savagery" of some of the early stories as well as their apparent obsession with death, but suggests that these have much more to do with technique and style than meaning. Summarizing his view, he claims that Mann's "early stories . . . are the work of a writer who . . . imbued with 'modern' ideas and modern literature, but lacking in an abundance of first-hand material, has produced glittering but brittle samples of virtuosity." T. J. Reed, *Thomas Mann: The Uses of Tradition* (Oxford, 1974), 36. Reed's assumption here seems to be that experience is a matter of event rather than feeling and fantasy.

30. T. Mann, "Fallen," in *Sämtliche Erzählungen* (Frankfurt a. M., 1963), 32.

31. T. Mann, *Stories of Three Decades*, trans. H. T. Lowe-Porter (New York, 1951), 12; *Erzählungen*, 71. The English translation makes a number of the question marks into exclamations, a not insignificant change in emphasis.

32. T. Mann, *Stories*, 22; *Erzählungen*, 82. I have modified the English translation.

33. T. Mann, *Stories*, 58, 60; *Erzählungen*, 132, 135.

34. Böhm, *Selbstzucht*, 170, 176–77.

35. But see my remarks on this issue in the previous chapter.

36. K. Harpprecht, *Thomas Mann: Eine Biographie* (Leck, 1995), 42–43.

37. Ibid., 64.

38. T. Mann, *Royal Highness*, trans. A. C. Curtis (Berkeley, 1939, 1992), 49.

39. T. Mann, *Stories*, 53; *Erzählungen*, 113.

40. T. Mann, *Stories*, 57; *Erzählungen*, 118.

41. T. Mann, *Buddenbrooks: The Decline of a Family*, trans. J. E. Woods (New York, 1994), 55.

42. G. Lukacs, "In Search of Bourgeois Man," in *Essays on Thomas Mann*, trans. S. Mitchell (London, 1964), 20–21.

43. T. Mann, *Reflections*, 99.

44. Ibid., 98.

45. T. Mann, *Buddenbrooks*, 25.

46. For the view of Romanticism on which these remarks are based, see my *Impossible Individuality: Romanticism, Revolution and the Origins of Modern Selfhood, 1787–1802* (Princeton, 1992).

47. The disparaging "superficialities" is not to be taken at face value; it is the dismissive disenchantment of one who would like to believe in what he no longer finds realistic. In his notebook a few years later, after a performance of Mozart's *Magic Flute*, Mann wrote, "The Magic Flute. The spirit of mild and cheerful humanity, which speaks from music and action. 'Virtue', 'Duty', 'Enlightenment', 'Liebe', 'Humanity',—those happy people still believed in it. Today all of that is corroded and eaten away." *Notizbücher 7–14*, 90.

48. T. Mann, *Reflections*, 49.

49. T. Mann, *Notizbücher 7–14*, 70.

50. See his letter to Heinrich of February 13, 1900, *Letters*, 21.

51. "I am not a writer but a poet, who also makes poetry of his life." *Notizbücher 7–14*, 112. "I am, after all, a lyric poet (fundamentally)." Letter to Kurt Martens, March 28, 1906, *Letters*, 47.

52. T. Mann, *Notizbücher 7–14*, 39.

53. Ibid., 44.

54. Ibid., 62.

55. Letter of June 29, 1900, *Letters*, 12–13.

56. T. Mann, *Notizbücher 7–14*, 47.

57. Letter to Heinrich Mann, April 1, 1901, *Letters of Heinrich and Thomas Mann*, 51.

58. Ibid., 87.

59. Ibid., 48. Italics in original.

60. Ibid., 56. Italics in original.

61. Ibid., 86.

62. Ibid., 60. Italics in original.

63. Ibid., 47. Italics added.

64. Letter of February 13, 1901, *Letters*, 21.

65. T. Mann, *Tonio Kröger*, in *Death in Venice and Other Stories*, trans. D. Luke (New York, 1988), 147.

66. T. Mann, *Stories*, 170.

67. T. Mann, *Tonio Kröger*, in *Death in Venice*, ed. Luke, 151.

68. T. Mann, *Stories*, 169–70.

69. T. Mann, *Tristan*, in *Death in Venice*, ed. Luke, 124–25.

70. T. Mann, *Tonio Kröger*, in *Death in Venice*, ed. Luke, 155.

71. T. Mann, *Tristan*, in *Death in Venice*, ed. Luke, 117–18.

72. Luke, *Death in Venice*, editor's introduction, xxv.

73. T. Mann, *Tristan*, in *Death in Venice*, ed. Luke, 118.

74. T. Mann, *Tonio Kröger*, in *Death in Venice*, ed. Luke, 156.

75. T. Mann, "Bilse und Ich," *Essays*, vol. 1, 47.

76. Letter to Heinrich Mann, December 3, 1903, *Letters of Heinrich and Thomas Mann*, 57–58.

77. T. Mann, "Gutachten Über Frank Wedekinds 'Lulu,'" *Essays*, vol. 1, 167.

78. "Because of its poetic greatness and beauty," Wedekind wrote, "'Fiorenza' has long de-

served to be a repertory piece on any stage that claims to be a refuge for the arts." "Fiorenza," in *Schauspielkunst: Ein Glossarium,* in *Frank Wedekind: Werke in zwei Bänden,* vol. 1, ed. E. Weidl (Munich, 1990), 327.

79. T. Mann, *Fiorenza, Stories,* 211.

80. Letter of early June 1904, *Letters,* 33.

81. Letter of late August 1904, *Letters,* 40.

82. Letter of early September 1904, *Letters,* 42.

83. T. Mann, *Royal Highness,* 147.

84. Letter to Heinrich, November 8, 1913, in *Letters of Heinrich and Thomas Mann,* 119.

85. T. Mann, *Notizbücher 7–14,* 97.

86. Ibid., 74.

87. Ibid., 71.

88. T. Mann, *Death in Venice,* in *Death in Venice,* ed. Luke, 200.

89. My emphasis differs from that of T. J. Reed, who in a carefully detailed if still hypothetical reconstruction of the genesis of *Death in Venice* suggests that Mann was originally inclined to a more celebratory view of Aschenbach's intoxication with Tadzio, and that a more positive sense of the Platonic sublimation of Eros is an undercurrent even in the final "critical" version of the story. I find even Reed's genesis problematic on the basis of the early working notes I have cited, and the interpretation as a whole, though consistent with Reed's analysis of Mann's trajectory, incompatible with the development I have traced. Anthony Heilbut, in a somewhat related view, suggests that Mann's more positive view of the creative possibilities of homosexual passion in an essay on Michaelangelo four decades later was the expression of possibilities latent even in *Death in Venice* that it took Mann forty years to declare (265). While the creative implications of homosexual passion are of course central to Mann's whole *Weltanschauung,* this way of putting things ignores, I think, the important transformation that Mann's "feminine" view of homosexuality had to undergo before he could take a more evenhanded approach to it.

90. "Working Notes for *Death in Venice,*" in T. Mann, *Death in Venice,* trans. C. Koelb (New York, 1994), 71.

91. Ibid., 76–77.

92. T. Mann, Princeton lecture "On Myself," 1940, quoted in editor's introduction, *Death in Venice,* ed. Luke, xlv.

93. Letter to Heinrich, November 11, 1913, *Letters of Heinrich and Thomas Mann,* 119.

94. T. Mann, "The Hunger," *Stories,* 172.

95. N. Hamilton, *The Brothers Mann: The Lives of Heinrich and Thomas Mann, 1871–1950 and 1875–1955* (London, 1978), 158.

96. T. Mann, "Gedanken im Kriege," *Essays,* 190.

97. T. Mann, "Friedrich und die grosse Koalition," *Essays,* 167.

98. T. Mann, *Reflections,* 24.

99. T. Mann, *Buddenbrooks,* 375–76.

100. Ibid., 179–80.

101. F. K. Ringer, *The Decline of the German Mandarins: The German Academic Community, 1890–1930* (Cambridge, Mass., 1969).

102. T. Mann, *Reflections,* 208.

103. T. Mann, "Von Deutscher Republik," in *Von Deutscher Republik: Politische Schriften und Reden in Deutschland* (Frankfurt a. M., 1984), 123.

104. T. Mann, *Confessions of Felix Krull, Confidence Man (The Early Years)*, trans. D. Lindley (New York, 1955, 1992), 173–81.

Chapter Three

1. W. Kandinsky, "Self-Characterization," in *Complete Writings on Art*, eds. K. C. Lindsay and P. Vergo (Boston, 1982), 431. (Cited as *CW.*)

2. J. Hahl-Koch, *Kandinsky*, trans. K. Brown, R. Harratz, and K. Harrison (New York, 1993), 184. Not until the painting was rediscovered in 1989 could it be certain what painting Kandinsky referred to and the claim verified.

3. J. D. Fineberg, *Kandinsky in Paris, 1906–1907* (Ann Arbor, 1984), 84. The significance of Symbolist theory for Kandinsky's development was first emphasized by R.-C. W. Long, *Kandinsky: The Development of an Abstract Style* (Oxford, 1980), 42.

4. D. Kuspit, "A Freudian Note on Abstract Art," *Signs of Psyche in Modern and Postmodern Art* (Cambridge and New York, 1993), 103. For a succinct statement of the ideological origins of the artistic avant-garde since its appearance in Europe in the 1820s in reaction to the new financial and industrial capitalist order, see C. Jencks, "Postmodern vs. Late-Modern," in *Zeitgeist in Babel: The Postmodernist Controversy*, ed. I. Hoesterey (Bloomington, 1991).

5. Kandinsky, "Reminiscences," *CW,* 367–68.

6. Kandinsky, *On the Spiritual in Art, CW,* 175.

7. Ibid., 192.

8. Ibid., 181–83.

9. Ibid., 193. Italics in original. In a wide and generally persuasive survey of the anti-psychologistic thrust of Modernism, Martin Jay uncritically accepts Antoine Compagnon's claim that in the mind of the first abstract painter, abstraction was supposed to make individual psychology extinct. It is certainly true that on occasion Kandinsky dismissed psychological interpretations of his paintings—"I have no intention of painting psychic states," he once said. "Mein Werdegang," in *Kandinsky: Die Gesammelte Schriften, Bd. I*, ed. H. K. Roethel and J. Hahl-Koch (Bern, 1980), 58. But his objection was to the kind of reductionism that made the elements of painting nothing but arbitrary signifiers for a reality outside itself. Above all, psychological interpretation meant to Kandinsky the kind of denigrating "explanation" that, like Max Nordau's notion of degeneration, attacked the "sickness of the modern school of art" and attributed it to "the psychological derangements of contemporary artists." "Critique of Critics," *CW,* 43. The formal elements of painting, color and line, were not simply arbitrary signifiers of emotion but pictographic embodiments of them, just as the shape of a letter of the alphabet had both "practical purposive . . . form," signifying a particular sound, and a "corporeal form," which produced impressions of emotions or intentional states. "On the Question of Form," *CW,* 245. It is certainly not the case, as Jay also suggests, following Greenberg, that the point of Kandinsky's "anti-psychologism" was to make "formal pictorial qualities . . . their own ends." "Modernism and the Specter of Psychologism," *MODERNISM / modernity* 3.2 (1996): 101. The point of a painting was to elevate and sublimate the clashing discords of psychic conflict into a timeless harmony.

10. Kandinsky, "Reminiscences," *CW,* 360.

11. Ibid., 361.

12. Unpublished letters of Wassily Kandinsky to Gabriele Münter, Gabriele Münter- und

Johannes Eichner-Stiftung, Lenbachhaus, Munich, September 9, 1903. Referred to hereafter as *Letters*. All translations are by the author.

13. Kandinsky, "Cologne Lecture," *CW,* 394.

14. Kandinsky, "Reminiscences," *CW,* 375.

15. Ibid., 382.

16. Joanna Hubbs points out that the maternal epithet was transferred very early from the land of Russia to its physical features, including man-made ones, like cities, roads, and churches. *Mother Russia: The Feminine Myth in Russian Culture* (Bloomington and Indianapolis, 1988), xiii.

17. R. Felski, *The Gender of Modernity* (Cambridge, Mass., 1995). Kandinsky's figuration of feminine nature was closer to the more powerful and anxiety-provoking image of the mother and her body discerned by some feminist art historians examining Modernist developments in England and France. Commenting on the contrast in Toulouse-Lautrec's work between pale upper-class femininity and the "bacchanalian animal energy" of his lower-class dancers, Griselda Pollock argues that "it is that mother who must be seen as the structuring absence which creates the necessity for the incessant re-engagement with the bodies of the 'other' and the stylistic deformations from bourgeois realism which then become the formal hallmark of a modernist oeuvre." G. Pollock, "Fathers of Modern Art, Mothers of Invention," *Differences* 4.5 (1992): 97. See also her *Avant-Garde Gambits, 1888–1893: Gender and the Colour of Art History* (New York, 1993); and L. Tickner, "Men's Work? Masculinity and Modernism," *Differences* 4.5 (1992): 1–37.

18. For an overview of the traits and figures on which the rubric is based, see "The New Woman," in *Changing Lives: Women in European History Since 1700,* B. G. Smith (Lexington, Mass., 1989), chap. 8.

19. Kandinsky, "Reminiscences," *CW,* 358. The first memory is of being taken by his mother to kindergarten in Florence in a black coach. On the meaning of black, see *On the Spiritual in Art*: "Black has an inner sound of nothingness bereft of possibilities, a dead nothingness as if the sun had become extinct, an eternal silence without future, without hope." *CW,* 185.

20. O. Weininger, *Sex and Character* (London and New York, 1906), 286.

21. Ibid., 9.

22. A. Janik and S. Toulmin, *Wittgenstein's Vienna* (New York, 1973), 71–75.

23. J. Le Rider, *Modernity and Crises of Identity: Culture and Society in Fin-de-Siècle Vienna,* trans. R. Morris (New York, 1993), 114–15.

24. Weininger, *Sex and Character,* 65.

25. E. Naiman, "Historectomies: On the Metaphysics of Reproduction in a Utopian Age," in *Sexuality and the Body in Russian Culture,* eds. J. T. Costlow, S. Sandler and J. Vowles (Stanford, 1993), 262.

26. I. Paperno and J. D. Grossman, eds., introduction, *Creating Life: The Aesthetic Utopia of Russian Modernism* (Stanford, 1994), 5.

27. L. Engelstein, *The Keys to Happiness: Sex and the Search for Modernity in Fin-de-Siècle Russia* (Ithaca, 1992), 4.

28. Ibid., 98.

29. Paperno and Grossman, eds., introduction, *Creating Life,* 7.

30. I. Paperno, "The Meaning of Art: Symbolist Theories," in *Creating Life,* eds. Paperno and Grossman, 17.

31. O. Matich, "The Symbolist Meaning of Love: Theory and Practice," in *Creating Life,* eds. Paperno and Grossman, 30. See also R. E. Peterson, *A History of Russian Symbolism* (Philadelphia, 1993), 36–37.

32. Costlow et al., eds., introduction, *Sexuality and the Body,* 20.

33. Vladimir Solovyov, *The Meaning of Love,* in *Russian Philosophy,* vol. 3, eds. J. M. Edie, J. P. Scanlan, M.-B. Zeldin (Chicago, 1965), 85.

34. Ibid., 94–95.

35. Ibid., 96.

36. Paperno, "Symbolist Theories," in *Creating Life,* eds. Paperno and Grossman, 19.

37. Paperno and Grossman, eds., introduction, *Creating Life,* 2.

38. Kandinsky, "On Stage Composition," *Blaue Reiter Almanac, CW,* 257–58.

39. Kandinsky, "Schönberg's Pictures," *CW,* 225.

40. Kandinsky, "Content and Form," *CW,* 87.

41. Engelstein, *Keys to Happiness,* 4.

42. This aspect of their thought is not exclusively Russian, as Engelstein seems to think, but has strong affinities with the attitudes of the German *Bildungsbürgertum,* whose political situation to some extent resembled that of the educated Russian elites, as well as with liberals elsewhere in Europe who aligned themselves with an ideal of "individuality" against self-interested "individualism" within the liberal tradition.

43. A. Walicki, *Legal Philosophies of Russian Liberalism* (Oxford, 1987), 2. Walicki points out that the preference for customary law, which is typical of pre-industrial societies, was also strengthened in Russia by the Western critique of capitalism in both its left- and right-wing forms. The convergence of the two further accounts for the "conservative" resonance of Kandinsky's liberalism.

44. Kandinsky expressed his preference for Russian peasant law in his early legal writings and repeated it in even stronger terms years later in his "Reminiscences." See, e.g., "Über die Strafe in den Urteilen der Bauerngerichte im Bezirk Moskau," in *Gesammelte Schriften, Bd. I,* eds. Roethel and Hahl-Koch, 86–87; and *CW,* 362. In the early work, Kandinsky was even critical of the materialistic aspects of peasant law, pointing out that the reconciliation process often undermined moral responsibility in favor of material gain.

45. Engelstein, *Keys to Happiness,* 6–7 and *passim.* Amusingly, despite his deep skepticism about scientific rationality, Kandinsky did not escape the professional mentality even as an artist. Early on he wrote witheringly of the amateurism that passed as art criticism in Russian periodicals: "Can any Tom, Dick or Harry really resolve all the problems of art? . . . In matters of this kind we usually listen to, and take note of, only the opinions of . . . the so-called specialists." "Critique of Critics," *CW,* 36.

46. Engelstein, *Keys to Happiness,* 254. Much of her book is concerned with the ambivalence displayed in the legal and medical literature of the Russian fin de siècle toward sexual liberation and the effort to regulate it through scientific and cultural authority rather than old-fashioned coercion.

47. Naiman, "Historectomies," in *Sexuality and the Body,* eds. Costlow et al., 261.

48. Costlow et al., eds., introduction, *Sexuality and the Body,* 24–25.

49. P. Weiss, *Kandinsky and Old Russia: The Artist as Ethnographer and Shaman* (New Haven and London, 1995), 29.

50. The comment appears in the Russian edition of the "Reminiscences," *CW,* 895.

51. Kandinsky, *CW,* 848.

52. Hahl-Koch, *Kandinsky*, 104.

53. A. Hoberg, ed., *Wassily Kandinsky and Gabriele Münter, Letters and Reminiscences, 1902–1914* (Munich and New York, 1994), 31.

54. Ibid., 35.

55. Kandinsky, "Autobiographical Note," *CW,* 343.

56. See H. K. Roethel and J. K. Benjamin, *Catalogue Raisonné of the Oil-Paintings, Volume One, 1900–1915* (London, 1987), 51–85; and V. E. Barnett, *Kandinsky: Watercolors. Catalogue Raisonné, Volume One, 1900–1921,* (Ithaca, 1992), 71–80. While it can't be absolutely certain that all the work from the earliest period survives, the catalogues have done a thorough job of hunting down references even to paintings that can no longer be located. Fineberg, following Brisch, includes the "Old Russia" paintings in the "anecdotal" category, but his classification takes 1907 as the terminus of Kandinsky's first period. He does note that the Russian theme paintings begin around 1903 and represent a stylistic change from what had come before. *Kandinsky in Paris,* 30–32. The failure to note the great change in Kandinsky's work after 1902, shared by virtually all commentators, gives a skewed impression of his earliest work and of his development.

57. Quoted in G. Kleine, *Gabriele Münter und Wassily Kandinsky: Biographie eines Paares* (Frankfurt a. M., 1990), 147.

58. In the letters to Münter written while he was trying to separate from Anna, Kandinsky alluded to the fact that he had had a number of affairs before he met Münter, which he had freely discussed with his wife.

59. Irit Rogoff describes her disappointment upon discovering that Münter was not the self-confident autonomous female pioneer of the avant-garde she had hoped to encounter in her research, but this, as she herself came to recognize, was an ahistorical judgment derived from contemporary feminist standards. Looking at gender relationships within the Munich avant-garde of the early twentieth century in the context of its struggle for recognition, Rogoff comments shrewdly about the situation of women, whether themselves artists or not, experiencing the tension between their own agency and creativity and the desire to support their embattled men emotionally and intellectually. "Tiny Anguishes: Reflections on Nagging, Scholastic Embarrassment, and Feminist Art History, *Differences* 4.3 (1992): 38–65, esp. 38, 54–55.

60. The biographical information about Münter is largely from Kleine, *Münter und Kandinsky,* chapters 1–4.

61. Hahl-Koch, *Kandinsky,* 82.

62. See p. 167.

63. *Letters,* October 17, 1902. For Münter's reaction in those early months of the relationship, see her letter of October 10 in Hoberg, *Kandinsky and Münter.* Hoberg believes she never sent it—it appears as a kind of diary entry—but Kandinsky's letter of October 17 seems to respond to it quite directly.

64. The editors of Kandinsky's *Complete Writings* refer to the "Werther" pose of his early letters to Münter and claim that "only when we look past it do we discover the human [!] dimensions of the man." *CW,* 14–15. It can only be assumed that this odd judgment reflects the desire to protect Kandinsky's reputation, as if his deep and tortured emotions detract from his aesthetic achievement. The unfortunate result of dismissing Kandinsky's emotional life as a pose, however, is to forfeit a crucial key to understanding his art.

65. Barnett, *Watercolours,* 76.

66. Kleine, *Münter und Kandinsky,* 183.

67. Kenneth Lindsay suggested in 1981, before Kandinsky's letters were available, that the couple in *Trysting Place* reflects the beginning of the relationship between the two. The correspondence, with its documentation of numerous trysts and their perils, lends a good deal of substance to his argument. K. Lindsay, "Gabriele Münter and Wassily Kandinsky: What They Meant to Each Other," *Arts Magazine* (December 1981): 54–62.

68. Münter to Kandinsky, January 6, 1904. Quoted in Kleine, *Münter und Kandinsky*, 178.

69. Münter to Kandinsky, Christmas 1903. Quoted in Kleine, *Münter und Kandinsky*, 191.

70. Münter to Kandinsky, July 24, 1903. Quoted in Kleine, *Münter und Kandinsky*, 191. Hahl-Koch describes Münter from the beginning as being "coolly fascinated by her teacher" and claims that "she was reluctant to commit herself, was often cold to her lover and repeatedly asked him not to press her, saying she wanted to think things over." Hahl-Koch, *Kandinsky*, 104. This quite tendentious portrayal of Münter's feelings is an attempt to defend Kandinsky against what Hahl-Koch perceives as Kleine's criticism of him not only for the failure of the relationship but for the stunting of Münter's talents. Kleine's is a much more perceptive and better balanced account of the relationship.

71. Kandinsky and Anna, as cousins, were by law not allowed to marry, and there had been irregularities in the marriage documents.

72. The quotes and lengthened vowels suggest that Kandinsky is citing a line from a song or catechism, but I have been unable to locate its source.

73. Kandinsky's mother was worried about one of her sons who was serving in the army. He was killed in the Russo-Japanese war a short time later.

74. "I suffer unspeakably sometimes when I think about my crime against my wife." *Letters*, September 8, 1904.

75. Italics in original. The word before the question mark cannot be made out.

76. In effect, he reconstructed the triangle he had been in with his mother and his aunt—the absentee Russian woman he visited with and the "German" woman—his aunt Elizabeth, a Balt, was German-speaking—that he lived with.

77. He described one episode of repeated visits to an empty mailbox in obsessive detail in a letter of September 29, 1905.

78. For a detailed discussion of these developments, see Fineberg, *Kandinsky in Paris*, especially chapter 6.

79. I owe this observation to my colleague Max Okenfuss. While commentators have sometimes taken the town to be at least partly a representation of Moscow, none so far as I know have drawn attention to the tower, which appears in so many of Kandinsky's paintings. Peg Weiss's insistence on finding only Vologda towns in every such representation seems to me overdone, though nothing precludes multiple determination.

80. Quoted in Weiss, *Kandinsky and Old Russia*, 42.

81. Ibid., 50.

82. Kleine, *Münter und Kandinsky*, 254.

83. He first mentioned it in the letter to Münter of February 21, 1907. The argument for the centrality of theosophy and the occult to Kandinsky's work has been made most extensively by Sixten Ringbom in *The Sounding Cosmos: A Study in the Spiritualism of Kandinsky and the Genesis of Abstract Painting* (Helsinki, 1970). It is also the guiding assumption of the 1986–87 exhibit at the Los Angeles County Museum of Art entitled "The Spiritual in Art: Abstract Painting 1890–1985"; see the catalogue of the exhibit by the same title, which contains essays by Ringbom and others on the subject.

84. Fineberg's book is based on the thesis of the importance of the Paris stay. Kleine emphasizes Werefkin's theoretical inclinations along with Jawlensky's more empirical color sense (*Münter und Kandinsky,* 327, 329); Hahl-Koch, the decisive effect of living in the country (*Kandinsky,* 124), though in fact the "pure" Murnau landscapes date from a year earlier.

85. Kandinsky, *On the Spiritual, CW,* 197.

86. Ibid., 131. Italics added.

87. See Griselda Pollock's use of the same notion in a much more specific sense to explain the prominence of the dancer's cocked, black-stockinged leg in many of Toulouse-Lautrec's posters, especially those of Jane Avril. Pollock, "Fathers of Modern Art," 111.

88. Kandinsky, *On the Spiritual, CW,* 166.

89. Kandinsky, "Letters from Munich," *CW,* 68.

90. Ibid., 70.

91. Macke to Kandinsky, December 12, 1911. Quoted in Kleine, *Münter und Kandinsky,* 414.

92. Kandinsky, "Letters from Munich," *CW,* 68.

93. Ibid., 87.

94. Ibid., 74.

95. Münter to Kandinsky, October 30, 1910, in *Kandinsky and Münter,* ed. Hoberg, 78.

96. The letters carry the dates of both the Julian and Gregorian calendars. The date given is the European date.

97. Despite his public praise of Picasso, Kandinsky was privately contemptuous because his Cubism represented only a halfhearted break with representation and still clung to the external world.

98. Münter to Kandinsky, December 5, 1910, in *Kandinsky and Münter,* ed. Hoberg, 95.

99. Alexander Kojevnikov, Kandinsky's half-brother, had been killed in the Russo-Japanese war. It was Lidia's worry over him five years before that Kandinsky had pleaded as his excuse for not telling his mother about his desire to divorce Anna.

100. Kandinsky to Schönberg, January 18, 1911, in *Arnold Schönberg, Wassily Kandinsky: Letters, Pictures and Documents,* ed. J. Hahl-Koch, trans. J. C. Crawford (London, 1984).

101. Kandinsky to Schönberg, January 26, 1911, Ibid.

102. Kandinsky to Schönberg, April 9, 1911, Ibid.

103. Kandinsky, "Cologne Lecture," *CW,* 398. Italics added.

104. C. Greenberg, "Avant-Garde and Kitsch," in *Art and Culture: Critical Essays* (Boston, 1968), 6.

105. Kandinsky, "Reminiscences," *CW,* 360.

106. Kandinsky, "Reminiscences," *CW,* 372.

107. In her book, Long refers generally to the attitude prevalent among intellectuals in Munich, Saint Petersburg, and Moscow at the time that sex was a way to communicate with cosmic forces. *Kandinsky,* 104. In a later article, she gives more detail on these circles, mentioning the Polish writer Przybyzewski and the Russian Symbolist Merezhkovsky, among others, though not in this connection Solovyov. "Kandinsky's Vision of Utopia as a Garden of Love," *Art Journal* (spring 1983): 50–60.

108. Roethel and Benjamin, *Catalogue Raisonné,* 405.

109. This is the central contention of Peg Weiss's *Kandinsky and Old Russia: The Artist as Ethnographer and Shaman.* Her detailed analysis links concrete images in Kandinsky's work with his observations of the customs, traditions, and art of the Zyrians of the Vologda region

of Russia, made during an expedition to the region sponsored by the state Ethnographic Society while he was still a student at the university.

110. See the preface to M. Dabrowski, *Kandinsky's Compositions* (New York, 1995), published in conjunction with the exhibition of all of Kandinsky's extant *Compositions* at the Museum of Modern Art in New York that same year. Dualism also seems to be a central formal feature of *Composition II*, but the destruction of the first three *Compositions* in World War II, which are now represented by black-and-white photographs and a few preliminary color works, makes interpretation difficult.

111. Kandinsky, "Composition 4," *CW*, 384.

112. Dabrowski, *Kandinsky's Compositions*, 36.

113. *Letters*, February 10, 1912. Underlined in the original.

114. Kandinsky, "Composition 6," *CW*, 387.

115. H. K. Roethel, *Kandinsky* (New York, 1979), 109–10.

116. Weiss, *Kandinsky and Old Russia*, 125.

117. Hahl-Koch, *Kandinsky*, 245.

118. Quoted in Kleine, *Münter und Kandinsky*, 431.

BIBLIOGRAPHY

General

Berg, C., F. Durieux, G. Lernout, eds. *The Turn of the Century: Modernism and Modernity in Literature and the Arts.* Berlin and New York, 1995.

Berghahn, V. R. *Imperial Germany, 1871–1914: Economy, Society, Culture and Politics.* Providence and Oxford, 1994.

Blackbourn, D., and R. J. Evans, eds. *The German Bourgeoisie.* London, 1993.

Bradbury, M., and J. McFarlane, eds. *Modernism, 1890–1930.* London, 1976.

Butler, C. *Early Modernism: Literature, Music and Painting in Europe, 1900–1916.* Oxford, 1994.

Dykstra, B. *Idols of Perversity: Fantasies of Feminine Evil in Fin-de-Siècle Culture.* New York and Oxford, 1986.

Eley, G., ed. *Society, Culture and the State in Germany, 1870–1930.* Ann Arbor, 1996.

Erhart, W., and B. Hermann, eds. *Wann ist der Mann ein Mann: Zur Geschichte der Männlichkeit.* Stuttgart, Weimar, 1997.

Evans, R. J. *The Feminist Movement in Germany, 1894–1933.* London, 1976.

Eysteinsson, A. *The Concept of Modernism.* Ithaca, 1990.

Felski, R. *The Gender of Modernity.* Cambridge, Mass., 1995.

———. "Modernism and Modernity: Engendering Literary History." In *Rereading Modernism: New Directions in Feminist Criticism,* edited by L. Rado. New York, 1994.

Fogel, G. I., F. M. Lane, and R. S. Liebert. *The Psychology of Men: New Psychoanalytic Perspectives.* New York, 1986.

Frevert, U. *"Mann und Weib, und Weib und Mann:" Geschlechter-Differenzen in der Moderne.* Munich, 1995.

Gay, P. *The Education of the Senses.* Vol. 1, *The Bourgeois Experience: Victoria to Freud.* New York, 1984.

———. *The Cultivation of Hatred.* Vol. 3, *The Bourgeois Experience: Victoria to Freud.* New York and London, 1993.

Gilbert, S. M., and S. Gubar. *The Madwoman in the Attic: The Woman Writer and the Nineteenth-Century Literary Imagination.* New Haven, 1979.

Bibliography

Gilmore, D. D. *Manhood in the Making: Cultural Concepts of Masculinity.* New Haven, 1990.

Greenberg, C. *Art and Culture: Critical Essays.* Boston, 1968.

Greenberg, D. F. *The Construction of Homosexuality.* Chicago, 1988.

Heisserer, D. *Wo die Geister wandern: Eine Topographie der Schwabinger Bohème um 1900.* Munich, 1993.

Hobsbawm, E. J. *The Age of Empire, 1875–1914.* New York, 1989.

Hoesterey, I., ed. *Zeitgeist in Babel: The Postmodernist Controversy.* Bloomington, 1991.

Horkheimer, M., et al. *Studien über Autorität und Familie.* Paris, 1936.

Huyssen, A., and D. Bathrick, eds. *Modernity and the Text: Revisions of German Modernism.* New York, 1989.

Izenberg, G. *Impossible Individuality: Romanticism, Revolution, and the Origins of Modern Selfhood.* Princeton, 1992.

Janik, A., and S. Toulmin. *Wittgenstein's Vienna.* New York, 1973.

Jay, M. "Modernism and the Specter of Psychologism." *MODERNISM/modernity* 3.2 (1996): 93–111.

Kafka, F. *Letter to His Father.* Translated by E. Kaiser and E. Wilkins. New York, 1953.

Krafft-Ebing, R. von. *Psychopathia Sexualis: A Medico-Forensic Study.* Translated by H. E. Weddeck. New York, 1965.

Le Rider, J. *Modernity and Crises of Identity: Culture and Society in Fin-de-Siècle Vienna.* Translated by R. Morris. New York, 1993.

Mauge, A. *L'Identité masculine en crise au tournant du siècle, 1871–1914.* Paris, 1987.

McLaren, A. *The Trials of Masculinity: Policing Sexual Boundaries, 1870–1930.* Chicago, 1997.

Merrick, J., and B. T. Ragan, eds. *Homosexuality in Modern France.* Oxford and New York, 1996.

Mommsen, W. J. *Bürgerliche Kultur und Künstlerische Avantgarde, 1870–1918: Kultur und Politik im deutschen Reich.* Frankfurt a. M. and Berlin, 1994.

Mosse, G. L. *The Image of Man: The Creation of Modern Masculinity.* New York and Oxford, 1996.

———. *Nationalism and Sexuality: Respectability and Normal Sexuality in Modern Europe.* New York, 1985.

Nicholls, P. *Modernisms: A Literary Guide.* Berkeley and Los Angeles, 1995.

Parr, L., ed. *Lesbianism and Feminism in Germany, 1895–1910.* New York, 1975.

Pollock, G. *Avant-Garde Gambits, 1888–1893: Gender and the Colour of Art History.* New York, 1993.

———. "Fathers of Modern Art, Mothers of Invention." *Difference* 4.5 (1992).

Ringer, F. K. *The Decline of the German Mandarins: The German Academic Community, 1890–1930.* Cambridge, Mass., 1969.

Rubin, W., H. Seckel, and J. Cousins. *Les Demoiselles d'Avignon, Studies in Modern Art.* Vol. 3. New York, 1994.

Showalter, E. *Sexual Anarchy: Gender and Culture at the Fin de Siècle.* New York, 1990.

Smith, B. G. *Changing Lives: Women in European History Since 1700.* Lexington, Mass., 1989.

Steakley, J. D. *The Homosexual Emancipation Movement in Germany.* New York, 1975.

Strindberg, A. *The Father: A Tragedy in Three Acts; and, A Dream Play.* Translated by V. Anderson. Arlington Heights, Ill., 1964.

Tickner, L. "Men's Work? Masculinity and Modernism." *Differences* 4.5 (1992).

Toews, J. E. "Refashioning the Masculine Subject in Early Modernism: Narratives of Self-Dissolution and Self-Construction in Psychoanalysis and Literature, 1900–1914." *MODERNISM/modernity* 4.1 (1997): 31–67.

Van Casselaer, C. *Lot's Wife: Lesbian Paris, 1890–1914*. Liverpool, 1986.

Weininger, O. *Sex and Character.* London and New York, 1906.

Widdig, B. *Männerbünde und Massen: Zur Krise männlicher Identität in der Literatur der Moderne.* Opladen, 1992.

Frank Wedekind

PRIMARY SOURCES

Die Büchse der Pandora: Eine Monstretragödie. Edited by H. Vinçon, Pharus III. Darmstadt, 1990.

Diary of an Erotic Life. Edited by G. Hay and W. E. Yuill. Oxford, 1990.

The First Lulu. Edited by E. Bentley. New York, 1994.

Gesammelte Werke. Edited by A. Kutscher and R. Friedenthal. Munich, 1920, 1921.

The Lulu Plays. Translated by C. R. Mueller. New York, 1967.

The Marquis of Keith. In *Masterpieces of Modern German Theater,* edited by R. W. Corrigan. New York, 1967.

Prosa, Dramen, Gedichte. Edited by H. Maier, 2 vols. Munich, 1964.

Spring's Awakening: Tragedy of Childhood. Translated by E. Bentley. New York, 1995.

Die Tagebücher: Ein erotisches Leben. Edited by G. Hay. Munich, 1990.

Der Vermummte Herr: Briefe Frank Wedekinds aus den Jahren 1881–1917. Edited by W. Rasch. Munich, 1967.

Werke: Kritische Studienausgabe. Bd. III, 1. Edited by H. Vinçon. Darmstadt, 1996.

Werke: Kritische Studienausgabe. Bd. III, 2. Edited by H. Vinçon. Darmstadt, 1996.

Werke in drei Bänden. Edited by M. Hahn. Berlin and Weimar, 1969.

Werke in zwei Bänden. Edited by E. Weidl. Munich, 1990.

SECONDARY SOURCES

Austermühl, E., A. Kessler, and H. Vinçon, eds. *Frank Wedekind: Texte, Interviews, Studien.* Pharus I. Darmstadt, 1989.

Best, A. *Frank Wedekind.* London, 1975.

Boa, E. *The Sexual Circus: Wedekind's Theatre of Subversion.* Oxford, 1987.

Bovenschen, S. *Die imaginierte Weiblichkeit: Exemplarische Untersuchungen zu kulturgeschichtlichen und literarischen Präsentationsformen des Weiblichen.* Stuttgart, 1979.

Firda, R. A. "Wedekind, Nietzsche and the Dionysian Experience." *Modern Language Notes* 87.5 (October 1972): 720–31.

Florack, R. *Wedekinds "Lulu": Zerrbild der Sinnlichkeit.* Tübingen, 1995.

Gittleman, S. *Frank Wedekind.* New York, 1969.

Hilmes, C. *Die Femme fatale: Ein Weiblichkeitstypus in der nachromantischen Literatur.* Stuttgart, 1990.

Höger, A. *Frank Wedekind. Der Konstruktivismus als schöpferische Methode.* Königstein, 1979.

Jakubowski, M., and N. Braund. *The Mammoth Book of Jack the Ripper.* New York, 1999.

Jelavich, P. "Art and Mammon in Wilhelmine Germany: The Case of Frank Wedekind." *Central European History* 12 (1979): 203–36.

———. *Munich and Theatrical Modernism: Politics, Playwriting and Performance, 1890–1914.* Cambridge, 1985.

245
■

Bibliography

Kieser, R. *Benjamin Franklin Wedekind: Biographie einer Jugend.* Zurich, 1990.

Kieser, R., and R. Grimm, eds. *Frank Wedekind: Yearbook 1991.* Bern, 1991.

Kutscher, A. *Wedekind; Leben und Werk.* Munich, 1964.

Lewis, W. B. *The Ironic Dissident: Frank Wedekind in the View of His Critics.* Columbia, 1997.

Mennemeier, F. N. "Frank Wedekind." In *Handbuch des Dramas,* vol. 2, edited by W. Hinck, 360–73. Düsseldorf, 1980.

Pickerodt, G. *Frank Wedekind: Frühlungs Erwachen. Grundlagen und Gedanken zum Verständnis des Dramas.* Frankfurt a. M., 1984.

Text+Kritik. "Frank Wedekind." Vol. VII (131/132). 1996.

Vinçon, H. *Frank Wedekind.* Stuttgart, 1987.

Wagener, H. *Frank Wedekind.* Berlin, 1979.

Wedekind, T. *Lulu: Die Rolle meines Lebens.* Munich, 1969.

Thomas Mann

PRIMARY SOURCES

Buddenbrooks: The Decline of a Family. Translated by J. E. Woods. New York, 1994.

Confessions of Felix Krull, Confidence Man (The Early Years). Translated by D. Lindley. New York, 1955, 1992.

Death in Venice. Translated and edited by C. Koelb. New York, 1994.

Death in Venice and Other Stories. Translated by D. Luke. New York, 1988.

Diaries 1918–1939: 1918–1921, 1933–1939. Edited by H. Kesten. Translated by R. and C. Winston. London, 1982.

Essays, Band I: Frühlingssturm. Edited by H. Kurzke and S. Stachorski. Frankfurt a. M., 1993.

Gesammelte Werke, 13 vols. Edited by H. Bürgin and P. de Mendelssohn. Frankfurt a. M., 1990.

Letters of Heinrich and Thomas Mann, 1900–1949. Translated by D. Renau. Berkeley, 1998.

Letters of Thomas Mann, 1889–1955. Translated by R. and C. Winston. Berkeley, 1975.

Notizbücher 1–6. Edited by H. Wysling and Y. Schmidlin. Frankfurt a. M., 1991.

Notizbücher 7–14. Edited by H. Wysling and Y. Schmidlin. Frankfurt a. M., 1992.

Reflections of a Nonpolitical Man. Translated by W. D. Morris. New York, 1983.

Royal Highness. Translated by A. C. Curtis. Berkeley, 1939, 1992.

Sämtliche Erzählungen. Frankfurt a. M., 1963.

Stories of Three Decades. Translated by H. T. Lowe-Porter. New York, 1951.

Tagebücher: 1918–1921. Edited by P. de Mendelssohn. Frankfurt a. M., 1979.

Tagebücher: 1949–1950. Edited by I. Jens. Frankfurt a. M., 1991.

Von Deutscher Republik: Politische Schriften und Reden in Deutschland. Frankfurt a. M., 1984.

SECONDARY SOURCES

Baumgart, R., et al. *Thomas Mann und München: Fünf Vorträge.* Frankfurt a. M., 1989.

Bloom, H., ed. *Thomas Mann.* New York, 1986.

Böhm, K. W. *Zwischen Selbstzucht und Verlangen: Thomas Mann und das Stigma Homosexualität, Untersuchungen zu Frühwerk und Jugend.* Würzburg, 1991.

Ezergailis, I. M. *Male and Female: An Approach to Thomas Mann's Dialectic.* The Hague, 1975.

Hamilton, N. *The Brothers Mann: The Lives of Heinrich and Thomas Mann, 1871–1950 and 1875–1955.* London, 1978.

Bibliography

Härle, G. *Männer Weiblichkeit: Zur Homosexualität bei Klaus und Thomas Mann.* Frankfurt a. M., 1988.

Harpprecht, K. *Thomas Mann: Eine Biographie.* Leck, 1995.

Heilbut, A. *Thomas Mann: Eros and Literature.* New York, 1996.

Heller, E. *Thomas Mann: The Ironic German.* New York, 1973.

Lehnert, H., and P. C. Pfeiffer, eds. *Thomas Mann's 'Doctor Faustus': A Novel at the Margins of Modernism.* Columbia, S.C., 1991.

Lukács, G. *Essays on Thomas Mann.* Translated by S. Mitchell. London, 1964.

Prater, D. *Thomas Mann: A Life.* Oxford, 1995.

Reed, T. J. *Thomas Mann: The Uses of Tradition.* Oxford, 1974.

Reiss, G. *'Allegorisierung' und moderne Erzählkunst: Eine Studie zum Werk Thomas Manns.* Munich, 1970.

Ridley, H. *The Problematic Bourgeois: Twentieth-Century Criticism on Thomas Mann's* Buddenbrooks *and* The Magic Mountain. Columbia, S.C., 1994.

―――. *Thomas Mann—Buddenbrooks.* Cambridge, 1987.

Rudloff, H. *Pelzdamen: Weiblickheitsbilder bei Thomas Mann und Leopold von Sacher-Masoch.* Frankfurt a. M., 1994.

Swales, M. *Buddenbrooks: Family Life as the Mirror of Social Change.* Boston, 1991.

Winston, R. *Thomas Mann: The Making of an Artist, 1875–1911.* New York, 1981.

247
∎

Wassily Kandinsky

PRIMARY SOURCES

Barnett, V. E. *Kandinsky: Watercolors. Catalogue Raisonné, Volume One, 1900–1921.* Ithaca, 1992.

Hahl-Koch, J., ed. *Arnold Schönberg, Wassily Kandinsky: Letters, Pictures and Documents.* Translated by J. C. Crawford. London, 1984.

Hoberg, A., ed. *Wassily Kandinsky and Gabriele Münter, Letters and Reminiscences, 1902–1914.* Munich and New York, 1994.

Kandinsky, W. *Complete Writings on Art, Vol. One (1901–1921).* Edited by K. C. Lindsay and P. Vergo. Boston, 1982.

―――. *Kandinsky: Die Gesammelten Schriften, Band I.* Edited by H. K. Roethel and J. Hahl-Koch. Bern, 1980.

―――. Unpublished letters to Gabriele Münter. In the Gabriele Münter- und Johannes Eichner-Stiftung, Städtische Galerie im Lenbachhaus. Munich.

Lankheit, K., ed. *Wassily Kandinsky–Franz Marc: Briefwechsel.* Munich, 1983.

Roethel, H. K., and J. K. Benjamin. *Kandinsky: Catalogue Raisonné of the Oil-Paintings, Vol. One, 1900–1915.* London, 1987.

SECONDARY SOURCES

Costlow, J. T., S. Sandler, and J. Vowles, eds. *Sexuality and the Body in Russian Culture.* Stanford, 1993.

Dabrowski, M. *Kandinsky's Compositions.* New York, 1995.

Edie, J. M., J. P. Scanlan, and M.-B. Zeldin, eds. *Russian Philosophy.* Vol. 3. Chicago, 1965.

Eichner, J. *Kandinsky und Gabriele Münter: Von Ursprüngen Moderner Kunst.* Munich, 1957.

Bibliography

Engelstein, L. *The Keys to Happiness: Sex and the Search for Modernity in Fin-de-Siècle Russia.* Ithaca, 1992.

Fineberg, J. D. *Kandinsky in Paris, 1906–1907.* Ann Arbor, 1984.

Grohman, W. *Wassily Kandinsky: Life and Work.* New York, 1958.

Hahl-Koch, J. *Kandinsky.* Translated by K. Brown, J. Harratz, and K. Harrison. New York, 1993.

————. Review of Kleine, in *Kunstchronik* 46 (1993): 1, 32–37.

Hubbs, J. *Mother Russia: The Feminine Myth in Russian Culture.* Bloomington and Indianapolis, 1988.

Kleine, G. *Gabriele Münter und Wassily Kandinsky: Biographie eines Paares.* Frankfurt a. M., 1990.

Kuspit, D. *Signs of Psyche in Modern and Postmodern Art.* Cambridge and New York, 1993.

Lindsay, K. "Gabriele Münter and Wassily Kandinsky: What They Meant to Each Other." *Arts Magazine* (December 1981): 54–62.

Long, R.-C. W. *Kandinsky: The Development of an Abstract Style.* Oxford, 1980.

————. "Kandinsky's Vision of Utopia as a Garden of Love." *Art Journal* (spring 1983): 50–60.

Overy, P. *Kandinsky: The Language of the Eye.* New York, 1969.

Paperno, I., and J. D. Grossman. *Creating Life: The Aesthetic Utopia of Russian Modernism.* Stanford, 1994.

Peterson, R. E. *A History of Russian Symbolism.* Philadelphia, 1993.

Reynolds, D. *Symbolist Aesthetics and Early Abstract Art: Sites of Imaginary Space.* Cambridge, 1995.

Rieber, A. J. *Merchants and Entrepreneurs in Imperial Russia.* Chapel Hill, 1982.

Ringbom, S. *The Sounding Cosmos: A Study in the Spiritualism of Kandinsky and the Genesis of Abstract Painting.* Helsinki, 1970.

Rogoff, I. "Tiny Anguishes: Reflections on Nagging, Scholastic Embarrassment, and Feminist Art History." *Differences* 4.3 (1992): 38–65.

Walicki, A. *Legal Philosophies of Russian Liberalism.* Oxford, 1987.

Weiss, P. *Kandinsky in Munich: The Formative Jugendstil Years.* Princeton, 1979.

————. *Kandinsky and Old Russia: The Artist as Ethnographer and Shaman.* New Haven and London, 1995.

West, J. L., and I. A. Petrov, eds. *Merchant Moscow: Images of Russia's Vanished Bourgeoisie.* Princeton, 1998.

INDEX

253
■

256
■